Third Edition

BABIES with
DOWN SYNDROME

Third Edition

BABIES with
DOWN SYNDROME

A New Parents' Guide

Edited by Susan J. Skallerup

Woodbine House ▪ 2008

Cover photo taken by Johanna Mattern Allen

Library of Congress Cataloging-in-Publication Data

Babies with Down syndrome : a new parents' guide / edited by Susan J. Skallerup.
-- 3rd ed.
     p. cm.
  Includes index.
  ISBN 1-890627-55-0
  1. Down syndrome--Popular works. 2. Children with mental disabilities--Care. I.
Skallerup, Susan J.
  RJ506.D68B33 2008
  618.92'858842--dc22

                                                                    2008033377

Manufactured in the United States of America

10   9   8   7   6   5   4   3   2   1

■■
TABLE

OF

CONTENTS

Foreword

Mitchell Levitz

My name is Mitchell Levitz and I have Down syndrome. I think that at the time I was born my parents fell in love with me. They told the doctors that they wanted me to be home with my family. For the past 37 years my life has been very enriching and fulfilling because I had lots of love, caring, supports, and guidance. In looking back on my entire life, I feel very lucky to have had the success that I was able to build for myself.

Congratulations to all of the expecting and new parents who are starting to read this book about Down syndrome. I am sure your baby will have a life of happiness and joy, and will accomplish his or her hopes and dreams—just like me. Life is precious and we should live every day to the fullest. When you have a family who cares and loves you, you will be able to have a long-lasting relationship with them.

I have wonderful relationships with my family, friends, colleagues, and people in my community. I enjoy all of our family outings when we spend time together like going to parks, parties, family get-togethers, trips, and holidays.

Growing up with Down syndrome gave me opportunities to be part of my community. I think it is important for young kids to explore the adventures of getting involved in community activities. This is how to discover interests, hobbies, and what you prefer doing in your own neighborhood or town. One of the many ways is to join clubs with others that you have things in common with such as the boy scouts or girl scouts. When I was young, this was a great experience for me to have fun and make good friends. When I joined the boy scouts, I learned how to earn badges doing projects, sometimes with my father, and we had lots of fun working on them together. Another great way to explore the nature of outdoors and be active is to be with friends playing sports like soccer. This was very exciting for me. What better way is there to be with your buddies than to play sports with them? And it gives you a great work out! The good thing about all of this is that it is another opportunity to make new friends and spend time with other kids with and without disabilities.

People with Down syndrome, like me, enjoy having friends and spending time with each other. We want to be able to find new friends. One way to meet new people that we can be friends with is to join a social group. I have been involved in my own social and travel groups while I was growing up and also now. We go to movies, attend sporting events, go dancing, go out to eat, and take trips. Wow! For me and other people with developmental disabilities, that has been a great way to meet new people that we can call our friends.

I had tons of supports from close family who especially helped me get through some tough times in my life fitting in because of my disability. That was because people did not know me that well. But when they got to know me better, people treated me the same as any other person. Sometimes we became friends in school, camps, and community activities, and when I started having jobs, we had good work relationships.

Basically, what I am saying is that people should see and talk about the person first, then their disability, because each individual is unique in his or her own way. This is what is described as "people-first" language. I think that we need to educate others to think about and talk about individuals with Down syndrome with respect and dignity. Each of us has different abilities, skills, knowledge, interests, and achievements. I have learned that all of us should have choices about our everyday lives and be treated as equals because we should have the same rights and opportunities to be able to live a successful and meaningful life.

For me, education has given me a sense of knowledge, experience, opportunities, and direction. I went to the same schools with my siblings and friends and it was an enriching time that we spent together. That is why I enjoyed being in the same classes with my friends. I took the required courses I needed to learn skills and determine what type of an education I needed to receive.

First, when I was very young, I was involved with early intervention and then preschool. My teachers taught me how to take the first steps in learning how to count, walk, and speak so I could say my first words. With guidance and support from my teachers in elementary school and my family, I was able to take my very first steps in becoming a smarter, bright, and friendly person. When I was in speech and language classes, I learned how to speak clearly and slowly so that people would understand my ideas and thoughts.

Throughout my years in school, I took several courses that I needed to become a good student. In middle school and high school, I took courses in computers, business, English, social studies, and math for independent living. When I took a computer class, I learned how to type and how to operate a computer. I learned all about business and gained the skills so that some time I would be able to work in the business community. I also enjoyed taking a theater class—it was a wonderful experience. I learned how the theater industry works and how people perform. It was very exciting.

I think it is important that all students should attend their own Individualized Education Program (IEP) meetings. It gave me a chance to speak up for myself and advocate for myself about what classes I wanted to take. When you are at these meetings, you can discuss how to handle teasing and peer-pressure from other students. People can give you some good advice on how to deal with these experiences. They might suggest some strategies that you may use in these situations. As an example, I learned I could walk away, ignore, or talk to the guidance counselor, teacher, or my family. For parents with a son or a daughter with a disability, it is important for you to be part of these planning meetings by having a voice in determining what type of an education your child should receive.

I was lucky to have different opportunities to further my education throughout my life. This gave me the chance to gain the skills that I needed to pursue my future living on my own, as I now do. This also helped me to establish a direction for my future goals besides living on my own. Training on public policy, education, and employment gave me an opportunity to work more in the disability field and to have a job and receive a paycheck to work. Having a job makes me feel more independent and gives me a chance to do more in my community. It also allows me to be a better self-advocate, to teach other people to speak up for themselves, and to give professionals something to think about when they work with individuals with disabilities.

My life is great! I have a wonderful family that supports me in the decisions that I make. So, in conclusion—as you can see, all of us, including myself, should have hope, love, honest caring, and an open heart to everyone. We should cherish each other. Always remember to think positive and have high hopes for you and your baby with Down syndrome.

ACKNOWLEDGEMENTS

This book builds on the superb groundwork laid by the previous two editions of *Babies with Down Syndrome*. Woodbine House would therefore like to thank everyone who provided input into the design or content of the earlier works and express our gratitude to them for helping to make this book a touchstone for parents' guides to disabilities. In particular, we would like to acknowledge the tremendous contributions of Jake and his family, who were at the heart of it all.

Our sincere appreciation also goes to the parents, professionals, and parent-professionals who contributed chapters to this book. Four of the authors have been involved with the book from its outset over two decades ago: Marian Jarrett, Dr. Chahira Kozma, Joan B. Riley, and Marilyn Trainer. We are very grateful to them for agreeing to be a part of this endeavor in the early 1980s when nobody really knew if it would succeed, and for graciously consenting to revise their original chapters for new editions of the book. Five of the authors are contributing to the book for the first time: Sue Buckley, Jean Nelson Farley, Dr. Len Leshin, Jo Ann Simons, and Mary Wilt. We are grateful to them for their willingness to share their hard-won expertise and experiences with a new generation of parents and for adding some fresh perspectives to this work.

We also thank Mitchell Levitz for so eloquently sharing his insights about what it is like to live with Down syndrome and for his excellent advice to new parents. And thanks to Emily Kingsley for allowing us to reprint one of the most widely disseminated and best-loved pieces ever written about Down Syndrome: "Welcome to Holland."

In addition, we appreciate the information and guidance we received from Dr. George Capone and Pat Winders, and the reprint permissions granted by Vanessa Quick at the National Down Syndrome Society, Greg Richards, and J. K. Morris.

Last, but not least, we would like to acknowledge the many parents and other family members who have helped to make this book as reader-friendly and helpful as possible for families of children with Down syndrome. That includes the many unnamed parents and parent groups who have given us feedback about earlier editions of the book, and, most especially, the families who have generously allowed us to print their parent statements and the photographs of their beautiful children in the pages that follow. We thank you all, on behalf of the many families who will benefit from your contributions.

INTRODUCTION

Susan J. Skallerup

My daughter dreams of owning a time machine. Specifically, she would like to have one with a "flux capacitor," like Marty McFly pilots in the *Back to the Future* movies. She has watched the movies in the series many times, drinking in the consequences of trying to undo past mistakes or glimpsing your own future. I think she has been surreptitiously choosing the years that she would visit, given the chance. "What year were you a freshman?" she's asked me. "How about Dad?" And, "Were you alive in 1885?" I find slips of paper under her bed with mysterious years written on them in pink gel pen: 2027, 1971, 1998.

The reason I bring up my daughter's fascination with time travel is that fourteen years ago, when I was in your place, I could have really used a time machine. I was struggling with my daughter's diagnosis of Down syndrome and didn't like the place where I was.

On the one hand, I kept wishing that I could somehow undo what had happened. If only I had gotten married sooner or had tried to have kids when I was younger, I probably would have had a baby with the usual number of chromosomes. On the other hand, I wanted to vault beyond the confusion and uncertainty of the present and just be done with all the messy coping and adjusting. If only I could see what our lives would be like in the future, maybe I could stop worrying that the smallest thing I did or didn't do today could have a profound and irreversible effect on my daughter's well being.

If I'd had a time machine, I could have used it to see which of my worries were valid and which were really laughable. For example, there was the day my husband and I were driving down the highway with our tiny, fuzzy-headed newborn asleep in her car seat. To fill the weary silence that yawned between us, we had the radio tuned to a classical station. The station switched to a jaunty French horn concerto, and suddenly my eyes filled with tears at the thought that my daughter would probably never share my appreciation of good music. If I could have jumped ahead a few years, I would have seen what a ridiculous concern this was.

My daughter definitely appreciates good music, but her idea of good music is not the same as mine, thank goodness. "Your music is boring, Mom!" she objects whenever I play one of my antiquated classical CDs. "It doesn't have any words." She has a voracious and age-appropriate appetite for popular songs, which she expertly downloads to her iPod herself. She revels in her ability to identify tunes that I cannot, and pores over teen magazines for news of her favorite singers. Like any normal teenaged girl, she wants and *needs* to listen to songs with lyrics like "You're beautiful, you're beautiful, it's true," and even, "I'll stop the world and melt to you."

Of course, there are still occasionally times when I wish I could go back and undo things and make them come out better. For instance, there are times I wish that my husband and I had made different decisions related to our daughter's education, or been more assertive, or known then what we know now. But I can no longer conceive of life without my witty, creative, kind-hearted daughter to grace it. And I stopped worrying so much about the future years ago.

The truth is, I have discovered that my daughter's (and my family's) ultimate destination is not fixed in place, but somewhat under our control. It turns out that many of the things my husband and I do actually *can* affect my daughter's future—and I'm glad of that now. With our help, our daughter has mastered thousands of skills we deliberately set out to teach her—to walk and to ride a bike, to eat with a spoon and to tie her shoes, to label colors and to write a polite thank-you note. She has also mastered many other things we had no idea she was learning—to make a peanut butter and whipped cream sandwich, to find online fan clubs for her favorite singers and actors, to reel off the names and special powers of the 151 original Pokemon, to get out of math class by claiming that she has a headache or aching molar....

In many respects, raising our daughter has been akin to scattering a big handful of wildflower seeds across a rich patch of earth. We may not always know what will come up and when, but everything that has emerged has been exquisite and well worth the wait.

At this point, it may reassure you to know that many parents, like me, have fallen in love with their baby with Down syndrome and discovered that raising their child is indescribably rewarding. Or your feelings may be too raw right now for you to care much about other parents' experiences. Then again, perhaps you have deliberately chosen this path for your family, and you are impatient to get on with your new life.

In any case, I am sure you could use a trustworthy, knowledgeable guide to help you get your bearings as you begin to explore what Down syndrome will mean for you and your family. That is what *Babies with Down Syndrome* is meant to be for you. Since this book was first published in 1985, it has empowered tens of thousands of parents, equipping them with information and guidance essential to meeting their child's special and not-so-special needs. (For the record, I was not the editor of the previous two editions, so I am not boasting—just stating a fact.)

There is no way to show you now exactly what your child's life will be like in one year, five years, twelve years. But there is a lot of information available to help you envision the future you would like for your child and to show you how to work toward that vision, step by step. This information can give you confidence in making choices and decisions that are right for you and your family, and help you avoid missteps or decisions that you might want to undo later.

This book covers information that should be most helpful to families of children from birth through about age five. The chapter authors include parents of children with Down syndrome who have first-hand experience in living with children with Down syndrome, as well as professionals who have spent their working lives helping children with Down syndrome and their families. (In fact, six of the chapter authors are parents of children or adults with Down syndrome.) As in the previous two editions of this book, all of the information has been carefully selected to represent what is considered best practice in caring for and raising a child with Down syndrome.

Perhaps you wonder why you should even read a book on Down syndrome when so much information is easily and instantaneously accessible on the Internet. One reason is that there *is* so much information out there. It can be overwhelming to read through pages of often contradictory information and not know which websites to trust. Another reason is that, sadly, there is still a lot of outdated and overly negative information about Down syndrome out there. Some of it is even disseminated by geneticists, obstetricians, educators, and other professionals who obviously know very little about Down syndrome and the potential of people who are born with it

You should know that *Babies with Down Syndrome* was originally written *because* there was so little positive, up-to-date information available for parents a quarter century ago. In fact, Woodbine House was founded to remedy that situation. Rest assured that the contributors to this edition are motivated by the same empathy for new parents and passion for helping children with Down syndrome achieve their best that motivated the publication of the first edition.

Babies with Down Syndrome is designed to give parents of babies and young children with Down syndrome a comprehensive picture of the most important issues facing them. This means that it delves into some medical and developmental issues that not all new parents wish to tackle at first. Educating yourself about these topics, however, may be vital to your child's well-being—especially if the professionals working with you are not experienced in these areas. We therefore believe it would be unethical not to cover this information. Please don't feel as if you have to read everything in the book at once, though, if that feels too overwhelming at present. Take things at your own pace.

Glance over the table of contents and look for the topics that you are wondering about *now*. Perhaps at the moment, you don't much care about the causes of Down syndrome, but you want to read the Daily Care chapter to make sure you are on the right track with feeding or bathing your baby. Or maybe you have no concerns about daily care, but want to read the Early Intervention chapter to find out how instruction and therapies can help maximize your child's developmental progress. Once you are familiar with the contents of the book, you can come back to the information you need when you are ready to read about it.

As you page through the book, you will notice we use the personal pronouns "he" and "she" in alternate chapters to refer to children with

Down syndrome. This is because Down syndrome occurs equally in boys and girls.

You will also notice the Parent Statements at the ends of the chapters. This was an innovation introduced in the first edition of *Babies with Down Syndrome* by the originators of the "Parents' Guide" format. The Parent Statements were conceived as a way to help new parents see that they are not alone with their feelings, questions, and concerns, and to benefit from the advice of dozens of seasoned parents. Reading these comments by other parents can be something like sitting in on a support group. You may agree with some of the thoughts and opinions and disagree with others, but you will certainly come away with a better idea of what it's like to raise a child with Down syndrome.

At the back of the book, you will find lists of books for further reading and organizations and websites that can give you additional information on Down syndrome, special education, and related subjects. Again, you can find a lot of information of this nature on the Internet. But the resources listed in this book are ones that we know to be reputable, so they may be good ones for you to begin with as you widen your search for helpful information and support. There are, of course, many other excellent resources besides those we have listed. The Resource Guide is just meant to get you started on your quest for knowledge and support.

Maybe you don't feel quite ready to begin your quest, and maybe you never wanted to go on such a quest to begin with. After all, by the time we are old enough to be parents, most of us have a pretty clear picture of who we are and what we want our lives to be like. We do not want to be hijacked by sudden change and taken off in a new direction without our consent. But since you find yourself on this quest, try to remain open to suggestions and advice from guides who have traveled this road before you—whether you meet those guides in person, on the Internet, or in the pages of books like this one.

I will not presume to predict what your journey into the world of Down syndrome will be like, or what your child's future will be. I will let the authors of this book tell you about the nature of Down syndrome, the best ways to deal with its effects, the amazing capabilities and gifts of children with Down syndrome, and the many people who can help your child reach her individual potential. I think what you read will hearten you.

In time, you will be able to set your sights on the future you would like for your child, and then work in the present to make that future a reality. Hopefully, there will also be many times when you can simply savor the moment without feeling that you must rush along to see what lies ahead for your family. My advice: Take plenty of photos and keep a journal. If your experience is anything like mine, you will treasure your memories of your child's first years and want to revisit them often.

May your family's journey with your child be filled with love, happiness, and moments of serendipity.

1

WHAT IS
DOWN SYNDROME?

Chahira Kozma, M.D.

The best way to understand Down syndrome—what it means to your baby and what it means to you—is to get the facts. The worst enemy facing parents of babies with Down syndrome is ignorance. Before you do anything or decide anything about your baby, learn about Down syndrome.

This chapter addresses the basic questions parents have about Down syndrome and how it affects young children. It gives the foundation of knowledge you need to begin properly caring for your baby.

No one would tell you that raising a child with Down syndrome (or any child, for that matter) is easy. The thousands of parents who have done it successfully could tell you that a lot of hard work and patience are involved. But they could also tell you that your hard work will pay off with significant rewards for you, your child, and your family. Today, growing knowledge and rising expectations are shattering the myths and stereotypes that unfairly limited opportunities for children with Down syndrome in the past. Children with Down syndrome and their families now have options that enable them to become vital, welcomed parts of their communities and to look forward to satisfying and fulfilling futures.

▪▪ What Is Down Syndrome?

If you are like most people, you probably had little understanding of what Down syndrome meant before your baby was diagnosed. Basically, Down syndrome means that your baby has a genetic condition

resulting from the presence of one extra chromosome in some or all of his or her millions of cells. Instead of having two copies of the twenty-first chromosome, your baby has three. As a result, he has a total of 47 chromosomes in his cells, instead of the usual 46. For more information about the genetic basis of Down syndrome and why it occurs, see "What Causes Down Syndrome?" below.

Because chromosomes and the genetic material they carry play an essential part in determining your child's characteristics, this extra chromosome will affect his life. His appearance will be slightly different from other children's, he may have some unique medical problems, and he will likely have some degree of intellectual disability. The severity of any of these problems, however, varies tremendously from child to child. In general, children with Down syndrome are usually smaller, and their physical and mental development is slower, than youngsters who do not have Down syndrome

The word "syndrome" refers to a set of signs and symptoms that tend to occur together and which reflect the presence of a particular disorder or an increased chance of developing a particular disorder. Down syndrome is called a "syndrome" because it produces a recognizable pattern of differences in different areas of the body. For instance, the bridge of the nose is often flattened and the eyes have an upslanted instead of a horizontal appearance; the back of the head is flattened; and fingers are often shorter than usual and there may be a wide gap between the first and second toe. Not everybody who has Down syndrome has exactly the same combination of differences, but these differences occur together often enough that they are considered characteristic of Down syndrome.

Although the physical features can help in making the diagnosis of Down syndrome, they do not cause any disabilities and no emphasis should be put on these characteristics otherwise. And, even though individuals with Down syndrome have distinct physical characteristics, they are usually more similar to their siblings and the average person in the community than they are different from them. The section called "What Are Babies with Down Syndrome Like" describes the most common differences.

Two things about Down syndrome are clear. First, parents do not cause Down syndrome; nothing you did or did not do before or during pregnancy caused your baby to have Down syndrome. Second, like other children, each baby with Down syndrome is unique, with his own personality, talents, and thoughts. There are few absolutes governing your baby's destiny. Like other children, he is an individual and will grow to become a distinct personality.

▪▪ How Common Is Down Syndrome?

Recent figures from the Centers for Disease Control (CDC) place the frequency of Down syndrome in the United States at about 1 in 733 births. This means that over six thousand babies with Down syndrome are born in the United States every year and thousands more in other countries. It is one of the most common congenital disorders, occurring in all races, ethnic groups, socio-economic classes, and nationalities. It can happen to anyone, although women over age 35 have a higher risk of having babies with Down syndrome (see below). Slightly more males than females are born, with the male-to-female ratio being approximately 1.15:1 in newborns with Down syndrome.

▪▪ What Are Babies with Down Syndrome Like?

Doctors are often able to spot babies with Down syndrome immediately after birth. Typically, newborns with Down syndrome have differences in their faces, neck, hands and feet, and muscle tone. The cluster of these features triggers the doctor's suspicions and suggests the diagnosis. After examining your baby, the doctor will usually order chromosome studies, called a karyotype, to confirm the diagnosis, as discussed under "Some Genetics Basics." A karyotype is an organized

profile of someone's chromosomes. The chromosomes are arranged and numbered by size, from largest to smallest. This arrangement helps scientists to identify chromosomal alterations that may result in a genetic disorder such as Down syndrome.

The following characteristics are most commonly associated with Down syndrome. Bear in mind, however, that there is tremendous variety among babies with Down syndrome; not every baby possesses all of the characteristic features. Most importantly, no connection has been shown between the number of Down syndrome features a baby has and that baby's cognitive or other abilities.

Low Muscle Tone

Babies with Down syndrome have low muscle tone, also known as hypotonia. This means that their muscles appear relaxed and feel "floppy." Low tone usually affects all the muscles of the body. It is a significant physical feature that alerts doctors to look for other signs of Down syndrome. More importantly, low muscle tone affects your baby's movement, strength, and development.

Most of the physical features linked to Down syndrome do not affect your baby's ability to grow and learn, but low muscle tone can complicate all areas of development. For example, low muscle tone affects the development of gross motor skills such as rolling over, sitting, standing, and walking. Since the muscles of the mouth have low muscle tone, the development of feeding and speech skills can also be affected. Hypotonia also results in increased mobility between the joints.

Hypotonia cannot be cured. That is, your child's muscle tone will likely always be somewhat lower than other children's. Often, however, it can improve over time, especially with the help of physical therapy. Accordingly, great importance is placed on good physical therapy to help children with low muscle tone develop properly, especially when they are very young. Physical therapy is discussed in Chapter 7.

Facial Features

Your baby's face may have some or all of the features characteristic of Down syndrome:

Nose. Your baby's face may be slightly broader and his nasal bridge may be flatter than usual. Often, children with Down syndrome have noses that are smaller than other children's because of an underde-

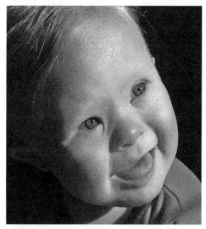

veloped nasal bone. The nasal passages may be smaller as well, and can become congested more quickly. Problems with nasal congestion are discussed in Chapter 3.

Eyes. Your child's eyes may appear to slant upward. (This somewhat Asian appearance is one reason Down syndrome was formerly called "mongolism.") Your doctor may call these "upslanting palpebral fissures." The eyes may also have small folds of skin, called epicanthal folds, at the inner corners. The outer part of the iris (or colored part) of each eye may have light spots called Brushfield spots. These spots are more commonly seen in children with blue eyes and do not affect your baby's sight. It is very important to have your baby's eyesight checked, however, because vision problems tend to be more common in children with Down syndrome than in other children. This is discussed in more detail in Chapter 3.

Mouth. Your baby's mouth may be small, and the roof of his mouth may be shallow. When these features are accompanied by low muscle tone, the tongue may protrude or appear large in relation to the mouth.

Teeth. Your child's teeth may come in late and in an unusual order. Most babies get their teeth in the same sequence, but the teeth of babies with Down syndrome seem to have a sequence all their own. The teeth may also be small, unusually shaped, and out of place, and these problems may continue when your child gets his permanent teeth. Good dental care and routine visits to the dentist should start in early childhood.

Ears. Your baby's ears can be small and the tops may fold over. Small or absent ear lobes are common. Sometimes, the ears are set slightly lower on the head. The ear passages tend also to be smaller, which can make it very difficult for your pediatrician to check your baby's ears for infection. The size of the ear canals improves with growth. Because the ear canals are narrow and small, the ear passages can become blocked, contributing to a hearing loss. For this reason it is important to include early hearing exams in your infant's check-up schedule. Ear and hearing problems are discussed in Chapter 3.

Head Shape

Babies with Down syndrome have smaller than normal heads. Usually their head size falls within the lower 3 percent on standard growth charts for children. This is technically called microcephaly. The difference in size, however, is not usually noticeable. Studies have shown that the head, while smaller than average, is still within a normal range relative to the rest of the body. The back of the head may be flatter and shorter (brachycephaly). Also, the neck may appear shorter, and in newborns there may be loose folds of skin on the back of the neck, but these folds tend to disappear with growth. The soft spots of the head (fontanels), which are present in all babies, may be larger in babies with Down syndrome and may take longer to close in the normal course of development.

Stature

Babies with Down syndrome are usually of average weight and length at birth, but they usually do not grow as fast as other children do. For this reason, special growth charts for boys and girls with Down syndrome are used. During routine checkups, your doctor will measure your baby and plot the height and weight on the growth chart to make sure he is gaining weight nicely and growing well.

According to the most recent study in the United States, the average adult height for males with Down syndrome is about 5 feet, 2 inches (156 cm) and the average adult height for females is about 4 feet, 9 inches (144 cm). (See the growth charts at the end of Chapter 4.) However, more recent studies from European countries found a final average height of about five feet, three and a half inches (161.5 cm) for males and four feet, ten inches (147.5 cm) for females.

Hands and Feet

Your child's hands may be smaller, and his fingers may be shorter, than other children's. The palm of each hand may have only one crease across it (a transverse palmer or simian crease). The fifth finger may curve inward slightly and have only one crease. Usually the feet of babies with Down syndrome appear normal, but there may be a gap between the first and second toes. Frequently there is a deep crease on the sole of the feet in this gap. Flat feet are common.

Babies with Down syndrome also have unique "dermatoglyphics"—that is, finger and palm prints. These do not affect your baby's development in any way, but may be mentioned to you as one of the diagnostic signs of Down syndrome.

Other Physical Features

Chest. Your baby's chest may be somewhat funnel shaped (when the chest bone is depressed) or pigeon breasted (bowing out of the chest wall). Neither of these differences in shape results in medical problems.

Skin. Your child's skin can be mottled, fair, and sensitive to irritation. Skin care is discussed in Chapter 4.

Hair. Children with Down syndrome often have hair that is thin, soft, and sparser than usual. In addition, some children with Down syndrome have a condition known as alopecia areata, which causes the hair to fall out in patches. (See Chapter 3 for more information.)

Most newborns with Down syndrome do not have all of the physical features described here. In general, the most common features are the low muscle tone, the upwardly slanting eyes, flatter mid-face, small, flat nose, small ears, short fifth finger, and wide gap between first and second toes. With the sole exception of low muscle tone, these features will not hinder either your baby's health or his development. There are, however, some medical conditions associated with Down syndrome that can affect your baby's health. These are discussed in detail in Chapter 3.

Because your baby with Down syndrome has the extra chromosome, he may have some features that resemble those of other babies with Down syndrome. However, because your baby also has twenty-two sets of completely normal chromosomes, he will also resemble his parents, brothers, and sisters, and will possess his own unique characteristics.

▪▪ What about My Baby's Intelligence?

Children with Down syndrome almost always have some degree of intellectual disability. That is, they learn more slowly and have difficulty with complex reasoning and judgment. The degree of intellectual impairment, however, varies tremendously. Your baby will learn, and what he learns, he will not "lose." Most importantly, remember that

both the intellectual and the social skills of babies with Down syndrome are maximized when they are raised in a supportive environment with their families.

Intelligence has been measured for many years by standardized tests. These tests gauge a child's ability to reason, conceptualize, and think. Scores are often computed into a measurement called an intelligence quotient or IQ.

Among the general population, there is a wide range of measured intelligence (IQ). Studies find that ninety-five percent of the population have what is called "normal" or average intelligence, with IQs in the range of 70 to 130. Two and one-half percent of the population have what is called superior intelligence, with IQs over 130, and, two and one-half percent have intelligence below the average range, with IQs of less than 70. In the U.S., individuals who score below the average range are technically considered to have mental retardation. However, you should know that that terminology is falling further and further out of favor, and you are likely to hear other terms used instead, such as intellectual disability or cognitive disability.

Just as there is a range for average intelligence, there is also a range for mental retardation (intellectual disability), called degrees. A person is considered to have mild intellectual disabilities if his score on an IQ test falls between 55 and 70. Moderate intellectual disabilities means an IQ range of between 40 and 55. Severe intellectual disabilities means an IQ range of between 25 and 40. Most children with Down syndrome score within the mild to moderate range of intellectual disability. Some children have a more significant level of disability, and some possess intelligence in the near average or even average range.

Scientists do not yet understand how the extra chromosome in Down syndrome affects mental ability. Research indicates that the excess genetic material prevents or interferes with normal brain development. Both the size and structural complexity of the brain are different in babies with Down syndrome, but just how this affects mental functioning remains unknown. Some scientists theorize that a certain gene interferes with the transport of an important brain chemical into a certain part of the forebrain. Others theorize that one or more genes on the 21st chromosome lead to abnormalities in the structure and function of the gaps between brain cells (the synapses) and, as a result, the brain cells can't communicate properly with each other.

In general, differences in chromosomes, such as in Down syndrome, affect the brain and central nervous system, resulting in developmental delays or intellectual disabilities. (For more information about possible brain differences, see the section "Why Does One Extra Chromosome Alter Development?")

Keeping "Intelligence" in Perspective

If your child is given an IQ test, you may want to take the results with a grain of salt. First, IQ tests are not considered accurate until the child is about age seven. Standard IQ tests that depend heavily on language tend to underestimate the abilities of children with Down syndrome, who frequently have language difficulties that make it difficult for them to respond to the types of questions on standard IQ tests. Never forget that your child's IQ scores do not preclude him from taking care of himself, performing productive work, and, most importantly, learning. One of the myths that has long plagued children with Down syndrome is that because of their relatively lower IQ scores they cannot learn. This is simply not true.

Intellectual disabilities have been misunderstood for centuries. As a result, society has consistently underestimated the intellectual potential of children with Down syndrome. Today, however, with appropriate treatment for medical conditions, early infant intervention, better education, and higher expectations, mental achievement for children with Down syndrome is on the rise. Watch out for old studies and statistics about the mental ability of children with Down syndrome (usually gathered from people in institutions where there was no special education or early intervention). These studies tend to indicate lower intelligence than more current studies show. In the past, low expectations tended to yield low performance. We know today that this negative cycle is both unfortunate and avoidable. With early intervention, advanced medical care, better education, and greater social acceptance, children with Down syndrome are functioning at increasingly higher levels.

How might intellectual disabilities affect your child? Although the effects are different in each child, they will generally slow development. Your child will likely learn most new skills more slowly than other children. He will find it more difficult to pay attention for extended periods of time, his memory may not function as well as other children's, and he will have more trouble applying what he learns in one setting to another (called generalization). He will also find learning advanced skills harder. Skills requiring fast judgment, intricate coordination, and detailed analysis will be more difficult for him. This does not mean he can never develop advanced skills, but it will be harder and will take more time for him to learn these skills. The effect of an intellectual disability on your baby's development is discussed in Chapter 6.

Parents often want to know precisely what skills their child will master. Will he be able to read? Will he learn to write? What will his schooling be like? None of these questions can be answered unequivocally for any child. Many children with Down syndrome learn to read and write, some of them quite well. Although higher mathematics skills are generally harder for children with Down syndrome to learn, many master the practical computation skills needed on a day-to-day basis in real-life situations, especially when taught to use a calculator. Many children with

Down syndrome are included in regular classes during all or a portion of their school years. Remember that "normal" children also have a wide range of abilities, just as children with Down syndrome do.

▪▪ What Causes Down Syndrome?

To understand what has caused your child to have Down syndrome, you need to have some understanding of simple genetic facts, specifically about genes and chromosomes, and about how cells divide and grow. You also need to understand the three types of genetic mechanisms that can result in a baby being born with Down syndrome.

Some Genetics Basics

Genes

Every person has genes located in every cell of the body; they are the blueprint of life. Genes are made up of a special material called DNA (deoxyribonucleic acid). The genes provide the cells with instructions for growth and development. If you imagine the human body as a computer, the genes are the software that tells the computer what to do. Almost all of a person's traits—from eye color to hand size to the sound of his voice—are coded in the genes. Every person has millions of them.

Genes come in pairs, with one member of each pair coming at conception from the father and the other from the mother. For example, both the father and the mother contribute a number of genes that control hair color, and it is the combination of these genes that their children inherit. The tremendous diversity that exists among people is due to the vast number of ways that the genes from both parents can be combined.

Chromosomes

Genes are located on microscopic, rod-shaped bodies called chromosomes inside our cells. (See Figure 1 on the next page.) The

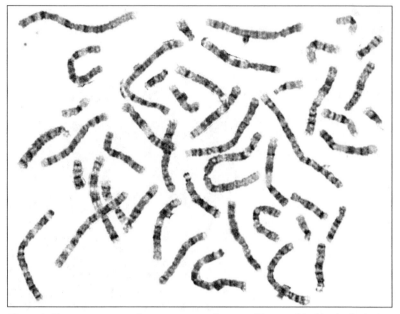

Figure 1. Chromosomes—*A chromosome spread prepared from a white blood cell which has been stained with the Giemsa-banding technique. (Courtesy of Dr. Jeanne Meck, Director of the Cytogenetic Laboratories, Georgetown University Hospital, Washington, DC.)*

chromosomes are the packages that contain the genes. Usually, there are 46 chromosomes in each cell of our bodies. Chromosomes come in 23 pairs with one member of each pair donated by each parent via the sperm (father) or the egg cell (mother). Only one of the 23 pairs of chromosomes is created differently. They are the X and the Y chromosomes. These are the chromosomes that determine sex.

Figure 2 shows a picture of normal chromosomes called a karyotype. Such pictures are made from blood samples. The white cells inside the blood samples are cultured and allowed to grow in a petri dish. The chromosomes are then isolated by a microscope or camera. In humans, each cell normally contains 23 pairs of chromosomes, for a total of 46. Twenty-two of these pairs, the so-called autosomes, are numbered from 1 to 22 according to their size. The autosomes look the same in both males and females. The twenty-third pair, the sex chromosomes, differs between males and females. Females have two copies of the X chromosome, while males have one X and one Y chromosome.

When they are karyotyped, chromosomes are stained to help in identifying them and to detect small structural abnormalities, such

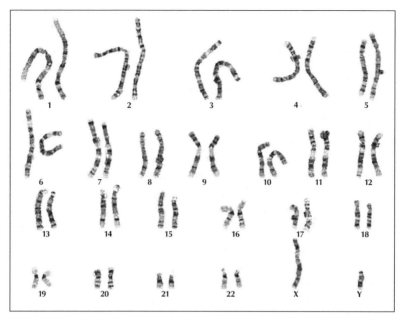

Figure 2. Karyotype of Normal Chromosomes—*A human male karyotype with Giemsa banding. The chromosomes are arranged in a standard classification, numbered 1 to 22 in order of length, with the X and Y chromosomes shown separately (46, XY). (Courtesy of Dr. Jeanne Meck, Director of the Cytogenetic Laboratories, Georgetown University Hospital, Washington, DC.)*

as loss or duplication of chromosomal material. Fluorescence In Situ Hybridization, or FISH, is a new process which vividly paints chromosomes or portions of chromosomes with fluorescent molecules in order to help detect a particular chromosome or gene with the help of fluorescence microscopy. FISH can be used to test for additional or missing chromosomal material.

The larger the chromosome, the more genes it contains. For instance, chromosome 1 is the largest human chromosome and comprises approximately 10 percent of the human genome. On the other hand, chromosome 21 is the smallest of human chromosomes, and contains roughly about 1 percent of the human genome, or about 330 genes. (Strictly speaking, chromosome 21 should be numbered chromosome 22, since it is the autosome with the fewest genes, but when the chromosomes were first categorized and numbered, chromosome 22 was believed to be smaller.)

Chromosomes are believed to function in tandem, with each set carefully balanced. If, for some reason, an extra chromosome is present, the genetic balance is thrown off. If an extra one of the larger chromosomes is present, the baby cannot survive. Babies born with an extra one of the smaller chromosomes, such as number 21, however, are more likely to survive. This may be why Down syndrome is the most common chromosomal abnormality in humans.

Cell Division

A human life begins as a single fertilized egg called a *zygote*, which develops into a complex organism containing billions of cells. Body tissues grow by increasing the number of cells that make them up. In adulthood, most cells reproduce in order to replace dead ones. Therefore, the processes of development and replacement require the production of new cells. One cell doubles its contents and divides into two. Two cells become four, and so on.

Mitosis. Most cells reproduce themselves exactly through a process called *mitosis*. During mitosis, the original cell (called a parent cell) duplicates its contents, including its chromosomes, and splits to form two identical "daughter" cells with each containing the exact 46 chromosomes of the parent. Cell division is a fundamental process for life, and the steps of mitosis are carefully controlled by a number of genes. When mitosis is not regulated correctly, health problems such as cancer can result. Figure 3 shows the process of mitosis.

Meiosis. Almost all of the cells in the human body reproduce themselves through mitosis, with the important exception of the sperm and egg cells. Before they are fully developed, egg and sperm cells originate from cells containing 46 chromosomes. As they mature, they undergo *meiosis,* a special division that reduces their chromosome count to 23.

Meiosis is two-step process. The two steps are referred to as meiosis I and meiosis II. In the early stages of meiosis I, the cell contents, including the chromosomes, duplicate themselves. However, each pair of chromosomes splits or "disjoins" from each other, and the two daughter cells receive only one chromosome from the original pair. This is why meiosis I is called the reduction division. During meiosis II, the two daughter cells undergo a regular mitotic division and divide themselves equally into four cells. Each of the resulting cells has 23 chromosomes. Thus, at conception the sperm and egg that join together each contain only 23 chromosomes, half the usual number. Figure 3 shows how meiosis occurs.

Meiosis proceeds on a different timetable in men and women. A man produces millions of sperm cells during his life, beginning at

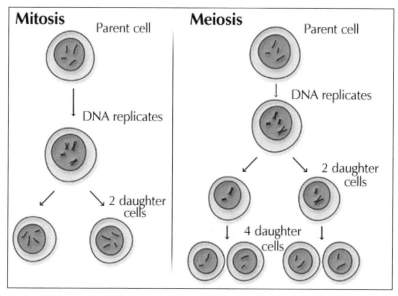

Figure 3. Mitosis and Meiosis (Courtesy of U.S. National Library of Medicine.)

puberty. Since sperm die every day, they need to be continually produced. Therefore, the processes of meiosis I and meiosis II are ongoing
throughout a man's life. Women, on the other hand, are born with all
the eggs they will ever have. A baby girl's eggs actually begin the process
of meiois I when she herself is still a fetus. The process, however, is not
completed and remains suspended and dormant until the girl reaches
puberty. Meiosis I is completed in teenaged girls and women during
ovulation in the middle of the menstrual cycle, when an egg is released.
The egg undergoes meiosis II only if it is fertilized by a sperm cell.

Meiosis generally ensures that humans have the same number of
chromosomes in each generation. When the sperm and egg cells unite
at conception, each usually contributes 23 chromosomes and the resulting embryo has the usual 46. Errors in chromosome division during
meiosis are very common, however. For instance, more than half of all
spontaneous miscarriages during the first trimester of gestation have
chromosomal abnormalities. In the general population, the incidence of
chromosomal abnormalities is about 7 in 1,000 (0.7%) of live births.

Fertilization

When a baby is conceived, a sperm cell and an egg cell combine,
typically yielding one fertilized egg with a complete set of 46 chromo-

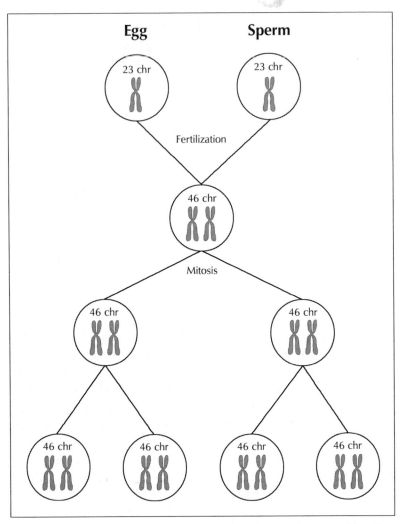

Figure 4. During fertilization, the 23 chromosomes from the egg and sperm combine. The resulting fertilized egg ordinarily has 46 chromosomes.

somes, 23 from the mother and 23 from the father. Figure 4 shows what occurs during fertilization. Soon after fertilization, the fertilized egg begins to grow and develop through mitosis. First it forms two identical new cells, and it continues mitosis until there are billions of cells. As cells duplicate, their genetic material is also duplicated so that each new cell receives the exact same chromosomal material as the original fertilized cell. Because all cells duplicate the genetic structure of that first fertilized egg, its genetic content determines the genetic makeup of the baby.

A large number of abnormal events or mistakes can occur during meiosis and affect a child's growth and development. Some of these mistakes can lead to Down syndrome as a result of faulty chromosome distribution.

The three ways that Down Syndrome can result are through:
1. nondisjunction,
2. translocation, and
3. mosaicism.

These types of errors in cell division or chromosome rearrangements result in the generally recognized types of Down syndrome discussed below.

The Types of Down Syndrome

1. Nondisjunction

Down syndrome usually results from what is called *nondisjunction,* or failure of one pair of chromosomes to separate evenly during meiosis. In nondisjunction, one daughter cell receives 24 chromosomes and the other cell, 22 chromosomes. A cell with only 22 chromosomes (missing an entire chromosome) cannot survive and cannot be fertilized. On the other hand, an egg or sperm cell with 24 chromosomes can survive and be fertilized. When this occurs, the resulting fertilized egg has 47 chromosomes instead of the normal 46 chromosomes. Doctors call this condition *trisomy,* referring to having three copies of one of the chromosomes. Figure 5 on the next page shows how nondisjunction occurs.

In Down syndrome, it is the number-21 chromosome that does not separate properly. This is referred to as trisomy 21, which is another term for Down syndrome. In 88 to 90 percent of individuals with Down syndrome, the additional chromosome comes from the mother. About 70 percent of the time, these maternal errors occur during meiosis I, while the other 30 percent occur during meiosis II.

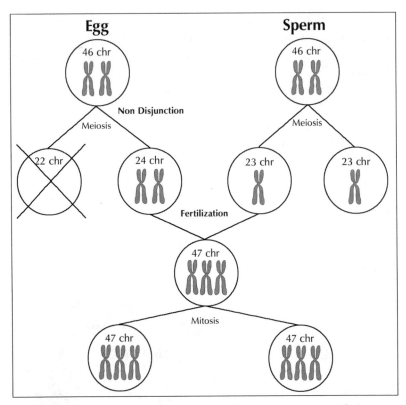

Figure 5. *Nondisjunction is the failure of the pair of chromosomes to separate during meiosis, resulting in both number-21 chromosomes being carried to one daughter cell and none to the other. Upon conception, the fertilized egg contains 47 chromosomes, leading to Nondisjunction Trisomy 21.*

In trisomy 21, incorrect chromosome division during meiosis results in the fertilized egg having three number-21 chromosomes instead of two. As the newly created embryo begins to grow by dividing and duplicating itself, the extra chromosome is also copied and transmitted to each new cell. The result is that all of the baby's cells contain the extra number-21 chromosome.

Figure 6 is a karyotype of the chromosomes of a baby with Down syndrome, and shows the extra number-21 chromosome. On a genetic report, this karyotype would be expressed as 47, XX, +21 for a girl (47 chromosomes, female, extra chromosome-21) or 47, XY, +21 for a boy (47 chromosomes, male, extra chromosome-21). This is in contrast to the normal female karyotype of 46, XX and the normal male karyotype of 46, XY.

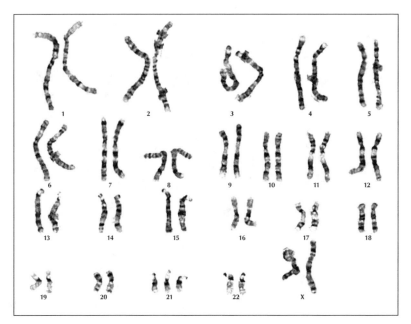

Figure 6. Karyotype of Chromosomes with Nondisjunction Trisomy 21—A karyotype of a female with nondisjunction trisomy 21 (47, XX, +21). (Courtesy of Dr. Jeanne Meck, Director of the Cytogenetic Laboratories, Georgetown University Hospital, Washington, DC.)

About 95 percent of babies with Down syndrome have nondisjunction trisomy 21.

2. Translocation

About 4 to 5 percent of babies with Down syndrome have translocation trisomy- 21. Translocation occurs when a piece of a chromosome or a whole chromosome breaks off during meiosis and attaches itself to another chromosome. When it is a number-21 chromosome that *translocates,* or breaks off and attaches itself to another chromosome, the resulting fertilized egg has Down syndrome or translocation trisomy 21. In this case, chromosome 21 attaches to another chromosome (usually 14) forming a single chromosome, referred to as chromosome t(14;21). All the cells in the body have two copies of chromosome 21, one of 14, and one of t(14;21). This means that there are effectively three copies of chromosome-21, which results in Down syndrome (see Figure 7 on the next page).

About three-fourths of translocations occur spontaneously during fertilization. The other one-fourth of translocations are inherited from

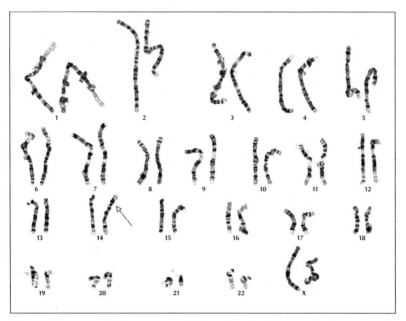

Figure 7. Karyotype of Chromosome with Translocation Trisomy 21—A karyotype of a female with 14-21 translocation trisomy 21. (Courtesy of Dr. Jeanne Meck, Director of the Cytogenetic Laboratories, Georgetown University Hospital, Washington, DC.)

a parent. This is the only type of Down syndrome that is inherited and can result from a condition in a parent's chromosomes. In this situation, the "carrier" parent has the typical number of chromosomes. But two of his or her chromosome pairs are stuck together. As a result, his or her total chromosome count is 45 instead of 46. He or she is unaffected because there is no loss or excess of genetic material; the usual amount is present, but with two chromosomes fused together. Doctors refer to a parent like this as a balanced carrier.

Usually, a baby with translocation trisomy 21 has an entire extra chromosome in all of his cells, even though part of the extra chromosome is translocated to another cell. Therefore, translocation Down syndrome usually has the same effects on a child as nondisjunction Down syndrome. The exception is with rare cases of partial trisomy 21 (see page 23).

Knowing whether your baby has a translocation is important because if he does and you or your partner is a balanced carrier, your risk of having another baby with Down syndrome is higher than in the general population. The karyotype or chromosome count of your baby will reveal whether or not he has translocation trisomy 21. If he does, then both parents are advised to have their karyotypes done as discussed in the section toward the end of the chapter on "Future Babies."

3. Mosaicism

The least common form of Down syndrome is known as mosaicism (or mosaic Down syndrome). Chromosomal mosaicism means that different cells within an individual have different chromosomal makeup. Typically, there are some cells with 46 chromosomes and other cells with an altered number or structure of chromosomes. In Down syndrome mosaicism, the individual has some cells with the typical number of chromosomes (46) and some cells with an extra chromosome 21, for a total of 47 chromosomes.

Using standard karyotype procedures, only about 1 percent of people with Down syndrome are found to have this type of trisomy 21. Recently, however, researchers using the more sophisticated genetic testing called FISH have found that the number of children who are mosaic may be higher.

In mosaicism, most commonly a faulty cell division occurs in one of the earliest cell divisions after fertilization. As in nondisjunction trisomy 21, something causes the chromosomes to divide unevenly. But when this occurs in the second or third cell division, only some of the cells of the growing embryo contain the extra chromosome. As a result, not all the cells have the extra chromosome, and the baby may have fewer of the usual physical features, as well as higher intellectual abilities. Mosaicism can also occur when the fetus starts out with an extra copy of chromosome 21 and then loses the extra chromosome in a mitotic division. In summary, the mosaic form of Down syndrome can occur in one of two ways:

1. The fertilized egg starts out with 46 chromosomes, but during early cell division, a mistake occurs in one of the cells during mitosis, resulting in a cell with 47 chromosomes. All cells that are derived from that cell also have 47 chromosomes. The rest of the cells will have 46 chromosomes. (See Figure 8.)

2. The fertilized egg starts out with 47 chromosomes, but then one of the dividing cells corrects the mistake and loses the extra chromosome at cell division, leaving 46 chromosomes in that cell. All cells that are derived from that cell will have 46 chromosomes. The rest of the cells will have 47 chromosomes.

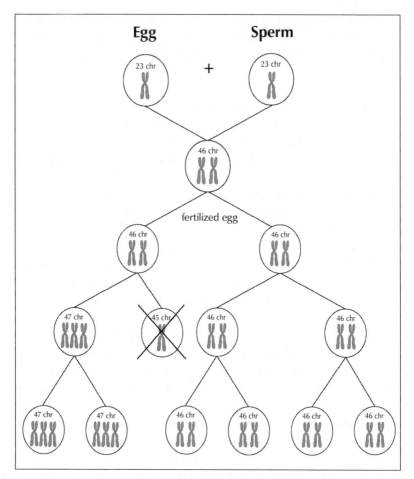

Figure 8. *Mosaicism can occur when a fertilized egg begins to divide normally, but then nondisjunction occurs in one cell line. This results in an individual with both normal and trisomy cell lines.*

How a baby is affected by mosaicism depends not on the number of "normal" cells he or she has, but on where these cells are in the body. For instance, even if only a small proportion of cells have the extra chromosome, if these cells are concentrated in the brain, the child may have the same neurological and developmental disabilities as the typical child with nondisjunction or translocation trisomy 21. Of course, the reverse is also true. Even if the child has a relatively large proportion of cells with the extra chromosome, he may be less affected by Down syndrome than usual, depending on which body tissues the cells are located in.

The proportion of the different chromosomes found in a particular tissue (blood, for example) may not necessarily reflect the proportions present in other tissues or in the embryo during the early stages of development. This makes it impossible to predict from a karyotype how a child with mosaicism may be affected by Down syndrome. Generally speaking, however, the existence of some normal cells—especially if they are in the brain—can moderate the effects of the extra chromosome on physical and sometimes mental development.

Partial Trisomy 21

Very rarely, a baby is born with only part of an extra number-21 chromosome in his cells. For example, the baby might have two complete number-21 chromosomes plus only a part of the long arm of an extra chromosome-21. This so-called partial trisomy 21 most often occurs when there are complex chromosome translocations that involve chromosome 21 and other chromosomes.

Researchers study individuals who have partial trisomy 21 in an attempt to determine which parts of the extra chromosome-21 cause which features of Down syndrome. For instance, from studying the characteristics of people who are missing different parts of the extra chromosome-21, some scientists have concluded that there is a "Down syndrome critical region" (DSCR) located on the lower portion of the chromosome, within the area 21q22.13 to q22.2. (The q refers to the bottom or long arm of the chromosome.) Depending on which part of the extra chromosome is present in a child with partial trisomy 21, he may have fewer physical characteristics and developmental delays than other children with Down syndrome, or he may be indistinguishable from a child with typical trisomy 21.

One of the many myths surrounding Down syndrome is that a child can have only "a little" Down syndrome. With the exception of Mosaicism or very rare partial trisomies, a child either has Down syndrome or does not. It is simply all in the genes.

▪▪ Why Does One Extra Chromosome Alter Development?

Although babies with Down syndrome possess an extra number-21 chromosome, all of their other chromosomes are normal. In fact,

the material in the number-21 chromosomes is normal as well; there is just too much of it. Although scientists still do not know how, the additional chromosomal material causes a genetic imbalance that alters the normal course of growth and development. Certain organ systems appear to be more vulnerable to disruption, including the brain, the eyes, and the cardiovascular and gastrointestinal systems.

Some researchers believe that only the extra genes in a "critical region" at the bottom tip of the 21st chromosome are involved in causing the features of Down syndrome. Genes located on other chromosomes may also be involved in the process that results in Down syndrome.

Some scientists have speculated that the extra genetic material causes *incomplete* rather than abnormal growth and development. For example, the heart in people with Down syndrome is essentially normal, but the wall separating the two sides of the heart often is not completely developed. Similarly, the separation of the fingers is sometimes incomplete, resulting occasionally in webbed fingers.

When first mapped in the year 2000, chromosome 21 was estimated to contain 225 genes. Currently, the total is estimated to be close to 330 genes. Intense work is being done to identify the function of these genes, as well as their possible role in Down syndrome. Some of the genes that are believed to play a role in specific Down syndrome features include:

1. **Cell Adhesion Molecule gene (DSCAM)**—the overexpression of this gene (i.e., the extra copy) is thought to be central to the development of heart anomalies that are common in Down syndrome, as well as some of the neural (nervous system) differences.

2. **Drosophila Single-minded gene (SIM2)**—a gene that helps regulate the production of new nervous tissue.

3. **Amyloid Precursor Protein (APP)**—a gene that has a role in brain growth and development and has been liked

to Alzheimer's disease and other types of neurological disorders; disruption of this gene may interfere with a growth factor that brain cells need to survive.

4. **Superoxide Dismutase gene (SOD-1)**—some researchers believe the overexpression of this gene is responsible for accelerated aging in people with Down syndrome.

5. **DYRK/Minibrain (MNb) gene**—plays several roles during brain development and in adulthood; believed to be involved in the neurobiological alterations that result in cognitive disabilities and motor delays associated with Down syndrome.

6. **Glutamate Receptor Subunit 5 (GluR5)**—overactivity of this gene may cause damage to the neurons in the brain.

Scientists hope that someday, as the result of research into these and other genes on chromosome-21, gene therapy and other treatment modalities may be able to mitigate the effects of Down syndrome. Organizations and websites that can help you keep up with current research findings are listed in the Resource Guide at the back of the book.

:: Why Does *My* Child Have Down Syndrome?

Scientists have investigated the causes of Down syndrome for decades. So far, its exact cause—what makes the number-21 chromosomes stick together—has eluded discovery. Although many factors have been considered to be possible causes, the age of the mother (maternal age) is the only factor related to the likelihood of having a baby with Down syndrome that has been proven.

As explained above, women are born with a fixed number of eggs and do not produce new eggs during their life. The process of meiosis in the eggs starts while the woman is still herself a fetus. Each egg stays in a suspended state until meiosis is completed shortly before ovulation. It is possible that as eggs age and remain suspended in their meiosis for many years, something happens to cause the chromosomes to become sticky or to fail to separate properly. In fact, research has supported the view that older eggs are more prone to errors in cell division with increasing maternal age.

Figure 9 shows the likelihood of having a baby with Down syndrome based on the mother's age at delivery. As you can see, the chance increases dramatically as women age. Yet, many young women with no history of Down syndrome in their families have babies with Down syndrome. In fact, the majority of babies with Down syndrome are born to mothers under 35 years age because of the high number of pregnancies in this age group. However, since more and more women are putting motherhood off until after age 35, the number of pregnancies with Down syndrome in older mothers has increased as well.

In addition to maternal age, researchers have studied several environmental factors and personal habits to determine whether they play a role in the nondisjunction that results in Down syndrome. Tentative roles have been proposed for maternal smoking and use of oral contraceptives. One theory is that smoking diminishes the blood flow to the egg, resulting in hypoxia (too little oxygen), which could lead to difficulties in meiosis.

The role of abnormal folic acid metabolism and the incidence of Down syndrome has been investigated with conflicting results. One study found that a maternal mutation in a gene related to the metabolism of folic acid (the methylenetetrahydrofolate reductase or MTHFR gene) was linked to an increased risk of having a baby with Down syndrome. Subsequent studies, however, did not replicate these results. Likewise, researchers looking for a connection between the mother's exposure to radiation and an increased risk of having a baby with Down syndrome have come up with conflicting results.

There has been less research into possible causes linked to the father. Some scientists think, however, that some men may be genetically predisposed to "sticky" genes, even though a man produces new sperm throughout his adult life.

At present, the hard fact remains that we don't know why Down syndrome occurs and we don't know how to prevent it. Research into the cause of Down syndrome continues.

Figure 9. Likelihood of Having a Baby with Down Syndrome Based on Maternal Age

Mother's Age (Years)	Estimated Risk	Mother's Age (Years)	Estimated Risk
20	1:1476	36	1:266
21	1:1461	37	1:199
22	1:1441	38	1:148
23	1:1415	39	1:111
24	1:1381	40	1:85
25	1:1339	41	1:67
26	1:1285	42	1:54
27	1:1219	43	1:45
28	1:1139	44	1:39
29	1:1045	45	1:35
30	1:937	46	1:31
31	1:819	47	1:29
32	1:695	48	1:27
33	1:571	49	1:26
34	1:455	50	1:25
35	1:352	51	1:25

These figures show the predicted odds of having a baby with Down syndrome, in the absence of prenatal screening, based on data on births in England and Wales collected by the National Down Syndrome Cytogenetic Register from 1989 to 1998. Reprinted by permission from: Morris, J.K., Mutton, D.E., & Alberman, E. (2002). Revised estimates of the maternal age specific live birth prevalence of Down's syndrome. Journal of Medical Screening 9: 2-6.

❚❚ What about My Child's Future?

Generally speaking, children with Down syndrome can look forward to a great deal of independence in adulthood. Fewer and fewer adults with Down syndrome are remaining at home (except by choice). This is thanks to the trend toward community living options, such as group homes and apartments that foster independence and self-reliance, as well as increased options for postsecondary education. Adults with Down syndrome take care of themselves, hold jobs, and enjoy activities with family and friends. As Chapter 8 explains, federal laws protect all people with disabilities from the discrimination that formerly deprived them of so many opportunities. So, today there is real opportunity for learning, growth, and productivity throughout life. Achieving independence and self-reliance, however, takes a lot of effort. The essential foundation that will enable your child to grow into a capable adult is laid through hard work in the first years of life.

As children with Down syndrome grow up, parents often worry about their child's reproductive capacity. The concerns are different

for male and female children. Many, if not most men with Down syndrome are infertile, due either to lack of, or reduced numbers of sperm. However, there are two confirmed cases of men with Down syndrome fathering children. More studies are needed to better understand the exact incidence and causes of infertility in men with Down syndrome. Whether or not they are fertile, however, all males with Down syndrome grow and mature sexually.

Women with Down syndrome often have somewhat impaired, but still significant, fertility. A number of women with Down syndrome have carried pregnancies to term and delivered infants with and without Down syndrome. The eggs of fertile women with Down syndrome are likely to possess the extra number-21 chromosome. Consequently, when the egg cells divide during meiosis, there is a 50/50 chance that the daughter cell will get an extra number-21 chromosome. This means there is about a 50 percent chance that an egg that is fertilized will have an extra chromosome. Because miscarriages are more likely to occur if an embryo has trisomy 21, however, the chance that any baby carried to term will have Down syndrome is lower than 50 percent.

Babies born to mothers with Down syndrome are at increased risk for premature delivery, low birth weight, and other congenital disorders, in addition to the risk of Down syndrome. Sex education and proper birth control methods are important subjects for you to discuss with your child as he or she grows.

∷ Future Babies

Parents often wonder if their chances of having another baby with Down syndrome are higher after giving birth to a child with Down syndrome. The answer depends both on the type of Down syndrome your child has and on your particular family history.

In general, the risk of having another baby with Down syndrome after you and your spouse have already had one is 1 in 100. This represents an increased risk for mothers who are under 40. (The risk in the general population does not approach 1 in 100 until approximately age 40.) After the age of 40, the probability of having a baby with Down syndrome increases markedly for all mothers, regardless of whether they have already had one baby with Down syndrome. These figures apply to families with a child with nondisjunction trisomy 21, or roughly 95 percent of all families with a child with Down syndrome.

It is unclear why younger mothers who already have one child with Down syndrome have this increased recurrence risk. Some scientists theorize that there are genetic factors that predispose some mothers to nondisjunction. It is also possible that the recurrence risk is higher in some couples due to *germline mosaicism* in either the mother or the father. That is, perhaps one parent has some reproductive cells (egg or sperm) with the normal number of chromosomes and some cells with trisomy 21, even though he or she does not have Down syndrome. In other words, it may be that only some couples actually have an increased recurrence risk, while others continue to have the same risk as other parents their age.

For families who have a baby with translocation Down syndrome, the risk of recurrence is also about 1 in 100, unless one of the parents has a balanced translocation, as explained above. If a parent has a balanced translocation, the risk of recurrence is significantly higher than in the general population. In this case, the risk of recurrence depends on the type of translocation and the sex of the carrier parent. If the mother is the carrier, the risk is about 1 in 10; if the father is the carrier, the risk is about 1 in 20.

To find out exactly what type of Down syndrome your baby has, ask your geneticist. He or she can tell from looking at your baby's karyotype and will counsel you accordingly. If necessary, your chromosomes can be tested to determine whether or not you carry a balanced translocation. If you do have a balanced translocation, there is a chance that your other child/children might be balanced carriers as well. They may therefore want to seek genetic counseling when they begin to think about starting families of their own.

There is no need for parents or their other children to have their chromosomes karyotyped unless their baby has translocation trisomy 21. In the event a prospective parent does have a balanced translocation, assisted reproduction procedures have advanced to the point that it is possible to screen fertilized eggs for Down syndrome and other chromosomal problems, if desired, before attempting to implant them.

** Prenatal Tests to Detect Down Syndrome

Perhaps you are reading this section because you are pregnant, and a prenatal test has shown that your baby is at increased risk of having Down syndrome. Or perhaps you are pregnant or thinking of getting pregnant, and a doctor has recommended prenatal testing to you. Then again, perhaps you have already had one baby with Down syndrome, and you want to know how you can monitor any future pregnancies to determine whether you are carrying another baby with Down syndrome.

In any of these cases, you need to know what tests are available, how accurate they are, and what the risks associated with them are. This information may be very useful even for parents who have made up their minds that they will welcome any baby into their family. A prenatal diagnosis of Down syndrome has enabled many parents:

- to educate themselves about the nature of Down syndrome;
- to make contact with other parents or support groups in their community who can help them learn about Down syndrome and adjust to the diagnosis;
- to arrange for the proper medical personnel to be present when the baby is born (for example, if he is known to have a heart defect);
- to find out about early intervention and other supportive services available in their communities; and
- to emotionally prepare themselves, their friends, and family for their baby's birth.

Screening Tests

In the United States, it is standard procedure to offer all pregnant women screening tests to determine whether their fetus has an increased chance of being affected by Down syndrome or other disorders. Doctors usually use these tests to determine who should be recommended for additional diagnostic prenatal testing. Screening tests are not in and of themselves 100 percent accurate in detecting the presence of Down syndrome.

The types of screening tests commonly used are maternal blood tests and ultrasound. Although the American College of Obstetricians and Gynecologists (ACOG) now recommends that all pregnant women have both of these tests during the first trimester, women are free to decline all testing or to choose to have just one or the other of the screening tests.

Blood Tests

There are several prenatal blood tests that can detect fetuses that may be at higher risk for certain birth defects such as Down syndrome and neural tube defects (spina bifida). A quadruple screen is the one that gives the most accurate estimate of the chances that a fetus has Down syndrome. This is a simple maternal blood test that measures four things called alpha-fetoprotein, human chorionic gonadotropin, unconjugated estriol, and inhibin-A. Alpha-feta protein (AFP) is a protein produced by all fetuses during pregnancy. This protein is produced by the fetus and is spilled into the mother's blood and the amniotic fluid. A low level of AFP in the mother's blood can indicate the possibility of Down syndrome, and a high level can indicate spina bifida. AFP is thus called a *marker*. By measuring the amounts of four different substances in the mother's blood, doctors can get a more accurate estimate of the likelihood that the fetus has Down syndrome or another congenital disorder.

The quadruple test is offered to pregnant women between the fifteenth and twentieth week of gestation and is most accurate when given between sixteen and eighteen weeks of gestation. Remember, however, that the quadruple test is not a diagnostic test. It is only a screening test designed to calculate the probability of having a baby with certain genetic disorders. The screening test can alert the mother and her doctor that the baby is at an increased risk for a genetic disorder or it can reassure them that the baby is at a lower risk for these conditions.

When doctors calculate the results of blood screen tests, they take into account many factors, including gestational age, maternal smoking, chronological age, and the presence of two or more fetuses (twins or higher). If the results are outside the normal range, the physician frequently uses an ultrasound to verify the fetal age and to look for any anatomic abnormalities. If results of the blood test indicate that the risk of carrying a baby with Down syndrome is higher than average, considering the mother's age, an amniocentesis is recommended (see next page).

Because the quadruple test is a screening test, there is a chance of getting a false-positive test result. This means that test results suggest a possible genetic disorder when in reality there is none. False-positive test results are increasingly likely as the mother approaches age forty. False-positive results can be quite stressful and lead to unnecessary invasive testing, such as amniocentesis. Also, false-negative results can occasionally be wrong. This means that test results do not uncover an existing genetic condition. Many women have gone on to deliver perfectly healthy babies after a positive screening test, and others have gone on to deliver babies with Down syndrome after a negative test.

The accuracy of the quadruple test is approximately 86 percent. (Note that as this book went to press in 2008, there were reports that a new, more accurate blood test would be available shortly. If you are reading this in 2009 or later, your physician will undoubtedly have information about this new test.)

Ultrasounds

A pregnancy ultrasound is a method of visualizing the fetus and the mother's pelvic organs during pregnancy. It is considered to be a safe, noninvasive, accurate, and cost-effective way to examine the fetus. It has become a very useful screening and diagnostic tool, playing an important role in modern obstetrics and the care of every pregnant woman. The ultrasound machine sends out high-frequency sound waves. The information from the waves that bounce back off the body structures is gathered to create a picture on a monitor.

Prenatal ultrasound is widely used during pregnancy to assess the well being of the fetus, estimate gestational age, detect twins or higher multiples, assess the fetal heart, monitor growth, or screen for abnormalities. Fetal ultrasound is also recommended if results from a quadruple screen are outside the normal range.

Research has shown that fetuses affected with chromosomal disorders may have a skin fold at the back of the neck that is thicker than usual (increased nuchal translucency) and an underdeveloped nasal bone. During the first trimester, physicians can use ultrasound screening to measure the nuchal translucency by calculating the amount of fluid underneath the skin along the back of the baby's neck. Measurements that are more than 3 millimeters may indicate the presence of Down syndrome or another chromosomal disorder. This type of testing requires highly experienced sonographers and sophisticated high-resolution scanners and equipment. Current research in prenatal diagnosis and sonography is studying whether an underdeveloped nasal bone in the first and second trimesters can also be used as a marker and a screening tool for Down syndrome.

The majority of women who obtain an ultrasound during pregnancy (about 95 percent) receive normal results. If results are questionable, mothers can elect to have one of the prenatal tests discussed in the next section.

Prenatal Tests

In addition to the screening tests that are recommended for all pregnant women, there are also two highly accurate, but more invasive prenatal tests: amniocentesis, and chorionic villi sampling (CVS). Percutaneous blood sampling (PUBS) is also occasionally used. These prenatal tests are used to determine a fetus's chromosomes during pregnancy.

Until recently, these tests were routinely offered only to mothers over the age of 35. This is because at age 35, the age-related risk of having a baby with Down syndrome outweighs the risk of miscarriage or other major complications due to having the prenatal testing done. The ACOG recommendation is now that women of all ages should have the option of having these tests performed. Again, it is still a woman's right to refuse these tests, and a physician's obligation to respect the woman's decision about prenatal testing.

Amniocentesis

Amniocentesis is typically performed between fifteen and seventeen weeks of gestation, either in a doctor's office or in a hospital. Before the procedure, the doctor performs an ultrasound scan which shows the location of the uterus, placenta, amniotic fluid, and fetus. During the procedure, a very thin needle is inserted into the uterus through the mother's abdomen. A small amount of amniotic fluid is drawn out and analyzed. Because the amniotic fluid contains cells from the fetus, doctors are able to thoroughly examine the cells and count the chromosomes to determine whether the baby has Down syndrome or any other chromosomal disorder. The results of amniocentesis are highly reliable. It generally takes about twelve to fourteen days to obtain results.

Since its introduction in the late 1960s, amniocentesis has been performed during hundreds of thousands of pregnancies. Although amniocentesis is a very safe procedure and is almost considered to be routine, a small percentage of complications have been reported. These include miscarriages (less than 1 in 200), cramping, and bleeding.

Chorionic Villus Sampling (CVS)

Chorionic Villus Sampling (CVS) is a prenatal procedure that is done in the first trimester between ten and eleven weeks of gestation. Although a newer procedure than amniocentesis, CVS is considered to be safe and accurate when it is done by an experienced physician and when the tissue is analyzed by a laboratory with expertise in handling the sample.

As with an amniocentesis, the procedure begins with an ultrasound to look at the woman's anatomy and the location of the fetus. Then a thin needle is inserted either through the abdomen or through the vagina, and a small piece of chorionic villi (the projections of tissue from the placenta) is obtained. Because cells from the villi are fetal tissue, they can be cultured for their chromosome content in one week to ten days. Occasionally, there can be difficulty making a diagnosis with CVS due to "confined placental mosaicism"—mosaicism that is seen only in the placenta but not in the fetus.

CVS is slightly more likely than amniocentesis to be followed by miscarriage or other complications such as infection, bleeding, and leaking of amniotic fluid from the vagina. Because very early CVS has been linked to a few instances of limb anomalies such as missing fingers or toes, CVS is not done before ten weeks of gestation.

Percutaneous Umbilical Blood Sampling (PUBS)

PUBS is a procedure in which a blood sample is taken from the umbilical cord while the fetus is still in the uterus. PUBS is not a routine test and is considered to be invasive. It is mostly used for rapid chromosome analysis or to evaluate fetuses at risk for certain blood disorders. The results from PUBS are very accurate, but the procedure carries a risk of miscarriage. It is done late in pregnancy; usually after eighteen weeks of gestation.

The Parents' Role in Prenatal Testing

Which particular diagnostic test to use depends on personal preference, the available expertise in your area, and your medical history. Your doctor should be able to guide you to the appropriate procedure.

Although prenatal tests may permit you to learn the chromosomal makeup of your baby early in pregnancy, it is your decision as to whether to pursue this testing. All forms of prenatal testing for Down syndrome must be voluntary. Doctors are required to discuss options for prenatal testing with their patients, but they should remain objective about the pros and cons of such testing. The same holds true if tests show the presence of Down syndrome. Ideally, your doctor will help you find the information you need— perhaps by referring you to a geneticist or by helping you find a family who has been in your position. If not, you should seek out such information for yourself. (See the Resource Guide for organizations and Internet resources that can help you find information and support.)

It is very important for parents to understand that in seeking prenatal testing, they are under no obligation to terminate a pregnancy in the event a genetic diagnosis such as Down syndrome is made. Of course, the most intimate personal decisions are involved, and this book does not presume to recommend to you what to do about prenatal testing and diagnosis.

▪▪ The History of Down Syndrome

Well before the genetic link to Down syndrome was discovered, John Langdon Down, an English physician, described the condition as a distinct set of characteristics. In 1866, he distinguished Down syndrome from other conditions by noting some of the common features associated with it, such as straight, thin hair, a small nose, and a broad face. Down is also responsible for naming the condition "mongolism." This and other derogatory labels are no longer commonly used today, although some people still need to be reminded that Down syndrome does not refer to someone who is unhappy or inferior. It seems that too few people realize that Down syndrome is named for the man credited with first describing it.

In the twentieth century, advances in genetic research helped scientists begin to understand the cause of Down syndrome. By the early 1930s, some researchers began to suspect that Down syndrome might be caused by a chromosomal abnormality. In 1959, Jerome Lejune, a French geneticist, discovered that cells grown from individuals with

Down syndrome had an extra chromosome. Later, researchers determined that the extra chromosome was the twenty-first. These findings led to the discovery of the other forms of Down syndrome, including translocation and mosaicism.

Currently, scientists all over the world are conducting research into Down syndrome in hopes of developing treatments for Down syndrome. For example, in fall 2007, the National Institutes of Health (NIH) announced a ten-year research plan to advance understanding of Down syndrome and accelerate the development of new treatments. Among NIH's research goals are to study the aging process in Down syndrome, to better understand the genes that play a role in developing Down syndrome, and to develop a computer program to help people with Down syndrome learn. Other centers, such as the Center for Research and Treatment of Down Syndrome at Stanford University, are using mouse models to try to understand how genes contribute to intellectual and other disabilities in Down syndrome and to develop treatments for these effects. (A mouse model is a mouse that is specially bred to have characteristics similar to a person with Down syndrome.)

The medical treatment of people with Down syndrome has also advanced remarkably over the decades. Life spans have increased dramatically. In 1929, the average lifespan of a person with Down syndrome was nine years. Currently, the life expectancy is hovering around age sixty and will likely continue to rise with advances in medical care.

Educational opportunities for people with Down syndrome have also improved markedly. For years, children with Down syndrome were thought to have little potential to learn. Denied the opportunity to learn, they seemed to confirm society's mistakenly low estimation of their abilities. Since 1975, however, U.S. law has guaranteed children with Down syndrome a public education. And since about 1990, they have been increasingly taking their places in the same classrooms and schools as their siblings and neighborhood friends. Chapter 7 describes the educational and therapeutic programs available to children with Down syndrome from birth on. Thankfully, today's world is very different for children with Down syndrome than it once was.

■■ Conclusion

It is vital that you learn as much as you can about Down syndrome. Many books about Down syndrome, disabilities in general, and special education are available. But be careful: avoid books that are outdated. Also avoid Internet websites where the source of the information posted there is not clear. The Reading List at the end of this book contains a list of useful current publications. In addition, many of the organizations listed in the Resource Guide in the back of this book can direct you to useful materials.

Down syndrome has its own language. Understanding the terms used in connection with your child's care and development is important for good communication with doctors, teachers, and other professionals. The glossary at the end of this book will help. You will be surprised by how fast you will become an "expert" in Down syndrome and by how much a good understanding of Down syndrome will help you and your child.

∎∎ Parent Statements

We were really surprised to find out how common Down syndrome is. We thought it was just women over 40 who gave birth to babies with Down syndrome.

❧❧

When Josh was born, we wanted to pick up as much information as possible, as quickly as possible. Of course the biggest question is the one they can't answer: "What's causing this? How does Down syndrome make him the way he is?"

❧❧

I'd never known a child with Down syndrome, but my husband knew a family who raised their daughter with Down syndrome at home and he has followed her progress for many years. She is now about fourteen and does very well. Also, we had good information. We had a geneticist who explained the need for early intervention right from the beginning.

❧❧

We had talked about adopting a child with Down syndrome probably a year and a half before our daughter was born. I think we thought about it so hard we split a chromosome.

❧❧

My image of what Down syndrome was before our son was born was not very clear. I remember there was a boy with Down syndrome who lived in our neighborhood before Christopher was born, and he perplexed me because he seemed able to get about by himself, but he still looked like he had a mental disability.

❧❧

I knew the incidence of Down syndrome for mothers my age was about 1 in 600. That meant it wouldn't happen to me, right? Now I tend to think that when someone says to me there's a 1 in 600 chance, it's like saying, "Well, there's a great possibility that it will happen."

❧❧

It took me five years and tens of thousands of dollars in infertility treatments to get pregnant. So, even though I was 36 and knew I had an increased risk of having a baby with Down syndrome, I didn't have an amnio. I figured that, statistically, I was much more likely to have a miscarriage as the result of the amnio than I was to have a baby with Down syndrome. So much for playing the odds! The second time around, I didn't care about the risks of prenatal testing and had CVS as early as possible. The baby didn't have Down syndrome and I didn't have a miscarriage. I'm still not sure what we would have done if our second baby had turned out to have Down syndrome, too.

ঙ৻৻৽৽

Before Kevin was born, an ultrasound indicated "soft markers" for Down syndrome. (The ratio of the length of the top of his leg bone to the bottom of his leg bone was in the borderline normal range.) We had the amnio because we just didn't want to worry for the rest of our pregnancy. But after I had the test, the doctors and nurses we talked to would wait and stare as if they were waiting for us to say something. We didn't know they were waiting for us to say we were going to have an abortion. We were so naïve; that was never our intent.

ঙ৻৻৽৽

I had a couple of ultrasounds during my pregnancy, and they never picked up on anything the least bit unusual.

ঙ৻৻৽৽

I worked with kids with disabilities before our child was born. I just loved the kids with Down syndrome. I liked being with them and I liked their vivaciousness and just lots of things about them.

ঙ৻৻৽৽

The geneticist who examined our baby in the hospital was as upbeat as possible in pointing out the possible signs of Down syndrome to us—low muscle tone, head shape, up-slanting eyes, curved little fingers, a space between the first and second toes. But he left open the possibility that she really didn't have it, so we kept hoping that the results of the blood test would come back negative. But then the karyotype came back and we could see a picture of the extra chromosome, and there was no disputing it.

ঙ৻৻৽৽

Our baby has the most interesting, beautiful eyes. The Brushfield spots look like little copper stars sprinkled across the blue.

❧

The best way I can explain low muscle tone is that when I pick my baby up, she doesn't feel as tightly bundled together as other babies. She feels heavier because she isn't doing as much of the work of holding up her own arms and legs, but lets them dangle more.

❧

I know a lot of women who are well into their thirties. One of them was pregnant and close to forty. She was having her first baby, and was having prenatal testing. She came and asked me for counsel. I don't like to get into the abortion issue, but I was just real candid about the fact that our child is the joy of our lives. She's brought such an added dimension to our lives. She's not a liability; she's a definite asset.

❧

I think obstetricians are afraid of being sued, so they feel that it's in their best interest to urge parents to do the prenatal screening tests. That way it's not their "fault" if the test shows Down syndrome but the parents continue the pregnancy. Unfortunately, most OB/GYNs don't seem to have any training in supporting parents who get a positive result. It seems pretty irresponsible of the professional organizations to actively recommend testing without making sure that doctors are prepared to deal with the emotional repercussions.

❧

After Hope was born with Down syndrome, a few people had initial reactions along the lines of, "Oh, so you didn't have prenatal testing?" The implication was that we wouldn't have had our baby if we'd known in advance. I thought that was incredibly rude to imply.

❧

Right after the playwright Arthur Miller died in 2007, I read an article that revealed how he'd had a child with Down syndrome but never publicly acknowledged him. In fact, Miller had put his infant son in an institution and only rarely saw him. (Apparently, the baby is now a grown man, has a job, and is doing quite well, despite his father's ignorance and callousness.) So, even though we're now in the twenty-first century, there are still ordinary people—even quite well-educated ones!—walking around with terribly backwards ideas about people with Down syndrome. It's really shocking.

❦

After Sam was prenatally diagnosed, we saw a genetic counselor. It was helpful for us, but we had a most wonderful doctor. I can imagine that consulting a geneticist wouldn't be so good if the doctor wasn't a very compassionate and caring person.

❦

We were lucky because I was in the special education business. I had friends who had friends who could immediately refer me to knowledge-able parents and doctors and good books and websites. I think that a lot of parents don't know where to go for support and information at first.

❦

After we got the prenatal diagnosis, we felt a lot of pressure from the doctor to make up our minds quickly—when in reality, we had weeks to decide whether to keep our baby. It was almost as if the doctor didn't want us to have time to think. He told us several times how many parents decide to "terminate"—as if that should be the deciding factor for us. When I think about everything we would have lost out on if we had let this ignoramus tell us what to think, I still get all shaky inside.

❦

Genetic counseling was helpful to both my husband and myself. We went to counseling a few weeks after our daughter was born. Our genetic counselor was terrific at explaining what Down syndrome is and what we could expect in the next year with our baby. She gave us a starting point and much-craved information that we were able to share with our family and friends.

❦

The Internet helped us tremendously in learning about Down syndrome. I really didn't find a lot of misinformation. Most of what I researched was on mainstream-type websites for national organizations and it was very helpful. I now provide content for a website for our local Down syndrome association.

❦

If anything, there is too much information on Down syndrome out there on the Internet. You could spend years trying to read it all instead of getting out and meeting other parents who have kids with Down syndrome. Yes, I do use the Internet to gather information, but I mostly go to a few trusted sites. Plus, I belong to some listservs where I can ask questions and interact with other parents online. After a while, you get a sense of who knows what they're talking about.

≈≋≈

When my baby was first born, I thought of Down syndrome as a single monolithic thing that would alter my daughter's life in very predictable ways. But now that I've gotten to know other kids with Down syndrome, I can see that there is a huge range in what it means for any given child. I've been to a few national Down syndrome conventions and watched hundreds of people with Down syndrome and their families and they're all different and the kids are all their own little person.

≈≋≈

You learn day to day. I imagine we'll always be learning something new about our baby and what she can do. And you have to educate doctors, friends, and neighbors. We're still kind of new in this neighborhood. A lot of the neighbors are real interested, and that's nice, but it's a constant education process.

≈≋≈

When I look at my little boy and see how he takes my existence so absolutely for granted, it's impossible to imagine my not being there for him. It's not so much that he's mine, but that I'm his. He has no concept of belonging to me less than his sister just because he has Down syndrome.

■■ References

Capone, G.T. (2001). Down syndrome: Advances in molecular biology and the neurosciences. *Developmental and Behavioral Pediatrics 22:* 40-59.

Cronk, C., Crocker, A.C., Pueschel, S.M., Shea, A.M., Zackai, E., Pickens, G., & Reed, R.B. (1988). Growth charts for children with Down syndrome: 1 month to 18 years of age. *Pediatrics. 81 (1):*102–110.

Dutta, S., Nandagopal, K., Gangopadhyay, P.K., & Mukhopadhyay, K. (2005). Molecular aspects of Down syndrome. *Indian Pediatrics 42:* 339-44. (www.indianpediatrics.net.apr2005.339.pdf)

Gardner, R.J. & Sutherland, G.R. (2004). *Chromosome Abnormalities and Genetic Counseling.* 3rd edition. New York, NY: Oxford University Press.

Jorde, L., Carey, J., Bamshad, M., & White, R. (2005). *Medical Genetics.* Updated edition. St. Louis, MO: Mosby.

Lubec, G. & Engidawork, E. (2002). The brain in Down syndrome. *Journal of Neurology 249:*1347-56.

Morris, J.K., Mutton, D.E., & Alberman, E. (2002). Revised estimates of the maternal age specific live birth prevalence of Down's syndrome. *Journal of Medical Screening 9:* **2-6.**

Myrelid, A., Gustafsson, J., Ollars, B., & Anneren, G. (2002). Growth charts for Down's syndrome from birth to 18 years of age. *Archives of Disease in Childhood 87 (2):* 97-103.

Nussbaum, R., McInnes, R., & Willard, F.W. (2004). *Thompson & Thompson's Genetics in Medicine.* 6th edition. Philadelphia: Saunders Publishing Company.

Obstetric Ultrasound website. Measurements for Down syndrome. www.ob-ultrasound.net/xdown.html.

Roizen, N. & Patterson, D. (2003). Down's syndrome. *The Lancet. 361:*1281-1289.

Adjusting to Your Baby

Marilyn Trainer

It is painful beyond belief to be told that your precious new baby has Down syndrome. Instead of feeling that special sense of joy, you may feel as if your world has been turned upside down. Most likely, you didn't care whether you would have a girl or a boy—you just wanted a healthy baby. But it seems the baby you expected has not arrived.

Your baby has Down syndrome. And you may have another kind of syndrome: "Why Us?" It is a syndrome that strikes many families who have a child with Down syndrome.

It can't be real, you think. Something like this happens to other people—you hear or read about it all the time—but to us? It cannot be true; someone has made a mistake. That's it, isn't it? A mistake?

It may feel as if a stark, impenetrable wall has dropped from somewhere and with terrible force cut off the future, not only for the small, new baby, whom none of you yet really know, but for all of you in ways you cannot explain, but instinctively know are there. What you cannot grasp at this point, and are in no mood to think about anyway, is that the future you have been envisioning has been altered, no doubt about

it. There *is* a future, though, which, as it unfolds, can be life affirming and filled with a richness of spirit unimaginable to you now. Believe this, because it is true.

Right now you may well be in shock. In the minute or so after you first heard the term "Down syndrome," a strange, almost warm feeling may have enveloped you. Perhaps you feel as if you are sitting in a bubble; you can hear voices and you can respond to them. You may appear to be very calm. But somebody else is sitting in that bubble. The real you is outside, far above, watching and listening. The calmness is deceptive because you're trembling from head to toe. If you could just stay there above the bubble, if you could just stay there safe and untouched—but of course, you can't … and so reality begins.

This chapter addresses some of the many emotions that can go along with having a baby with Down syndrome and what you can do about these feelings. No one should tell you how to feel at this stage; there is no preprogrammed response to being told that your baby has Down syndrome. But eventually you will begin to notice all the little things that are just like any other baby—soft, warm skin, tiny fingers and toes, cries for Mom or Dad—and your need to care for your baby will take over.

❚❚ Your Emotions*

All kinds of emotions may well up at once: anger, despair, guilt, shame, rejection—yes, rejection of the baby—and perhaps most of all, as mentioned before, a terrible fear of the future. You wonder how, or if, you can cope with this overwhelming change to your life. I remember fantasizing about getting in the car alone and driving away. Where I would go, I had no idea—just away from it all.

---

* This section focuses on emotions typically experienced by parents after the birth of their baby. For insight into the range of emotions that often arise when parents are faced with a prenatal diagnosis and advice about coping with those feelings, please see the suggested readings listed for Chapter 2 in the Reading List at the back of the book.

Will life ever be even remotely light and carefree again? Will there always be a feeling of never-ending responsibility with no light at the end of the tunnel? Will there ever be laughter again or has the funny side of life been lost forever, along with happiness? In the days following the birth (or prenatal diagnosis) of a child with disabilities, many parents are haunted by these and other fears.

Grief

Often the first reaction to the news that your baby has Down syndrome is intense grief and sorrow. You may grieve the loss of that ideal baby you dreamed of or the loss of your family's "normalcy." You may not even know exactly why you are grieving. What you do know, however, is that sorrow sits on your chest like a ton of bricks. This sense of grief is, for parents who have received such shocking news, completely normal. And as with most parents, your grief will pass eventually.

But right now you may be feeling as if your heart will surely break. How could this have happened? How could it have happened to *you?* The unfairness of it is beyond comprehension. Worse, how will you face up to years of a responsibility that seems so totally overwhelming and one that you fear you cannot possibly handle? You may lie awake at night consumed with worry and if you do fall asleep your dreams may be so disturbing that you awake in panic. Are dreams any worse than reality, your tired mind may ask.

It is very easy at this point to let your grief rob you of the joyful feelings you can experience at your baby's birth. But remember this! You have achieved the miracle of life—your baby, alive and entirely trusting in you. Your love for your baby will grow spontaneously and will conquer your grief. Time is on your side.

Ego

Ego can be the biggest obstacle to accepting your child. Its interference is perfectly normal, and, as with other negative feelings, will diminish over time. I don't like to sound sexist here, but I have observed that men sometimes have a harder time with this than women, particularly if the baby is a son. But even these dads eventually come around and become crazy for their baby.

There is no denying that the birth or prenatal diagnosis of a child with an extra chromosome can be a tremendous blow to self-esteem. "How could we produce a child with a genetic abnormality?" some parents ask. "Other people have children with disabilities; we don't. It is simply not in our life plan. Along life's way, it may be that some of our own goals will not be met, but one thing is for sure: our children will be bright and beautiful and excel in all they do. When our children make it, we make it too."

One thing about Down syndrome, it does not discriminate. Rich or poor, average intelligence, brilliant scientist, ordinary appearance, movie-star gorgeous: a baby with Down syndrome can be born to anybody. From what I've noticed over the years, I would say that parents who have very high expectations—perhaps unrealistically high—for their children often have a really tough time of it. Raising a child whose intellect may not match their own seems truly overwhelming to them. But I would say to those parents—indeed, I would beg them—Give your baby a chance. Your love will grow naturally and you will realize your baby has true potential.

Children with Down syndrome work so hard to achieve. Rather than feeling a blow to your ego, you will feel tremendous pride at what your child accomplishes. It may take you awhile, but bide your time. It will be worth the wait.

Resentment and Depression

Parents often experience other painful emotions that they would consider less than noble. Jealousy, resentment, depression, and rejection are all common emotions in people who receive shocking news. You may resent parents with "normal" babies, begrudging them the joy you know they feel. You may even resent that they appear to take their baby's normalcy so much for granted. It can be especially difficult if others seem to treat the birth of your own baby as a catastrophe or a nonhappening. Instead of flowers sent to your room in the hospital, you may get silence or sympathy—no congratulatory cards or baby presents.

Years ago this was not uncommon; people simply didn't know what to say or do. Unlikely as it is now, if you should get such a reaction from someone, let it go. Today we live in much more enlightened times, for goodness sake, and Mom and Dad and baby deserve those cards and presents! Those who care about you—the ones who count anyway—know that. Enjoy the goodies that come your way!

Still, even though you wish you could feel unfettered joy over the birth of your baby, the pain may be intense. In a secret corner of your mind, you may even wish your baby would die. These feelings may strike you as contemptible. They are not; rather, they are your mind's way of coping with a situation you cannot fully grasp or control. Believe me, you are not the only parent who has grappled with such feelings. Again, I caution, time is on your side.

Anger

It is not unusual for some parents to feel a powerful anger and bitterness. Rarely is this directed at the baby. Rather, it is a lashing out at fate, circumstances, even God. "How could God do this to us when we've tried so hard to live by his commandments?" This sense of betrayal is no small anguish, but as time passes and parents allow themselves to learn about Down syndrome, they realize that raging against the supernatural is about as productive as raging against the extra chromosome that is the true cause of Down syndrome. "I'm going to get that blankety-blank chromosome and". . . what? . . . beat it to a pulp?

You may not like feeling angry and bitter, but in admitting these feelings you are being honest and realistic. And it is important to be realistic. In the long run your baby will be better for it.

If you are among those who feel anger, go ahead, be angry. But don't let that anger debilitate you and don't sit around waiting for miracles either. Create your own miracles by converting your anger into energy, and use that energy to seek and utilize every opportunity that comes your child's way. It's amazing what angry parents can accomplish when that anger is properly channeled. There is something you should keep in mind amidst the unsettling situation of this early period—and you are probably already aware of this, but it's important enough to be emphasized—as you live your daily life, you are going to be feeding, burping, and diapering a *baby,* not a condition.

Acceptance vs. Rejection

Some parents accept the news about their baby with calmness and equanimity. They may have questions, but don't seem overly concerned. To outward appearances, after their baby's birth, they are completely ready to gather him or her up from the hospital and go home. Only in the weeks or months following the baby's birth do they realize that they are going to have to become knowledgeable about Down syndrome if they want the best for their child. These parents of "the late wake-up call" often become very effective advocating not only for their own child, but for others with Down syndrome as well.

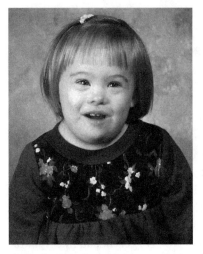

There are also other parents whose lifestyles, belief systems, or backgrounds truly enable them to have little or no negative feelings on hearing that their baby has Down syndrome. They may believe that a baby is a baby is a baby whose life they will enhance whenever possible and let the future take care of itself. These parents may choose not to have prenatal testing, or if they do and find that the fetus does, indeed, have Down syndrome, they opt to continue the pregnancy. It is their choice, their right to a choice. In my experience, these parents are a relatively rare breed. They are not denying the reality of the situation and they may not be jumping for joy, but they seem able to avoid the emotional turmoil that at least in part touches most of the rest of us.

Then consider the parents—and sadly there are a few—who either refuse to believe the diagnosis or who believe God will work a miracle and "take the Down syndrome away from our baby." They think Down syndrome has nothing to do with chromosomes, so they refuse to enhance opportunities for their baby's development; no infant stimulation, no early intervention, no participating in parent groups, no learning about Down syndrome—no consideration of the baby's future as a child with special needs because God will "cure it if it is His will." Months, even years pass; the parents wait for the miracle and the child loses precious ground that can never be made up.

I actually met a father like this, an authoritarian despot in my opinion, whose wife wanted to join our parent group and do right by her baby. He wouldn't let her. His attitude was that by trying to improve our babies' development, we were going against the will of God. To my way of thinking, this is a form of child abuse. (I have always hoped that his wife took the baby and left him.) Please note: Down syndrome of itself is not a tragedy, but there are those who can make it so.

Helplessness

To say that nobody gets through life without problems is as worn out a cliché as you'll hear, even if it happens to be true. Many a parent has stated that until the day they had a child born with Down syndrome there wasn't any problem that they hadn't been able to solve. Whether they avoided the problem, dispensed with it themselves, or waited until it was resolved over time, the problem eventually went away.

Down syndrome does not go away. When parents start thinking about this, they may feel very helpless and vulnerable. "How can we ever make it right?" "How can we fix it?" Obviously, nobody's going to "fix" it. But take heart, for as you read through this book you will find that where your baby is concerned, you will become anything but helpless. It may not seem possible now, but in a short while you will become knowledgeable about a multitude of ways to enhance your baby's development. You will probably also join with others to work for a brighter future for all people with Down syndrome. My husband, Allen, and I are by nature nonjoiners, at least as far as organizations are concerned. Who would ever have thought we would end up not only joining an active advocacy group but also founding one for parents of children with Down syndrome? We really surprised ourselves!

∷ How to Adjust

Address Your Emotions

Right now you may understand the term "emotional roller coaster" as you never have before. It probably never crossed your mind

that you would be riding this particular roller coaster, but here you are, like it or not. You are bringing a baby home feeling more than the usual newborn baby stress. The house is a mess, work responsibilities have fallen by the way, your other children need attention: there is always too much to do. Don't let the press of work prevent you from sifting your thoughts and emotions. Time spent on yourself now is essential.

Take Time to Adjust

You know best what you need to do first. Some people need to organize their lives. Others deal with their problems by jumping in headfirst. Still others need to be alone and withdrawn. Above all, take the time you need to adjust and recover. Don't make irreversible decisions immediately. You can't solve all the problems for your baby's life or your own life right away.

Don't Feel Personally Responsible

Do you torture yourself in the belief that you have somehow "given" your child Down syndrome? We have all heard of babies who are born with problems because of things mothers did or did not do during pregnancy. We've all read how drugs, alcohol, tobacco, poor nutrition, or lack of prenatal care can affect a baby. But Down syndrome is not caused by any of these. You are not personally responsible for your baby's extra chromosome any more than you are responsible for the last raindrops to fall in your neighborhood.

Underneath the feeling of personal responsibility is that old feeling of guilt that you are somehow at fault for producing a baby with Down syndrome. I remember dreaming, or maybe it was daydreaming, that somehow I should go back and "do it right." Have a "normal" baby.

Below the feelings of responsibility you may have feelings of guilt for rejecting this baby while longing for the baby that never was. It may hurt even more when you see or hear of a mother who didn't do everything "right" during pregnancy. Maybe she smoked, drank too many glasses of wine, or worse. Her baby turned out perfectly fine anyway. Your baby should have been born as fully endowed as any other baby. But fate or nature—call it what you will—cheated him or her, and in doing so cheated you too.

Quirks of nature or fate happen every day—often in worse ways than conceiving a baby with Down syndrome. You are no more responsible for your baby's Down syndrome than other parents are for their child's leukemia. So relinquish that guilt and put your energies where they are needed: in getting your strength back and helping your baby to reach his or her full potential!

Allow Yourself to Grieve

Perhaps right now all you want to do is cry. Spill all the tears you want. During the first few weeks of my son Ben's life, I was worried that

I would upset our three older children with my crying. So I would go take a shower and cry. My hair, of course, would become dripping wet and I was also dripping milk because I was still planning on nursing Ben, who had remained in the hospital. (Ben was not sick, but he was in a research program that required that he stay in the hospital the first month of his life.) I might have been very sad in those days, but I was also very clean, and with all that dripping and rushing water, the kids never heard me.

In addition to spilling tears, rant and rave, if that is your way: you have the right to do that too. Or go somewhere to lick your wounds alone.

Whatever you do, there is something you should keep in mind: hardly a parent of a child with Down syndrome has not experienced this anguish. And although you may find it impossible to believe right now, almost all of those parents would tell you that, despite the initial heartache, they would choose to have their child again, a thousand times over. It's almost a sure bet that in not too many months you will be saying the same thing.

Sometimes old truths do well by us: let some time pass. You will laugh again. Your baby will see to that.

** What You Should Do

Get to Know Your Baby

This might sound utterly banal considering what you are experiencing now, but ask yourself whether you are thinking more about the baby or more about the baby's condition. (I touched on this before, but it is very important.) When you look at your baby do you see your child or do you see Down syndrome? Take your cue from a young Ben, who, when told he was "a living doll," replied indignantly, "I'm not a doll, dumb-dumb—I'm a person!" Not too polite, maybe, but

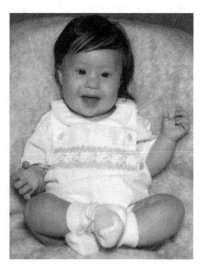

correct. That baby of yours is a person and as you come to know that little person, you will feel less grief.

As you take on the pivotal role of helping your baby to develop, wounded pride and bruised ego become irrelevant. As a matter of fact, expanded horizons often bring a mature kind of pride: pride in what your baby is achieving and pride in the part you play.

Tell Your Friends and Family

There is no doubt that one of your most difficult tasks is to break the news to friends and relatives, particularly grandparents. They may have grown up at a time when Down syndrome was considered in the most negative way. If so, they will feel hurt, just as you do, but may cast about for someone to blame, saying, "There's never been anything like this in the family before."

For example, it's not unheard of for grandparents to suggest that parents put their baby up for adoption. A few may ignore their grandchild, never mentioning the baby to friends, much less bragging about the baby as grandparents are wont to do. This attitude can be devastating to parents who are in a very vulnerable state themselves and are struggling to cope and to accept their child. But take heart, because grandparents with this mindset are fast fading into the past.

What you can do is give grandparents, aunts, uncles, brothers, sisters, and friends time to overcome their shock. Just as you needed some time to process the unexpected information, they need time to adjust as well. Their first reaction will probably not be their last.

Happily, today people with negative attitudes are in the minority. You must catch your breath, get your facts straight, and explain the situation in due time as forthrightly as possible. Give friends and relatives a book or a pamphlet to read that presents an accurate picture of Down syndrome. Or suggest that they visit the website of the National Down Syndrome Congress or National Down Syndrome Society (see the Resource Guide).

If they live nearby, by all means invite friends and relatives to come with you to medical appointments, or, once your baby starts early intervention, to sit in on therapy sessions. They may know absolutely nothing about Down syndrome or may have a distorted, outdated picture. Fortunately, people will take their cue from you and most will become sincerely interested and involved with you and your baby. A good number of advocates for children with Down syndrome are friends and relatives who have no children with special needs of their own.

With modern communications—email, blogs, voice messages, videos—it is easy to keep in touch with friends and family. You might want to keep those important to you up to date about your baby's progress, medical issues that might concern your baby, and yourself. Not only will you be giving out important information, but it will be therapeutic for you to actively do something on behalf of your baby.

It's possible that you may know a few people who may never "come around." They may always suffer from old myths and stereotypes, excess pity, or other emotions. These people cannot matter—you have more important things to do, more important people to care for, "darlings of your heart." Seek out those who will help you to cope.

Contact Other Parents

As stated previously, one of the very best sources of support is other parents of children with Down syndrome. Parent groups can be found in all parts of the country and throughout the world. Parents in the same boat can be tremendously helpful. Seek out an acquaintance, a small group, or an organization when you feel ready.

There are many ways to make contact. Call the national office of the National Down Syndrome Society or National Down Syndrome Congress and ask if there are any nearby chapters. You could also try calling your local chapter of the The Arc or Easter Seals, or your school system. Ask to speak with a staff member who works with parents of children with disabilities. These and other groups who can help are noted in the Resource Guide at the end of this book.

If you feel put off by the idea of suddenly becoming involved with an organization, be assured that parent-to-parent groups are usually small and informal, and no one is going to try to "recruit you." Tell them you need someone to talk to who can give you some basic information. Your greatest support will almost always come from other parents. No one is going to understand you better. It's just a phone call or email:

you have nothing to lose, and potentially a great deal to gain. Aside from gaining support and valuable information, many parents develop lifelong friendships with other parents because their children happen to have an extra chromosome in common.

You can also join Internet support groups (list services, mailing lists, etc.) to communicate with other parents "from a distance." These electronic support groups can be a tremendous source of information and advice, and you can usually find someone "listening" at any time of the day or night. If you don't feel like joining in at first, you can read what other parents have to say without posting any message of your own ("lurking"). Many parents these days get their strongest support through emailing other parents they may never even meet in person. However, a word of caution here. As with many situations, there are always those who would take advantage of parents who are seeking to do the best for their child with Down syndrome.

If you find someone on the Internet or right up the block who claims to have a "magic formula" to cure or greatly enhance the abilities of your child, watch out! Through the years there have been various therapies promulgated to "normalize" children with Down syndrome. Most of these have involved special diets with combinations of vitamins, proteins, off-beat foods, and supplements of one kind or another. (More than forty years ago, the "Retarded Grape" theory was briefly in vogue. The idea behind this was that those few grapes found withered on a bunch are that way because they did not get the proper nutrients, and that it is the same for children with Down syndrome. Somehow they did not get the proper nutrients or do not assimilate the nutrients they do get, hence, the disabilities associated with Down syndrome. Sorry, but I have never been able to visualize Ben as a grape!)

A point of interest: as an infant and toddler, Ben was in a research study run under the strict auspices of The National Institutes of Health. It was a double blind study (something the "Retarded Grape" researcher had refused to do) to determine whether a certain combination of an amino acid (tryptophan) could raise the serotonin level in the brains of children with Down syndrome, which in turn might enhance their intelligence level. The one overwhelming finding of this study was that children with cognitive disabilities who are stimulated from Day One definitely do better on every level than children who are not. It was not the medications that helped the children in the study; it was all the attention!

The bottom line is that if you come upon promises that sound too good to be true—on the Internet or anywhere else—check with one of the national Down syndrome groups to see what they have to say about it. Don't be hoodwinked by "anecdotal evidence."

Round Up Your Professionals

Get as much help for your baby as you can. When you have a baby without Down syndrome, you're often on your own. But when your baby does have Down syndrome, you will be surprised at the number of experts out there who can help you. In fact, some parents, after benefiting from the phalanx of professionals lined up to help their baby, say that they could use a little of this help for their other children.

Throughout the book we describe the different kinds of individuals who can help your baby, along with what they do. They include education professionals, therapists, and a wide variety of doctors. There are pediatricians, cardiologists, internists, geneticists, ear, nose and throat specialists, and ophthalmologists. Each plays a key role in screening your baby for possible problems and in helping ensure that he stays healthy.

You may find it helpful to use one doctor to coordinate the medical services your child might need. A doctor at one of the many Down syndrome clinics around the country who specializes in Down syndrome and other chromosomal conditions can be very helpful as a coordinator and information source. Ask your pediatrician, hospital, or obstetrician to refer you and your child. Nurses who work on the maternity floor are often up to date on Down syndrome information. A friend of mine is a neonatal nurse and the mother of Ben's best friend, who also has Down syndrome. She has greatly helped numerous parents of new babies with Down syndrome, as you can imagine.

This is highly unlikely, but be prepared in case a doctor expresses outdated negative and inaccurate information. Unbelievably, there are a few who still recommend institutionalization or inaction or who express horribly negative outlooks. (No excuse for this.) If your doctor is negative, change doctors. Parents are sometimes frustrated in trying to find a doctor who cares, but good doctors are out there. The search is worth the effort. Other parents are your best source of references to doctors who are good with kids and families with Down syndrome. Shop around, be picky, and get what is best for your child and for you.

Introducing Your Baby to the World

Few of us can resist smiling at tiny new babies and their parents when we encounter them at the drugstore, grocery store, or the

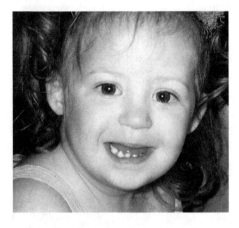

neighborhood park. Do you perhaps feel a bit leery about taking your baby out in public for the first time? Maybe someone will look at you "funny" or say something hurtful to you? It's an almost sure bet that the look you get will be a smile and the words you hear will be a comment on what a sweet baby you have. Most people will not recognize a baby with Down syndrome from any other baby and it wouldn't matter anyway. They only know a darling baby when they see one and your baby is that!

The more you and your baby go out and about, the more comfortable you will feel, and the more your fears about people staring at you will fade. Think of it this way: like any baby your baby gets to go places that are baby friendly: the park, the zoo, the swimming pool—maybe not a NASCAR race (not yet anyway) or a rock concert—but any place that is appropriate. Pick up and go and don't think twice about it!

There is something you should be aware of. It is not what other people may be thinking when they look at your baby, it is what you may be feeling. When Ben was six months old, we spent a week in West Virginia, at a cabin in the woods with a beautiful lake to swim in. One fine day we had set ourselves up on the sandy beach, the older kids jumping in and out of the water, thrilled and scared to see a water snake—just a really fun day. Ben was in his portable car bed/seat looking all around, content and happy. Allen and I were sitting next to him, watching the kids and relaxing, when I became aware of a family who had just arrived and was getting settled a few feet behind us. They had several children who made a beeline for the water and they also had a baby sitting up on a beach blanket.

The baby was about the same age as Ben and was very cute, and to all appearances, quite "normal." There was no dark cloud that came suddenly and covered the sun, but a cloud of sorts covered my heart when I looked at that baby. As I said, Ben was six months old. I thought I had gotten through the tears and pain—at least the pain that hurt the most. But I was wrong. Seeing that beautiful, typically developing baby on the beach and thinking how unfair it was that Ben wasn't the same really tore me up. I do not remember anything else about that vacation, but I remember that day on the beach in almost every detail, and the truth is, it still hurts in some kind of dim way—hurts, I would guess, for the person I was then. So I say to you, be prepared to be hurt now and again, but such a hurt will in no way diminish your life with your child. In fact, in a way it makes it more precious.

There is a phenomenon you should also be aware of and, in time, I guarantee you will experience it. This has to do with the built-in radar system that parents of children with Down syndrome are able to instantly use with one another almost at first sight. You might be at the mall, at the park, waiting in line somewhere and you see a child you recognize has Down syndrome. Immediately you look at the parent and if your own child is with you, there is almost instant recognition, a belonging, as if you've met before. Often there is a smile followed by conversation and even an exchange of names and phone numbers. Call it sisterhood, brotherhood.

What to do when your child is not with you and you see a parent with a child with Down syndrome? For this you follow your instinct. When I have been in this situation, I will compliment the baby or child and then quietly add that I have a son with Down syndrome. Usually the mother or father is interested and wants to continue the conversation. In the rare instances where someone looks at me as if I have crabgrass growing out of my head, I quickly turn and go about my business. There's no doubt that once in a while you will come across a parent who plain doesn't want to talk and will turn you off. But the overwhelming percent of the time you will find a parent who connects with you. It's an uplifting experience, even if you never see that parent again.

There is one thing I want to be honest about here. While it is true that your baby will garner smiles and admiration from strangers, sometimes an older child with Down syndrome—note, I said sometimes—will be scrutinized, and now and then in a rude and outrageous manner. I was once in a checkout line with Ben, who was standing quietly beside me minding his own business. A woman in front of us turned, spotted Ben, and stared at him with what I interpreted to be disdain or disapproval. Maybe the woman just had a face like a bulldog or a perpetual sneer, but I felt my hackles rise, or at least I think they were hackles. (What are hackles, anyway?) I put my arm around Ben's shoulders and stared defiantly back at her and she turned away. You should not worry about this sort of thing, though, because if and when it happens to you, by then you will be an old hand and able to handle it. Like me, you will become a tough cookie.

Remember, too, that today people with Down syndrome are everywhere in the community—going to school, attending movies, dining out, working at the neighborhood store. They are a part of the community, just as the rest of us are, as well they should be. Those who stare are the ones with the problem, not you and not your child.

Teach Your Baby Now

The importance of early intervention cannot be stressed enough. Neither can the fact that you can motivate your child better than anyone. Early intervention means parents and professionals beginning work with a child when that child is still an infant to help him or her reach the greatest potential. The typical developmental sequence of children is used as a guide. It's not just a matter of encouraging your baby to keep trying new and "harder" things, but to do them right. Early intervention requires professional help, but much of it can be done at home, and I will tell you without hesitation that good old common sense plays a role.

Under the law, your baby has a right to early intervention services, beginning at birth. Chapters 6 and 7 address some of the fundamentals of development and how important early intervention is for your baby. Chapter 8 explains your child's rights to early intervention and special education. At home, and with professional help, you can truly enhance your baby's potential.

The goal of early intervention is twofold: 1) to increase your baby's learning abilities every chance you get, and 2) to support families. There are learning opportunities everywhere in your baby's daily life, if you think about it. For example, a cat or a dog can be a great incentive for a child to move, or just to actively observe. We are a cat family—oh, are we ever. But none of our many cats was loved more than our ancient, diabetic cat, Diane The Fair, who as a frisky kitten enticed Ben to follow her—to roll, to hitch, to crawl, and then to walk, anything to catch up with her. To this day, Ben remembers Diane with love and affection, although she has been long gone.

Your brand new baby obviously is not going to be chasing the family cat. But a new baby can do exercises that strengthen muscles and improve tone, and can be introduced to playing games. Just remember that early intervention is crucial in the development of a child with Down syndrome and it should begin as soon as possible. But don't get nervous about it; work with professionals, use your common sense, and have fun with it.

Don't Despair

Above all, the experienced parent will want to tell you, "Don't despair." Don't even think of those things your child might not be able to do. At this point, there is almost nothing you can rule out of your baby's future repertoire. Focus on what your child can do now—all the better to help seemingly small achievements build toward future milestones.

It is important to keep your perspective and sense of humor. Minimize stress by having fun when you can. Get yourself a babysitter—a close friend might really enjoy the opportunity—and go out to dinner, a movie, whatever—regularly. A baby is a baby after all, and there's no reason yours won't be just fine with a reliable sitter. Babysitting is discussed more fully in Chapter 4.

∷ What about My Family?

Many parents ask whether a baby with Down syndrome will affect their other children. Chapter 5 addresses that question in detail, but the quick answer is a resounding yes! Siblings of babies with Down syndrome will most certainly be affected.

The day we brought Ben home from the hospital, I was sad, apprehensive, and plain scared. What was this going to mean for Doug, Ann, and Claire, who were ten, eight, and four at the time? They had so looked forward to the baby and then, to me, it seemed as if every-

thing had fallen apart. One thing was the same as when we had brought the other three home; we had the bassinet set up in our bedroom. So at Ben's homecoming, that's where he was placed, and the children gathered around to see their new baby brother. Baby Ben needed a diaper change, so I took off the wet diaper and was preparing to put on a fresh one when Ben let loose in a

beautiful streaming arc that hit the wall with uncanny precision and trickled on down. Those kids' eyes widened in undisguised admiration. "Wow! Look what he can do!"

Overcome by a tremendous sense of relief, I didn't know whether to laugh or to cry. It didn't matter in the least to my children that their baby brother had Down syndrome. In their eyes, he had performed a fantastic feat and was a wonder of a baby. They loved him and that was that.

Many years have passed since that wondrous and significant day, but none of us has ever forgotten it. Today that baby, our Ben, is a capable, high-functioning young adult, thanks in large part to his brother and sisters, who with each goal he achieved, said, "Wow! Look what he can do."

So yes, certainly the lives of your other children will be changed now and in the future because their sibling has Down syndrome. No one in life is immune to change, but children adjust to it surprisingly well. It becomes a natural part of their world. There may be times when they are annoyed, bothered, or even embarrassed by that pesky little kid with Down syndrome, but with good communication, understanding, and a lifetime of shared experiences, the deepest bonds will form. Chapter 5 discusses in detail the relationship of your baby and siblings.

It is no coincidence that many brothers and sisters who have siblings with Down syndrome grow up to be unreservedly compassionate and understanding human beings. Even during those tumultuous teenage years, youngsters who love and live with someone who has a disability exhibit insights about life—what is truly important, what is not—which their peers often sorely lack. Almost every brother and sister will tell you that their sibling with Down syndrome has enriched their lives beyond measure and they wouldn't trade him or her for the brightest, most beautiful child on the face of this earth. YOU'D BETTER BELIEVE IT!

‖ Your Work Will Pay Off

Kids with Down syndrome can do just about anything any other child can do. It might take them a little longer, but they can do it. As I stated before, they can learn to read, write, and use computers, and some parents report a positive genius in their children for reading logos and road signs that will take them to McDonald's or Pizza Hut. (Ben would be a great tour guide for this.) They have a persistence (and often excellent memories) that, with some delays, enables them to learn surprisingly much.

They play the piano, swim, ride horses, play basketball, baseball, and soccer, take ballet and figure-skating lessons—you name it. They do chores around the house, catch the school bus on their own, help the neighbor carry groceries, feed the family pet. And someday they will grow up, hold jobs, and be contributing members of society.

These things will happen. Your hard work with your baby and child will be rewarded. Just remember that your baby is first and foremost a child. And remember too that children with Down syndrome are more like typically developing children than unlike them. With your tenacity, encouragement, and—most of all—your love, that child is going to blossom.

While your child is growing and learning, so are you. If you gain nothing else, you will at least develop a point of view which might be somewhat different from the one you've held before. To some it will seem slightly askew, but it is nothing more than rejoicing at life's small victories.

I still remember the Sunday morning when we were all sitting around reading the paper, the kids on the floor browsing through the comics. Out of the blue, two-year-old Ben lost his temper, and, clearly enough to please Professor Higgins, shouted out, "Damn it! Damn it! Damn it!" And what do you think our reaction was to these less-than-proper words? Why, we all leaped to our feet, jumping up and down for joy, of course! Only hours later did we reflect that perhaps instead of jumping and celebrating Ben's increasing vocabulary we should have been saying, "No-no!" The truth is, we decided it was a whole lot better to hear him say a nice clear "Damn it!" than to not hear him say anything at all.

❖ The Future

As time passes, you will begin to look at your baby's birth very differently. Far from the grief and despair you felt at his or her birth, you will feel joy and pride. You will come to see the precious little baby you originally dreamed of, and Down syndrome will take on a different—and proper—prospective.

Many parents will tell you that if you are going to have a child with a disability, be glad it's Down syndrome. I don't want to sound like a Pollyanna here, but it's true. Compared to many other types of disabilities, Down syndrome can seem almost minimal. Children with Down syndrome are physically very capable, love and appreciate their families, and enjoy life in ways big and small. To my way of thinking, the emotional capabilities that almost all children with Down syndrome possess mitigate, at least in part, some of the difficulties usually associated with the syndrome.

Although the term "mental retardation" is falling out of favor, you will still hear it, and so it is important to note that the dictionary definition of the verb "to retard" is "to cause to move more slowly." Mental retardation (intellectual disability) does not mean "unintelligent," and those who think it does are often at a loss when they meet children with Down syndrome and find they do not fit their preconceived notions. Children with Down syndrome may have some limitations, but within those limitations they can be bright, inquisitive, and surprisingly erudite.

This was not always thought to be so. Perhaps no other group of people with developmental disabilities has been so stigmatized. Perhaps because of similar physical characteristics it has been easy to lump people with Down syndrome together and slap a label on them.

In the past, the diagnosis of Down syndrome was often a passport to an institution or a back room. (And let's be brutally honest here, the diagnosis was not termed Down syndrome—"Mongolism" was the operative word.) Sadly, these children then lived up to the dreadful images remembered from old biology textbooks or exposés of institutional life; they became victims of a self-fulfilling prophecy.

Today there is a new generation of children with Down syndrome who are leading very different lives. This is a generation of potential. Old stereotypes are fast being laid to rest. Your baby is of this new generation on which no one should be placing limits!

I must confess here that even the most experienced parent can be taken off guard by just how very perceptive and downright smart their child can be. For example, there was the time I took Ben to get his hair cut at the local Italian barbershop. We were waiting for Ben's turn when he suddenly stood up and at the top of his lungs—and dreadfully off key—started belting out "Figaro! Figaro!!" I didn't know whether to stare transfixed at the ceiling, deny all kinship and claim the quiet child in the corner as my own, or express the triumph I felt that Ben would and could equate grand opera with a happening in his own life.

The misgivings I felt about any possible ethnic misunderstanding, mixed with pride at Ben's perception, were dissolved when the barbers and patrons alike applauded as the impromptu performer climbed into the barber chair. How did Ben know about Figaro? It is true that I am an opera buff who listens to the Metropolitan Opera Broadcast every Saturday, if possible. And maybe at one time or another I explained something to Ben about the famous barber. But I really have no idea when or how he learned about Figaro. Which means I have no idea when he learned about other things too. The big lesson being: we should never underestimate these children of ours!

There is no getting away from it. Although generalizations can be as off with kids who have Down syndrome as with any others, the child with Down syndrome is often "the personality kid." Endearing, compassionate, exuberant, often stubborn, just as often mischievous, the child with Down syndrome has a genius for bringing out the best in people. Families who think they will never smile again find that life centers around their child in a joyous way they could not have dreamed possible when the baby was born.

When I think of the many youngsters I've known who have Down syndrome, the idea of "joie de vivre" comes to mind (the dictionary meaning is "a keen or buoyant enjoyment of life"). Again, I don't like to generalize, but from early childhood these kids have caught the meaning of that phrase. It enables them to get through life on a level the rest of us might envy. For one thing, they usually have no trouble accepting people just as they are. You don't have to be pretty, handsome, rich, or an outstanding athlete or scholar. You just have to be a nice person. This attitude goes a long way in explaining why people who have Down syndrome are able to make deep and long-lasting, indeed lifelong, friendships.

"Joie de vivre!" This ties in too with their knack for mischief making and just plain having fun, often at the expense of those of us who think we are "smarter."

One fine summer day when Ben was a toddler, he disappeared. One minute he was in the living room. The next minute he was nowhere in the house. The other kids went flying out the door to look for him, gathering other kids and their parents along the way. We live on a street that dead ends into woods, which made his disappearance even scarier. I headed for those woods and endured five minutes of pure and escalating panic before running back home to call the police.

By now the whole neighborhood was in an uproar, everyone running around calling Ben's name. "Ben! Ben! Where are you, Ben?!" Then, when I was really on the verge of losing it, my daughter Ann came rushing in to tell me that "Mrs. Larson's found Ben and he's OK!" I slammed the phone down and followed Ann to the neighbor's yard, two doors down, near the entrance of the woods. Sure enough, there was Ben behind a bush at the side of the house, holding one of our cats and grinning from ear to ear.

As our neighbor explained it, she had been making her second run past the bush when she heard giggles and peeked in to see Ben with the cat, laughing his head off at the commotion he was causing. I suppose this was one of those times when, as the saying goes, you don't know whether to kiss the kid or kill him. Ben was sorry, not for what he'd done

of course, but sorry that all the fun was over. He toddled home with me, the cat following, and there, waiting, were the police, two of them, and they had to make a full report. I felt like such a goofball.

Ben's escapade, though, impressed upon me, and not for the first time, what good neighbors we have and how many people care about him.

And how did the great escape artist get out of the house in the first place? We never found out. Ben and the cat weren't talking!

∷ Conclusion

Your baby has Down syndrome. It's a fact of her fresh little life and of yours. The birth of this baby has given a new challenge to your life, and, quite possibly, a new set of values as well. A different dimension has been added, partly frightening and partly sad, but also beautiful. You wish with all your heart that your baby had been born without Down syndrome; you wish it for the baby and you wish it for you. But you don't have time to dwell on that. Right now, above all else, your baby needs you. Someday, probably as you are giving a bath, spooning in the spinach, patting up a good burp, or even walking the floor in the wee hours, it will hit you how very much you need your baby.

∷ Parent Statements

I found out Amanda had Down syndrome right after she was born. The doctors were encouraging and gave me a little summary of what to expect. I remember they told me she'd be able to read. I was just so happy about having a baby that it didn't really hit me right away. I'd seen her when she was born and she was really healthy and everything.

⚜

My initial reaction was total shock, but soon after, I wanted information. What did this mean, what is going on, why? We realized we had to hold together for Abby, even though she was this minute-old baby. We felt that we had to put up a good front for other people who were going to take our lead on how we reacted and accepted her. We thought if we acted unaccepting, so would everybody else.

◆◆◆

We didn't want to tell anyone that our daughter might have Down syndrome until we had the results of the karyotype. So, the first few days she was home, we told people she was still in the hospital with jaundice. We didn't want anyone to come over to see her; we didn't want to have to put on happy faces when we were so worried. We almost got caught in our lie when my brother brought a casserole over for us. We hid the baby in the walk-in closet and then held our breaths, hoping she wouldn't cry and give us away. We had to be kind of rude to my brother to get him to leave right away.

◆◆◆

When the doctors told us that our son had Down syndrome, we both just felt as if the world had opened up and swallowed us right then.

◆◆◆

Initially my husband took the news harder than I did, but he rallied really well. I was disappointed, of course. I didn't want her to have Down syndrome. For a long time, when I would think about what her future might be like, I'd have a really hard time with it. But it never struck me as being a terrible tragedy. See, everybody was very accepting. They were very encouraging and told us how great it was we'd had our baby.

◆◆◆

We'd been told by several doctors, just on the basis of a quick examination, that Christopher probably didn't have Down syndrome. After we found out, the first things that came to mind were the worst images because we really didn't know anything about Down syndrome. We didn't know the mitigating factors.

◆◆◆

One part of me was extremely sad—I couldn't stop crying. And the other side of me wanted to be really happy and take Chloe for a walk and enjoy my new baby. It was a strange situation. Other people had a hard time because outwardly I looked really together and happy. Since then, some people have said to me that it was really weird. And it was.

❧

We thought it would be harder to tell people later. So we told everyone right away. The response from family and friends was just wonderful. They came to see us and showered us with everything under the sun. To us it really meant, "She's an important person and we're glad she's here." Because that's how we felt.

❧

When we first brought our baby home from the hospital, my husband didn't want to take any pictures of her homecoming. I didn't really feel like it either, but I insisted that he take some so we'd at least have some pictures to send to relatives. So, I managed a smile for the camera and held up our baby in her carrier. Now we're both really glad we have those photos because we love looking at her newborn pictures just as much as we love looking at her sister's.

❧

Everybody was just as nice as they could be when we told them the news. They didn't treat him or us weird. They didn't always know how to approach our baby, but I put myself in their position. I'd feel awkward too, so I wasn't offended.

❧

After my daughter's Down syndrome was confirmed, I called my sister to tell her the news. She said, "When you said you had bad news, I thought you were going to tell me something really awful, like that she has a fatal disease." That kind of put things in perspective for me.

❧

Most of our relatives have been very positive. With a couple exceptions, most of them have more than met our expectations and really looked on our son just like any other new relative. But one of Josh's cousins must have been told something negative about him because the child acted very different toward him. That hurt a lot.

❧

The first person we told about our daughter's Down syndrome reacted by saying, "Oh really?" My husband thought that was an inappropriate response. But really, what would an appropriate response be? You don't want someone to say, "That's terrible!" And you don't want them to say "That's great!" I truly don't know what I'd say if one of my friends had a baby with Down syndrome. You can't hold people's initial responses against them.

❦

After we got the news about our baby's Down syndrome, several people told me they thought I was a strong person who could handle this. I know they meant well, but they made me feel worse. I felt like they were minimizing the enormity of my problem—that they must think that finding out that your kid has Down syndrome is no big deal. But then again, I didn't want anybody's pity. For awhile, there probably wasn't anything people could have said that would have seemed "right" to me.

❦

When we found out we going to have twins—a boy and a girl—we thought we were going to have the perfect little family. Then when it turned out that our daughter had Down syndrome, it seemed like fate was laughing in our face for even daring to think that we were going to live happily ever after. We were crushed. After a while, though, we began to see the positive side of things. They could still be great playmates and friends, we realized, and our son could be a terrific model for our daughter to imitate. We would always know exactly where she stood developmentally by comparing her skills to his.

❦

The nicest times are when people treat Chris like any other baby. They say, "Oh, what a beautiful baby!" That makes me proud because he is a beautiful baby. One time we were in an airport and someone came up to us and said, "Down syndrome?" When I said yes, he said, "Wonderful children. I've got one myself." It was nice of him.

❦

Sometimes I have feelings of resentment. It's not against anyone specifically, but when I go to the store and I see a parent all concerned about some little thing about the kid's diaper not being on right, I feel like saying, "Come on, give me a break—save it for something really serious."

❧

We weren't particularly interested in why the cells didn't separate properly. We didn't really look back. Some people spend a lot of time asking "Why did this happen to me?" But we figured, he's here and he's got forty-seven chromosomes. Nothing is going to change that, so we may as well deal with him as he is.

❧

I think it made a big impact when people wanted to extend condolences to us and we came back at them very positive and optimistic. We let them know that it wasn't a sad moment for us and they kind of backed off with their condolences.

❧

My reaction now when I see a baby with Down syndrome is to think "Oh, how nice." But it makes me feel strange if people say, "Oh, they are wonderful children," because that is stereotyping. They aren't all wonderful all the time than any other children are.

❧

When our baby was born, some people initially acted like it was a tragedy. But I remember one guy who came in and he was all grins and congratulations and he shook my hand. It dawned on me that his reaction was different. He was reacting the way someone's supposed to act when you give birth to a child.

❧

It can take a long time to get used to other people looking at your child. But now that I've had another child, I realize that people look at any baby. They don't just look at your baby because she has Down syndrome. People stare at babies.

❧

I still have trouble telling people about my son. You know, I say "I have a child," and then I think, "Now do I have to tell them he has Down syndrome?" I don't want to introduce that to people I don't know.

❧

My daughter is going on two, and I still think about the fact that she has Down syndrome every day. I'll think, "Oh, she really looks (or doesn't look) like she has Down syndrome right now." Or, "I wonder if she's doing that because she has Down syndrome?" Or, "Wow—she seems so smart and inquisitive—how could she have Down syndrome?" I don't feel sad when I think these things, but I guess I haven't totally accepted her Down syndrome, either.

❧

My one neighbor had a little girl just about the same age as mine. I really had a hard time when that girl first sat up, when she crawled, when she walked. She was talking a blue streak in a year and that was really hard for me. It took me a long time to like that little girl—isn't that awful?

❧

One time someone I barely knew invited us to a new babies parent group that she'd just started. When I said Ethan had Down syndrome, she looked like she'd picked up a hot potato. She never got in touch with us afterwards. I always felt a bit bitter, but I thought she was pretty ignorant anyway to have that kind of reaction.

❧

I feel impatient with parents whose kids aren't quite perfect in some minor way. Like, people get all upset because their kid has an ear infection or because he needs glasses. When your kid has open-heart surgery and some other kid has a minor infection, you think, well, no big deal.

❧

Now that Chris is older, people ask, "How old is that lovely baby?" And I say "twenty months" and they say "ten?" And I say "twenty" and they say "oh." And then they say, "Can he say his name?" because he is so old. He doesn't walk yet and he doesn't talk well, so people notice. I don't feel embarrassed, just a little withdrawn.

❧

Initially we thought there would be a million decisions to make right away, but we found that the decisions were spread over a long period of time, like with any other child. The decisions aren't knocking at your door every day.

❦

I have an easier time sharing my concerns online with other parents than I do in person. You don't have to worry that you'll have to share more information than you want to, but if you do want to vent about something, you can always find a listening, sympathetic ear.

❦

When our daughter was about two months old, I started doing a lot of research on the Internet. One day I got into a chat room where the mothers were all talking about their teenage daughters and the different issues they were having with puberty. I swore I'd never go into another chat room again! Now I try to only go on websites that are run by reputable institutions or those that have been recommended to me by another parent, teacher, or therapist.

❦

My husband has never been that interested in the online listservs for Down syndrome, but I've found them to be a valuable source of information and, to a lesser degree, support. You have to watch out for controversial topics and just make up your mind to skip over the messages that get off topic or that you disagree with. I've evolved into the person in the family who usually goes online and asks questions about things we're both wondering about.

❦

We started going to a local parent support group when our baby was about nine months old. It was a good way to network and find out what kinds of early intervention services parents were getting in different parts of the county, and to compare notes about things like bottle nipples and sleeping problems and doctors.

3

MEDICAL CONCERNS
IN BABIES WITH
DOWN SYNDROME

Len Leshin, M.D.

▪▪ Introduction

One of the characteristics of Down syndrome is the variability in the way that medical problems affect babies and children with Down syndrome. With the presence of the third 21st chromosome in

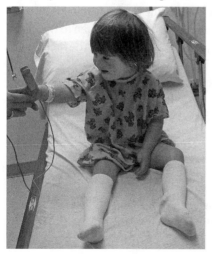

every cell, it is not surprising to find that every system in the body is affected in some way in people with Down syndrome. Parents of children with Down syndrome should be aware of these possible problems so the conditions can be diagnosed and treated quickly and appropriately. Therefore, the emphasis of this chapter is to outline conditions that parents of babies with Down syndrome may encounter.

If your baby has not yet encountered any medical problems, you may have some hesitation about reading this chapter. I certainly understand that a list of potential medical problems is scary to new parents. Please remember that not every infant or child with Down syndrome will have the same medical problems, and some have very few problems. It is in the best interest of your baby's health, however, that someone in the family be familiar with possible conditions so that you can identify any signs or symptoms and bring them to your doctor's attention.

‖ Heart Problems

Approximately 40 to 60 percent of all infants with Down syndrome have some type of heart defect. The most common defects are those of the septa, or walls, of the chambers of the heart. If the defect is in the wall between the upper chambers of the heart, it is called an atrial septal defect. If the defect is in the wall between the lower chambers, it is called a ventricular septal defect. These septal defects make up approximately 60 percent of the heart defects found in infants with Down syndrome. Occasionally the defect will involve the entire wall between the sides of the heart, and is called an atrioventricular canal or "AV canal." This type of defect occurs in approximately 35 percent of babies with the heart defects.

Some septal defects are mild and close on their own over several months. Other large septal defects, and the AV canal defect, require surgical repair. These defects are important to close, since if left untreated, the baby may have problems with too little oxygen to the body, fatigue, abnormal blood pressure, and even infection of the heart wall, which is called "endocarditis."

Other heart defects may occur in babies with Down syndrome but are far less common. One such condition is called a patent ductus arteriosus, or PDA for short. The ductus arteriosus is a blood vessel that carries blood from the right side of the heart to the aorta, bypassing the lungs, which is necessary in the heart of the baby before he is born. After birth, when the baby starts getting oxygen from his own lungs, the ductus arteriosus is no longer needed and is supposed to close down over the first three days of life. However, if this blood vessel stays open, then blood from the aorta goes backwards into the artery, going from the right side of the heart to the lungs.

Diagnosis and Treatment

While most cases of heart defects can be found during physical examination of the newborn, some babies with serious heart defects show no signs at all for weeks after birth. Because of this lack of signs and symptoms, it is recommended that every newborn with Down syndrome be evaluated with a sonogram examination of the heart, called an echocardiogram, soon after birth. The echocardiogram is much like the sonograms women have during pregnancy and is not painful. A sonogram may be done in the hospital before the baby goes home, or may be done in the doctor's office soon afterwards.

If your baby is found to have a heart defect, he will be evaluated by a pediatric cardiologist. This doctor will often need to look at the echocardiogram, chest X-rays, and an electrocardiogram (called an ECG or EKG) to evaluate the function of the heart. The ECG test requires placing several adhesive patches on your baby's chest. These patches are connected to wires that lead to a machine that measures the electrical activity of the heart. This test is painless and quick.

To decide whether or not an operation is necessary, the cardiologist may need to do a cardiac catheterization. This test involves inserting a small tube into a large blood vessel in your baby's leg and injecting dye into his blood system, which can help detail the specifics of the heart defect. If surgery is required, the cardiologist and a pediatric heart surgeon will explain what needs to be done and how the surgery needs to be performed.

Some children with heart defects need medication in order to keep the heart working efficiently. These medications may include diuretics, which keep fluid from building up in the body and overloading the heart, as well as medications that can improve the functioning of the heart muscle. How long a child needs the medications depends on the condition of his heart, but may be required for years or even throughout life.

Some heart defects are at risk for becoming infected, or developing endocarditis, even after being repaired. Children with these conditions will require a preventative dose of an antibiotic before medical or dental procedures that may put them at risk for exposure to the bacteria that cause endocarditis. If your baby has a heart condition, your cardiologist will inform you whether or not your child will need prevention for endocarditis.

If your children has a heart defects that puts him at risk for endocarditis, you must be alert to any infection that can lead to endocarditis.

If your child has such a defect, notify your doctor about any infection severe enough to cause a fever.

Any time a baby or child with a heart defect needs surgery, he should receive the surgery at a center that can provide optimal support. The center should include pediatric cardiologists, cardiothoracic surgeons, intensive care doctors, and skilled nursing staff.

Babies with Down syndrome who have heart defects have a very good recovery rate. Advances in surgical techniques over the last two decades have enabled many babies with heart defects to recover and live long, healthy lives.

▪▪ Gastrointestinal Problems

If your baby has trouble with spitting up, vomiting, poor feeding, or has difficulty having bowel movements, then he may have a disorder of the gastrointestinal, or "GI," tract. The GI tract includes the mouth, esophagus, stomach, and intestines.

Structural Defects

Babies with Down syndrome are more likely to have birth defects involving the GI tract. One defect is a partial or total block in the part of the intestine just beyond the stomach (the duodenum), which is due to improper formation of the GI tract during the pregnancy. These blocks are seen in 5 to 7 percent of babies with Down syndrome and require surgery to correct the problem. Babies who are born with this problem have vomiting which becomes more and more forceful in the first days of life.

Another defect that occurs more often in babies with Down syndrome is a connection between the esophagus and trachea, called a fistula. There can be several different types of these fistulas, all requiring surgery. A baby with a fistula frequently coughs during feedings, because when he swallows, formula or breast milk may move from his throat through the fistula and into his airway. Fistulas are diagnosed by having the baby drink a liquid that has barium in it, and then taking X-rays as the barium goes down the esophagus. This X-ray, called an "upper GI" test, shows the fistula. In severe cases, the esophagus does not connect to the stomach at all. This is called "esophageal atresia" ("atresia" means absence of a normal opening) and requires immediate surgery so the baby will be able to eat.

Reflux

A common condition in infants and children with Down syndrome is gastro-esophageal reflux (GER), meaning movement of stomach contents back up the esophagus. The cause is suspected to be due to decreased muscle tone at the point where the esophagus meets the top of the stomach.

This decreased tone allows stomach contents to move back up the esophagus, causing indigestion and spitting up or even forceful vomiting. Reflux can be diagnosed by the barium "upper GI" X-ray described above.

Reflux is a concern since it can cause chronic indigestion, which your baby may react to with frequent crying, or "colic." In severe cases, reflux may result in milk trickling into the airway. This can irritate the lungs and even cause aspiration pneumonia, which is infection of the lungs due to germs from the breast milk or formula.

If your baby is formula fed, you can reduce reflux by thickening his formula with cereal, since thickened formula refluxes less than regular formula. Breast milk does not thicken well with cereal, so doctors do not advise expressing breast milk to add cereal. Special positioning may sometimes help reduce reflux. This involves keeping your baby's head above his stomach, especially after a feeding. While these measures are enough to manage the reflux in some infants, often children need medications to control the reflux until they outgrow the condition.

Some infants have severe reflux that is not helped by thickening formula, positioning, or medication. If these children have problems gaining weight or frequent infections of the lungs from reflux, then surgical correction is required. The surgery involves tightening the upper part of the stomach around the lower part of the esophagus, an operation called a "fundoplication."

Constipation

Constipation, a very common problem in babies with Down syndrome, is also believed to be caused by decreased muscle tone of the intestinal tract. In many babies with Down syndrome, the intestine moves stool along the gastrointestinal tract more slowly, allowing extra water from the stool to be reabsorbed by the colon.

Constipation can sometimes be overcome through natural food laxatives such as juices or applesauce, but many babies require the routine use of stool softeners. Stool softeners are medications that increase the amount of water in the stool. Some stool softeners are available without a prescription, but you should always consult your doctor before using them. Laxatives, which are medications that stimulate the intestines to create a bowel movement, may be used occasionally, but are not recommended for longtime use. If used too often, the intestines tend to become dependent on the laxatives to have regular bowel movements.

Hirschsprung Disease

The biggest concern in the first weeks of life in children with Down syndrome who are chronically constipated is the possible presence of Hirschsprung disease. This condition, which is more common in infants with Down syndrome than other infants, is due to the lack of nerve cells in the part of the colon just above the rectum. This lack of nerve cells impairs the intestine's ability to move stool to the rectum and stimulate a bowel movement, causing severe constipation. If not diagnosed in a timely manner, the chronic constipation can cause the lower colon to stretch to the point that it becomes useless in moving stool at all.

Typically, babies with Hirschsprung disease do not have a bowel movement in the first 48 hours of life, while constipation shows up much later. When suspicions arise that an infant has Hirschsprung disease, a barium enema is performed. The barium enema is a special X-ray in which barium is introduced into the rectum via a tube, and then X-rays are taken to see how well the barium moves through the lower colon. If the X-ray shows any abnormalities, then a surgeon will biopsy the rectum to look for nerve cells. If there are no nerve cells, the diagnosis of Hirschsprung is made and the part of the colon without nerve cells must be surgically removed.

The traditional surgical treatment was performed in two stages: the first surgery attached the ending of the colon to an opening (colostomy) through the abdominal wall, allowing stool to be collected in a special bag outside the body, and then the rectum was reattached months later. More recently, many surgeons are removing the segment of colon without nerves and reattaching the good colon to the rectum in one procedure. Either technique solves the problem of constipation, though children without long segments of colon may need to be on special diets throughout life to avoid diarrhea and malnutrition.

Celiac Disease

The small intestine has many roles, one of which is to absorb nutrients from our food. Celiac disease arises when the lining of the small bowel becomes damaged from exposure to gluten, the protein found in wheat, barley, and rye. The small bowel becomes unable to absorb water and nutrients, causing a number of different symptoms.

Young children with Down syndrome have a higher risk of developing celiac disease than other children, though it still appears to be an uncommon occurrence. Babies are not at risk for developing celiac disease unless they have been eating one or more of these grains for several weeks.

Signs of celiac disease include failure to gain weight as expected, decreased appetite, bulky and foul-smelling stools, and in some cases, chronic diarrhea. Celiac disease is diagnosed by a biopsy of the small intestine, which involves inserting a tube down the child's throat while he is sedated. However, there are some blood tests that can determine whether a child is at risk for developing celiac disease or not. These blood screening tests look at antibodies that are elevated if celiac disease is a possibility. Whether or not children with Down syndrome should be screened routinely with these blood tests is still not determined. If you feel your child has any symptoms or signs that might indicate a problem in his GI tract, please talk to your pediatrician or a GI specialist.

Celiac disease is treated by removing all foods with gluten protein from the diet. While the gluten-free diet takes away many traditional foods in the cereal and bread group, many companies are now making tasty gluten-free food products.

▪▪ Umbilical Hernias

Many babies with Down syndrome are born with a gap between the muscles that lie just under the skin of the abdomen. This gap sometimes allows the belly button, or umbilicus, to protrude out. If the protrusion causes the umbilicus to appear large and swollen, this is called an umbilical hernia. This condition is not dangerous since nothing in the abdomen can become trapped in the hernia.

Most umbilical hernias go away by themselves in the first two years of life as the baby's muscles eventually grow together, closing the gap. If a large gap persists past your baby's second birthday, it can be closed by a simple surgical procedure. This surgery is not medically necessary, however.

▪▪ Epilepsy

A seizure is a sudden loss of control of the body by the brain. A sudden surge of electrical activity, in a pattern of no particular usefulness, takes over the brain for anywhere from one or two seconds to hours. There are several different types of seizures, but all of them interfere with the activity of the brain. When small children have seizures, they are usually of the type associated with fever. These seizures are short and rarely cause health problems or lasting side effects. However, if a child or adult has more than one seizure not associated with fever, then the condition is termed "epilepsy."

Epilepsy occurs in 5 to 10 percent of people with Down syndrome. The seizures tend to arise most often in two different age groups: the first two years of life and then in the late twenties. Epilepsy is diagnosed mostly by a history of seizures but also by the use of a test called an electroencephalogram, or "EEG." The EEG involves placing a cap with electrodes on the child's head and measuring brain wave patterns. The EEG is painless and is often done in a hospital or doctor's office. Children with epilepsy are typically diagnosed and treated by neurologists.

In babies with Down syndrome, the most common type of seizure is the infantile spasm, but other types can also occur. The infantile spasms commonly start between four and eight months of age and cause the baby's extremities and trunk to bend involuntarily in a forceful manner. Other seizures may involve rhythmic jerking of the arms or legs or even a sudden loss of muscle control, causing the child to drop to the ground. If you have seen any of these events in your child, you should call your doctor. Children who have a seizure that lasts for more than five minutes should be seen by a doctor immediately.

Children with Down syndrome who develop epilepsy are treated with the same anti-seizure medications, and usually respond better to the medications, than do children without Down syndrome.

▪▪ Orthopedic Problems

Orthopedic conditions involve the bones, muscles, joints, and ligaments. Most of the orthopedic problems encountered by children with Down syndrome are due to the laxity (looseness) of the ligaments between bones. This looseness causes problems with joints, but these problems are rare in babies.

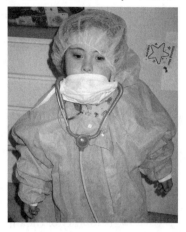

Atlantoaxial Instability

The most well-known orthopedic problem in Down syndrome is atlantoaxial instability (AAI)—too much movement between the first and second vertebrae in the neck. This condition is estimated to occur in about 15 percent of children with Down syndrome. The presence of AAI is a concern due to a presumed risk of spinal cord damage if there is pressing (or "impingement") on the spinal cord from one of the vertebrae.

AAI *without* impingement does not cause symptoms. AAI *with* impingement on the spinal cord may cause any of the following symptoms: easy fatigability, difficulties in walking, abnormal gait, neck pain, limited neck mobility, head tilt, incoordination and clumsiness, increased muscle tone to the point of spasms, and/or overexaggerated reflexes. Children with Down syndrome who have these symptoms, whether or not they have a previous diagnosis of AAI, need evaluation immediately. The treatment for this condition is surgical fusion of the two vertebrae.

There is controversy in the medical community over the likelihood of a child with nonsymptomatic AAI becoming symptomatic. Until this likelihood is known, it is still recommended that all children with Down syndrome be screened for AAI. The best way to screen presently is by taking lateral X-rays of the neck in the normal position, flexed, and extended. The first X-ray should be done around your child's third birthday. X-rays before then may be misleading due to the lack of enough calcification of the vertebrae to get accurate measurements. X-rays should be repeated when your child is 10 to 12 years of age.

If X-ray exam shows that your child has AAI, he should have an MRI of the neck to determine whether there is any injury to the spinal cord from the vertebrae and whether surgical treatment is necessary. Children with AAI that has been documented by X-ray but normal MRI scans should avoid activities that may cause strain on the neck: diving, gymnastics, and contact sports, for example.

An MRI scan is a painless procedure which is more in-depth than a standard X-ray. The MRI does require the child or adult to lie still for several minutes while the scan is being completed. Children who cannot remain still may need to be given medication to help them sleep through the scan.

Other Orthopedic Problems

There are other orthopedic problems common to older children and adults with Down syndrome.

- Scoliosis, which is curvature of the spine, is most often treated with back bracing, but may require surgery if the curve is severe enough to hamper lung or heart function.
- Instability of the hips can be caused by the thigh bone becoming too loose where it joins the pelvis, and may require casting or surgery to fix.
- Dislocation of the patella occurs when the patella, or kneecap, moves too far to one side, causing pain. This is repaired by either placing special bands about the knee to keep the patella in place, or by surgically tacking the kneecap down.
- Foot problems include flat feet, turning in or out at the ankles, and bunions, which are enlargements (bumps) of the bones or tissue at the base of the big toe, with the big toe often pointing inward toward the second toe. Flat feet are very common in people with Down syndrome due to the relaxed ligaments of the body, and may cause pain. Foot and ankle problems are often taken care of by either orthopedists or podiatrists.

** Ear, Nose, and Throat Problems

Upper Respiratory Infections

Many of the problems faced by children with Down syndrome are due to variations in the anatomy of the upper airway, which includes the ears, sinuses, nose, mouth, and throat. Specifically, children with Down syndrome have smaller midfacial areas, including nasal and sinus passages, which may contribute to frequent colds and sinus infections. The Eustachian tubes are also smaller, which may lead to more ear infections (see below). Some children with Down syndrome also have a decreased immune response to bacteria and viruses, which also plays a factor in the increased number of upper respiratory infections. While these

infections tend to be more common, severe infections such as pneumonia are not any more common in children with Down syndrome than in other children. As with all children, the number of upper respiratory infections decrease as the child becomes older.

Sleep Apnea

Another common problem is obstruction of the upper airway by large adenoids and/or tonsils. This obstruction may be constant or intermittent, and may lead to mouth breathing as well as sleep apnea. Obstructive sleep apnea (OSA) is the condition in which a child's airway is so blocked that he doesn't get enough oxygen during sleep. OSA is a common problem, occurring in up to 45 percent of all children with Down syndrome.

Children with OSA often snore, and parents can sometimes notice periods in which the child appears to stop breathing for five to ten seconds at a time. This can cause restless sleep and irritability in the mornings. If OSA results in chronic decreases in oxygenation of the blood during sleep, it can cause high blood pressure in the lungs, called pulmonary hypertension. This hypertension is bad for the heart, causing chronic damage.

Many times OSA can be diagnosed by a careful history and exam by your doctor. If in doubt, the doctor can order a polysomnography, or a "sleep study." Sleep studies involve attaching electrodes, as well as sensors to measure your child's oxygen intake, to his body and then

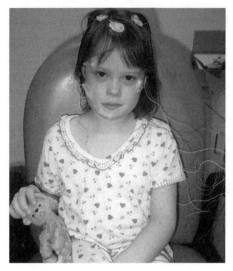

monitoring your child's brain waves and breathing patterns while he is sleeping. This study takes place overnight in a hospital or other monitoring center where specialists can determine whether your child is actually having periods where he stops breathing while sleeping, and in what stages of sleep they occur.

The treatment for OSA is usually removal of the adenoids, often with the tonsils as well. Some children may require more extensive surgical procedures. Children who are overweight and have OSA may also benefit from losing weight.

Hearing Loss

Approximately 50 to 60 percent of children with Down syndrome have some degree of hearing loss. This loss can be due to three reasons:

1. the presence of fluid in the middle ears for several months or longer; this is called "conductive" loss since the fluid interferes with the conduction of sound vibrations in the middle ear;
2. disruption of the transfer of sound from the inner ear to the auditory nerve, called "sensorineural" loss since it may involve disruption of the tiny bones or the nerves of the ear; or
3. a mixture of both types.

Hearing loss can result in delays in speech development. For this reason, hearing studies should be done on all newborns with Down syndrome, and should also be done yearly on children up through 12 years of age.

Many nurseries are now performing hearing screens on all newborns using an otoacoustic emission test (OAE). A small probe and microphone is placed into the sleeping infant's ear canals, and the test measures the responses from each cochlea, which is the part of the ear that interprets sound vibration and sends the message on to the brain. This test identifies babies born with a sensorineural hearing loss, but also wrongly identifies a small number of babies who actually have normal hearing.

A more accurate test for babies is the auditory brainstem response (ABR). The ABR requires a small microphone to be placed in the ear canals and electrodes to be placed on the baby's scalp, which then measure the brain's response to the sounds in the ear canals. The ABR is typically used if there are concerns about a baby's hearing after the initial OAE test. The ABR test is usually given in the office of an audiologist or ear-nose-and-throat doctor (ENT). Your child should have either OAE or ABR testing regularly until he is developmentally able to respond to behavioral hearing tests. Behavioral hearing tests require your child to make a response when he hears a sound, such as by looking toward the source of the sound, dropping a block in a bucket, raising his hand, or pressing a button.

Due to the increased risk of hearing loss, children with Down syndrome who have chronic fluid in the middle ears or recurrent ear infections should be treated aggressively. The accumulation of fluid in the middle ear is usually due to the inability of the Eustachian tube to drain fluid adequately to the throat. This fluid in the middle ear is the direct cause of conductive hearing loss.

Hearing loss due to middle ear fluid can usually be improved with tympanostomy tubes. The tympanostomy tubes, also called pressure equalization (or "PE") tubes, are small plastic tubes that are surgically inserted into the eardrums by an ENT, usually while the child is under general anesthesia. The tubes help equalize the air pressure on both sides of the eardrum, preventing the buildup of fluid in the middle ear. While placement of PE tubes may be technically difficult due to the smaller ear canals of children with Down syndrome, the procedure is usually very successful at preserving hearing.

Croup

Another common airway problem in children with Down syndrome is recurrent croup. Croup is the term given to inflammation and swelling of the trachea and larynx, with its resultant "barking" cough. Croup can be caused either by a virus or by allergies. Children with Down syndrome appear to be more prone to croup due to their smaller airways, so any swelling is more likely to cause breathing problems than in other children. Mild croup is treated with antihistamines and humidity, and moderate to severe cases may require treatment with steroids. If your baby or child is having a barking cough, he should be evaluated by a physician.

■■ Blood Problems

Several blood problems are more common in babies and children with Down syndrome. These problems most often occur in the newborn period or by the age of five.

Leukemia

Leukemia is cancer of the blood cells, usually the white blood cells. When the cancer starts in the type of white blood cell called lymphocytes, the cancer is called lymphocytic leukemia. When it starts in the white blood cells called monocytes or granulocytes, it is called myelogenous leukemia.

Leukemia occurs anywhere from 10 to 30 times more often in children with Down syndrome than in the general population of children. The initial signs of leukemia include easy bruising, a pale color to the skin, unexplained fevers, and fatigue. Leukemia is diagnosed through a blood test that shows abnormal white blood cells, followed by a bone marrow test that identifies the cancerous blood cells.

Most cases of leukemia occur in the first five years of life. In the first three years of life, myelogenous leukemia (AML) is the most common form of leukemia in children with Down syndrome. After age 3, approximately 80 percent of the cases are acute lymphocytic leukemia (ALL) and 20 percent are AML.

Both types of leukemia are treated with chemotherapy. Children with Down syndrome who develop AML generally seem to respond to chemotherapy better than do children without Down syndrome; with ALL, the response rate appears to be about the same.

Transient Leukemia

Newborns with Down syndrome have an increased risk of having a condition called transient leukemia. This condition resembles leukemia, but disappears on its own without treatment in just a few weeks or months. One study found that up to 10 percent of newborns with Down syndrome had evidence of transient leukemia on blood tests. When babies test positive for transient leukemia in blood tests, the number of white blood cells is greatly above normal and there are immature white blood cells, or "blasts," present.

Whenever a baby has transient leukemia, a specialist in leukemia should evaluate the test results to determine whether treatment is necessary. While this condition typically goes away without treatment, babies who have had transient leukemia have an increased risk of developing leukemia within the next years. Parents of children with transient leukemia should be vigilant for the appearance of pallor, easy bruising, or fatigue in their young children. The leukemia specialist will be able to advise whether any further blood testing is needed and, if so, for how long.

High or Low Platelet Counts

Another abnormal blood finding that is more common in newborns with Down syndrome is a low platelet count, called thrombocytopenia. The platelets are the blood cells that assist in clotting blood. Very low platelet counts will show up in a child as easy bruising or the development of bruises without trauma. Rarely, the platelet count may be so low that the baby needs transfusions of platelets to prevent bleeding problems. The reason for the thrombocytopenia is unknown, and it goes away without any treatment. Newborns with thrombocytopenia should be watched carefully for any other signs of transient leukemia.

On the other hand, some infants with Down syndrome show an increase in platelet numbers, called thrombocytosis. There is little risk to this condition and it goes away by itself.

▪▪ Thyroid Problems

Thyroid disorders are very common in people with Down syndrome. **Hypothyroidism,** or low thyroid levels, is the most common, and can be found at any age. In newborns with hypothyroidism, the most common cause is failure of the thyroid gland to develop correctly. In older infants and children, the most common cause is the body making antibodies against its own thyroid tissue.

The symptoms of hypothyroidism can be subtle, especially in people with Down syndrome: decreased growth rate, weight gain, constipation, lethargy, decreased muscle tone, and dry skin. Since it is easy to miss these symptoms, it is recommended that infants with Down syndrome be tested for hypothyroidism by blood tests that measure thryoid hormones at six months of age and one year, and then once a year thereafter for life.

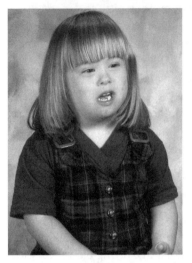

If hypothyroidism is diagnosed, it is treated by the lifelong replacement of thryoid hormone. Thyroid hormone is available as daily oral tablets that can be crushed if the child cannot swallow pills. Children who require thyroid therapy are monitored by either endocrinologists or pediatricians, and blood tests to evaluate the response to therapy are performed every six to twelve months

A common condition found while screening children with Down syndrome for hypothyroidism is to find normal thyroid hormone levels in the blood, but along with abnormally elevated thyroid stimulating hormone levels. This state may represent either a temporary condition or the first step of hypothyroidism. Often, finding antithyroid antibodies in the blood can help the physician diagnose early hypothyroidism. However, all doctors do not treat this the same way. Some doctors opt to treat the child with just enough thyroid hormone to bring the levels of thyroid stimulating hormone to normal, and other doctors opt to wait and retest thyroid levels three to six months later.

Hyperthyroidism, or high thyroid hormone levels in the blood, is also more common than usual in people with Down syndrome, though not as common as hypothyroidism. The symptoms include rapid heart rate, nervousness, sweating, decreased attention span, flushed skin, always feeling hot, and loss of hair. The diagnosis is made through blood tests and thyroid imaging studies. Hyperthyroidism is treated with medications that block the thyroid hormone's actions on the cells of the body, or by removing the overactive thyroid completely. If the thyroid is removed, the child then needs thyroid replacement therapy.

▪ Diabetes

Type I, or insulin-dependent, diabetes mellitus is more common in children with Down syndrome. In people with this type of diabetes, the pancreas does not produce enough of the hormone insulin. Early symptoms most often include increased urination followed by increased thirst. If the diabetes is not diagnosed, the child begins to lose weight and is constantly tired.

Diabetes is not common in children with Down syndrome during the first year of life, but may show up at any age. Doctors diagnose diabetes by first checking for sugar in the urine, and if found, testing the blood for sugar and insulin amounts. Children and adults with diabetes must be treated with injections of insulin throughout life.

■■ Eye Problems

Eye problems are very common in people with DS of all ages. Some are congenital, or present at birth, and some develop later in life.

Cataracts

Cataracts, which are abnormalities of the lens of the eye, are the earliest eye abnormality seen in Down syndrome and may be present at birth. The lens is a structure of the eye that focuses light from the pupil onto the back of the eyeball. If the lens has an area that is nontransparent, or opaque, then that will decrease vision. These opacities in the lens are called cataracts. All newborns with Down syndrome should be examined carefully by a doctor for cataracts. If found, the cataract is surgically removed and glasses are worn to correct any leftover visual problems.

Blocked Tear Ducts

Many infants with Down syndrome have blocked tear ducts (dacryostenosis). When a baby has a blocked tear duct, one or both eyes tend to tear up frequently, and he has frequent eye infections. If your child has blocked tear ducts, your doctor will show you how to gently massage the tear duct to remove the blockage, and will prescribe antibiotic eye drops for infection. If the blockage is still present at nine to twelve months of age, the ducts may need to be opened by an ophthalmologist. The ducts are opened with a small probe in the ophthalmologist's office.

Strabismus

Usually by the time an infant is three months old, his eyes are working together as a team: they move together to look left, right, up or down. This alignment of the movement of the eyes is what enables

us to see one image from two eyes, as well as to use depth perception. When the eyes do not move together, this is referred to as strabismus.

Strabismus is common in babies with Down syndrome. When strabismus is present, young children will see double images. Over time, their brains learn to suppress the image from the deviating eye so they can see a single image. If this problem is untreated, it may cause a loss of vision in the suppressed eye, called amblyopia.

Early treatment of strabismus involves patching the stronger eye or putting drops into the stronger eye to blur its vision, and sometimes glasses. Obstructing the vision of the stronger eye causes the child to use his weaker eye and strengthens its vision. Once vision has been equalized between the eyes, glasses may correct small deviations between the eyes. Surgery on the muscles of the eye is needed to correct large deviations.

Sometimes it may look as if a baby has strabismus when he really does not. The broad nasal bridge in infants with Down syndrome will often cause a baby to appear as if one or both eyes are turning inward toward the nose, when in fact the eyes are normal. An ophthalmologist will be able to determine whether strabismus truly exists.

Blepharitis

Blepharitis is a chronic infection of the edge of the eyelid that sometimes occurs in children with Down syndrome. It appears as redness and scaling along the edge of the eyelid, and you may see what looks like dust or dandruff in the eyelashes. Children with the condition are treated with antibiotic ointments applied to the eyelids along with special eyelid scrubs, and occasionally steroid drops.

Nystagmus

Nystagmus is a repetitive, involuntary movement of the eyeballs, usually involving both eyes. In most cases, the movement is side to side, but it may also be up and down. While many different conditions may cause nystagmus, usually no specific cause is found. Nystagmus may cause problems with vision, so if your baby or child has nystagmus, be sure that he is evaluated by an ophthalmologist.

Visual Acuity

Errors in visual acuity, or the ability to see clearly, are very common in children with Down syndrome. These errors include nearsightedness (myopia), farsightedness (hyperopia), and astigmatism (an irregularity in the shape of the eyeball). For this reason, it is recommended that children with Down syndrome have their vision evaluated for the first time when they are between six and nine months of age, and then once a year after that for life. Problems with visual acuity are treated with corrective lenses (eyeglasses) by an optometrist or ophthalmologist.

Dental Concerns

Teething is much more variable in children with Down syndrome than in other children. That is, the teeth do not always come in on a predictable timetable or in a predictable order. Very often the first teeth do not appear until beyond the child's first or even second birthday. When they come in, teeth may appear small or more pointed. Delayed teething rarely affects the choice of foods in the first year of life. Later on in your child's life,  you may notice that his other baby teeth are delayed or missing, and he may even be missing permanent teeth.

While cavities are not common in children with Down syndrome, there is an increased risk of gum disease. Children with Down syndrome should be evaluated by their second birthday by a dentist who is knowledgeable about the dental concerns of children with Down syndrome.

Skin Problems

Newborn Period

Newborns with Down syndrome frequently have blue hands and feet at birth and for several days afterwards. The term for this is acrocyanosis, and it is due to decreased circulation in the hands and feet. This is a harmless condition. Another condition found in newborns is a bluish mottling of the skin, called cutis marmorata. This mottled color is a response of the skin capillaries to cool temperatures and is normal in all newborns. Although the condition may persist for several months in some babies with Down syndrome, it is harmless.

Chronic Skin Conditions

Dry Skin. Children with Down syndrome may have dry, rough skin. This is often referred to as xerosis. While xerosis is often associated with vitamin A deficiencies in other children, this is not a common cause of xerosis in Down syndrome. Xerosis is best managed by using nondrying soaps, adding oils to the bath water, and applying moisturizers, especially right after bathing.

Chelitis. Chelitis is the presence of fissures or cracks and red, scaly skin at the corners of the mouth and lips. This is usually due to moisture collecting at the corners of the mouth, but can also be complicated by infection from bacteria or the yeast Candida. Treatment involves applying a mild steroid cream, along with treating infection when present.

Atopic Dermatitis. Atopic dermatitis, also known as eczema, is the presence of red, scaly, itchy skin. It most often appears on the cheeks, behind the ears, behind the knees, and in the elbow creases. Treatment is with steroid creams and oral antihistamines. In children with Down syndrome, it shows up mostly in the first years of life.

Seborrhea. Seborrhea is similar to eczema, but usually looks greasy and scaly and appears on the scalp and eyebrows. Dandruff shampoos or shampoos with either tar compounds or salicylates are used to treat seborrhea of the scalp. Sometimes antifungal preparations may be useful.

Infections

Folliculitis is the inflammation or infection of hair follicles of the skin, and appears as small red bumps or yellowish pustules. These can occur anywhere on the body but are more common on the buttocks. Most infections are due to the bacteria staphylococcus, though a fungal version is sometimes diagnosed in adults with Down syndrome. Folliculitis typically responds to either topical or oral antibiotics and to good cleaning with an antibacterial soap. When the staphylococcal infection is deep, it produces boils and abscesses, which require treatment with oral antibiotics.

Alopecia

Alopecia areata is the name for patchy hair loss which is not due to infection or drugs. The bald patches have distinct borders, with no hair thinning in other areas of the scalp. Alopecia is more common in children with Down syndrome than in other children, but it is still uncommon.

Alopecia is believed to be due to an autoimmune process, meaning the body is making antibodies against its own hair follicles. Alopecia is highly unpredictable. People with alopecia can have several episodes of hair loss and regrowth during their lifetime. The hair regrowth can be partial or complete, or there may be no regrowth at all. In most people, hair eventually grows back to some extent within one year. However, a small percentage of people can develop chronic alopecia.

Sometimes the hair loss covers the entire scalp, which is called alopecia totalis. In a very small percentage of people, hair loss occurs all over the body. This is called alopecia universalis.

There is no cure at present for alopecia. Treatment is currently aimed at helping hair grow back, but it cannot stop the spread of hair loss.

▪▪ Immunizations

It is recommended that all babies and children with Down syndrome receive the same immunizations and on the same schedule as other children. Infants with Down syndrome are not at risk for increased complications from the vaccines. Additionally, because Down syndrome can result in decreased immune function, it is recommended that babies and children with Down syndrome receive yearly flu vaccinations.

:: Doctors and Your Child

Pediatricians and family physicians vary widely in terms of experience and knowledge about the problems associated with Down syndrome. When choosing a doctor to help you take care of your baby, consider not only experience but also the willingness of the doctor to read and learn new things about Down syndrome. Your doctor should

be able to sit down with you and discuss all your questions and concerns to your satisfaction. He or she should also be willing to refer your child to specialists if necessary.

Doctors have access to two sets of guidelines which are useful in helping manage the medical care of people with Down syndrome. One set is written by the American Academy of Pediatrics and is available on their website at http://www.aap.org. The second set is written by a group of professionals known as the Down Syndrome Medical Interest Group, and it is also available on the Internet site of the Down Syndrome Research Foundation at http://www.dsrf.co.uk. If your doctor is not aware of these resources, consider printing them out and sharing them with him or her.

As with pediatricians and family doctors, the knowledge and experience of specialists is variable. Although many conditions that specialists treat occur in children other than those with Down syndrome, the specialists should be aware of any unique problems that may arise with your child. You should feel comfortable with your specialist's ability to care for your child's special needs.

At some times in his life, your child may be seeing more than one specialist. At these times, your pediatrician can be useful in acting as your child's case manager. The specialists will be concerned with their areas of expertise, but your pediatrician will be able to help concentrate on the overall wellbeing of your child. Your doctor should be obtaining letters from the specialists detailing their diagnoses and treatment plans and helping sort out any difficulties that may arise, as well as helping facilitate communication between the specialists if the need arises.

Several larger communities in the United States and a few in other countries have Down syndrome medical clinics. These clinics are associated with medical schools or large hospitals and are run by geneticists, behavioral pediatricians, or other specialists. The Down syndrome clinics generally have physical, occupational, and speech therapists on staff, and offer access to specialists who often deal with problems seen in children with Down syndrome. These clinics are beneficial to families who have children with multiple medical problems. Additionally, other families who live close to a Down syndrome clinic often find it reassuring to visit the clinic on an annual basis to check that their child's development is on track and that any health conditions have been properly diagnosed and treated. However, if you feel confident of your local doctor's knowledge and skills, going to one of these clinics may not be necessary.

You are your child's best advocate. Keep asking questions and accumulate as much knowledge as you can to ensure your child receives the best possible medical care. The more you know, the better it is for your whole family.

■■ Parent Statements

We have been quite pleased with the medical attention our son has gotten. The children's hospital is very understanding and proactive. They made sure he got tests for his heart, his hearing, and other things we wouldn't have known to request. They made sure he had the tests and then followed up on the results.

❧

When we found out that our daughter had a heart defect on top of Down syndrome, it almost didn't matter. What I mean is, we felt that we could take care of the heart problem—that we would be able to manage it better than the Down syndrome. As it's turned out, we have managed both things much better than we thought we would.

❧

Anthony has a big scar on his chest where he had open heart surgery. I look on it as his badge of courage. He was such a tiny little baby, but he was (and is) a fighter!

⋘⋙

If your child needs heart surgery, my advice is to look for a children's hospital with surgeons who have done the exact same surgery your child needs many times. Don't be afraid to ask them about their experience and success rate!

⋘⋙

Our little boy has hypothyroidism. We were so glad it was diagnosed early because we were able to start medication immediately. Otherwise, he'd have other problems on top of Down syndrome. But we caught it early enough, and now we just give him medicine once a day.

⋘⋙

Olivia really didn't get any colds until this year, when she started pre-school. Once she started being exposed to other kids, she started coming down with colds, which sometimes developed into ear infections.

⋘⋙

Jayden doesn't seem to get colds any more often than his little brother does. But when he gets one, it seems to last a little longer and he seems a little more miserable. Also, he can't seem to get the hang of blowing his nose. We'll put a tissue to his nose and say "Blow, Jayden," and sniff to show him what we mean. He'll try to blow but usually just ends up wrinkling his nose.

⋘⋙

When Hope was four months old, she had a lot of fluid in her ears. She didn't act as if her ears hurt, though, and we didn't notice any signs of hearing loss. Fortunately, our doctor had recommended she have a hearing test at around this age. The test detected a moderate hearing loss, so we took her to an ear, nose, and throat specialist. This doctor discovered the fluid in Hope's ears and monitored it for about three months. When the fluid didn't go away, the doctor recommended inserting tubes in her eardrums to drain the fluid and equalize the pressure in her ears. After the surgery, Hope's hearing was normal, and has remained normal for a year now. She's beginning to say real speech sounds now, which I doubt would be the case if we hadn't fixed her hearing problem so early.

✿

I think hearing should be checked in the same way that people vote in Chicago—early and often. Hearing is so essential for the development of communication skills. Ear infections and fluid can change your child's hearing very quickly and can really slow, or even reverse, progress he has made in communication skills. Our son has a mild hearing loss and wears hearing aids. Sure, they are a bother and expensive, but I would never take the chance of robbing him of something essential to his learning to communicate.

✿

The ENT says that Liam has "Eustachian tube dysfunction" and that is why he has so much trouble with fluid behind the eardrum. Basically, it's an anatomical problem and he may or may not grow out of it as he gets bigger. He got his first set of ear tubes put in when he was nine months old and another set about a year later. We are watching the situation like hawks so his hearing won't be affected.

✿

Our daughter's adenoids were really big and the doctor thought that could be contributing to the number of ear infections she had, and also to her mouth breathing. So, she had surgery to take her adenoids out and put ear tubes in. I was worried about the operation, since it involved anesthesia, but the whole procedure went very smoothly and quickly. It didn't seem like she had any pain afterwards and she wanted to eat normal food again as soon as we were home from the hospital, so it must not have hurt to swallow at all.

✿

Abby has always been a really restless sleeper. While she's sleeping, she'll turn around so her head is where her feet were, or sit up in her sleep and then flop over with her head in her lap, pancake-style. We had a sleep study done and found out she has something called "hypopnea." That means she doesn't get enough air when she's sleeping—something is blocking the airflow, but it doesn't completely stop. We got her tonsils *and adenoids taken out, which seems to have helped somewhat. She still sits up in her sleep sometimes, but not as much as before.*

❧

*If you go for a sleep study, make sure you go somewhere where they are used to testing **children**. We've had two studies done. The first time, our insurance would only pay for testing at a center that usually saw adult patients. They couldn't even find the right-sized equipment for testing our child, and didn't have enough staff working to monitor him properly. The results were inconclusive. Later we got testing at a children's hospital with a sleep study center. The difference in staff, atmosphere, and responsiveness was just like night and day!*

❧

Emily gets eczema in the winter time, especially behind her knees. We use hydrocortisone creams on it, which works pretty well.

❧

Sam has really dry skin, especially in cold weather. His cheeks are bright red and his little hands and feet are very rough. About the only thing that helps is those really expensive, petroleum jelly-based lotions for "severely dry" skin. We slather it on after his bath and throughout the day.

❧

Our daughter always wants to sit really close to the TV. I thought she must have a vision problem, but the eye doctor says she sees fine, although she has a touch of astigmatism. I guess she just likes to get up close to the action.

❧

We take Michael to see a pediatric ophthalmologist. They are good at getting the kids in and out of the office quickly. The doctor uses videos of cartoons, stuffed animals, and other kid-friendly "props" to get an idea of how well the child is seeing.

❧

Our daughter gets constipated pretty often. I think one reason is that we have trouble getting her to drink enough. When she was using a bottle, she always drank plenty of liquids, but since she's been using a cup, she just isn't that interested in drinking. The doctor gave us some kind of powdered laxative that you were supposed to mix in a lot of liquid, but of course she didn't want to drink the big glass of liquid, so that didn't help!

◈

We always ask Liam's doctors a lot of questions and don't let them get away with not answering or using medical jargon we can't understand. We're paying them to help our son and we need to understand what they're saying. People shouldn't be embarrassed to ask for an explanation.

◈

Our kids' dentist has a room with a couple of dental chairs in a row. We always schedule Chloe and her sister for appointments together, and they both sit in the chairs at the same time and get worked on together. I think that really helps Chloe see that going to the dentist is nothing to get worked up about.

◈

*It can take courage to change doctors. Maybe the pediatrician you have is the one the whole family uses, but he doesn't have a clue about the problems that can go along with Down syndrome. Or maybe he's patronizing or uses outdated terminology that sets your teeth on edge. If your doctor isn't willing or able to change, **you** have to make the change. Yes, it can be uncomfortable to terminate a doctor's services, but don't let that keep you from looking after the best interests of your child.*

◈

Health insurance can be a major concern. If at first you don't succeed in getting a certain service covered, keep trying. Sometimes the bureaucrat you deal with at one level doesn't understand, but the one at the next level does. Or maybe the services are not covered for a particular diagnosis, but if you get another diagnosis that is really the same thing but just said in a different way, your policy will cover it.

◈

When dealing with insurance companies, keep all your bills and insurance forms and keep submitting your documents. Keep going higher and higher up, because once you concede that something isn't covered, there's no going back. They expect you to give up, but if you persist, you might get lucky. You might get someone in the chain of command who will decide in your favor or get them to admit that your policy does cover a particular service.

❧

I think an important function of a pediatrician is to coordinate your child's care. He or she needs to be aware of what the speech therapist is doing, what the OT or PT is doing, what the ophthalmologist is doing, what the ENT is doing, etc. We found a pediatrician who reads everything he gets about our daughter, calls me if something doesn't jibe, and really is a coordinator. We wouldn't trade him for the world.

4

THE DAILY CARE
OF YOUR BABY

Joan Burggraf Riley, MS, MSN, CFNP
Jean Nelson Farley, RN, MSN, CPCP, CRRN

The daily care of your child with Down syndrome is very similar to the care you would provide to all babies. Perhaps this is why there is very little written

about the daily care of children with Down syndrome. However, because your baby may differ from typical children in some ways, her daily care will sometimes require special knowledge and effort. This chapter explores those areas of daily care that are unique to babies and young children with Down syndrome.

A tremendous amount has been written about childcare in general. Eating, sleeping, bathing, and diapering are extensively covered in hundreds of baby care books. Those general baby care books can be helpful, but their advice must be adapted to your child's special needs. Supplement those books with the information presented in this chapter.

Routine activities—eating, bathing, diapering, and dressing—are major events in a baby's or toddler's day. You can tailor your baby's activities to enhance her development simply by being aware of her developmental needs as you go through each day. But remember: Babies with Down syndrome are babies first and foremost. Care for her as you would any other baby. Follow your instincts, but in those areas where your baby has special needs, use the information in this chapter to deal with those needs effectively.

■■ Setting a Routine

One of the most important aspects of your baby's daily care is to set a daily routine. A routine allows your baby to learn what to expect in her daily activities. A routine sets an order to her day, and makes her feel safe. Having a routine within each daily activity provides security

and teaches your baby about the activity. For example, a bedtime routine of a bath and a storybook teaches her about how bedtime happens. Routines provide a child with the comfort of knowing what to expect. Later on, they will also allow your child to participate in daily activities with increasing independence.

Routines differ for each family because of family members' schedules and because of each baby's schedule. For example, some families give their babies a bath in the evening in order to help them calm down and relax, while other families bathe their babies in the morning because their babies get very excited splashing around and playing in the water. In either case, the consistency of your routine will benefit both you and your baby.

You may also need to reassess your family style in light of your baby's particular needs. Limit setting and consistency—discipline in general—are important for any child. But for a baby with Down syndrome, you may need to be more deliberate about it. Families with a child with Down syndrome often find it necessary to verbalize and repeat rules that other children in their family take for granted. For example, if your family dinnertime routine is very casual, you may have to structure your methods to your child's special needs. On the other hand, if your family routine tends to be highly structured, you might have to allow for more flexibility.

Most likely, your particular style is just fine. Just remember that it is important to be aware of how your daily activities, style, and expectations can affect your baby's development. Your goal in providing routine and structure is to create an environment in which your child will develop trust in the people in her life and in her surroundings. Other children may manage to get along well without this deliberate level of care, but if you optimize your baby's environment, you will help her reach her full potential.

Because your baby has special health and developmental needs, it may be easy for you to spoil her. Discipline and routine, however, are more important to her than to any other baby. You will be surprised at how clever she is at manipulating you. Your child will have to learn how to behave, and you won't be doing her a favor if you fail to enforce the do's and do-not's.

You want your child to be an active participant in her community. Appropriate behavior is a learned skill that is essential in order for your child to be included successfully in peer groups, social settings, and the community at large. If you allow your child to throw food at home or to hit her brother or sister, you cannot expect her to know that these behaviors are unacceptable. Simple, consistent, and clear directions will be the most helpful tools you can use to establish discipline guidelines for your child. As your child grows into the preschool and school age years, it will be important to teach her to observe how her peer group is behaving and to model her own behavior after theirs.

:: Holding Your Baby

Holding your baby will be your first interaction with her as parents. Although you might feel that holding your baby should be "second nature," this seemingly simple skill plays a significant role in establishing more normal patterns of development in the future. Children with Down

syndrome who move with correct posture, coordination, and position eventually can do more of the things other children can do, like climb, run, and play. How you hold your baby *now* will help her in these areas later in life. Remember, achieving developmental milestones is the result of careful attention to a number of small but very important details.

Therefore, it is very important for you to be conscious of how you position your baby, especially when holding her for social interaction and feeding. In addition to low muscle tone, babies with Down syndrome often have very loose joints. Loose joints allow their limbs to settle into positions that might lead to difficulties when they start to sit, crawl, and walk.

There are simple adaptations you can make to the way you instinctively hold your baby to stabilize her joints and provide needed support. For example, it helps to hold your baby securely with the joints of her neck, hips, and legs flexed. Avoid holding methods that require your baby to wrap her legs around your hips. This is important to prevent "frog legging" and other abnormal, low muscle tone motor patterns. An added benefit to using this flexed position while holding your infant is that it permits better eye contact with your baby. This eye contact allows her to watch and imitate your facial expressions and mouth and lip movements—skills that are crucial to your child's later language development.

In the early years, your child's healthcare provider will send your baby for an X-ray of her neck. This is done to assess your baby for atlanto-axial subluxation, as discussed in Chapter 3.

Consult with your baby's health care provider, physical therapist, or teacher for additional suggestions about holding and positioning your infant based on their professional assessment of her muscle tone, joints, and medical needs.

All this concern about how you hold your baby may sound intimidating. Unless your baby has a particular medical problem, however, don't handle her as though she were fragile. She will love physically active play, just as other children do. Not only is this activity good for sensory stimulation, it also sends to your baby and your other children the message that you intend to treat her as an equal member of the family. If you set this example, family and friends will follow your lead.

:: Hygiene

Good personal hygiene habits are as important for children with Down syndrome as for any other children. The foundation for good hygiene is established in early childhood. Getting your child into the pattern of washing, brushing, and caring for herself is a critical skill for her future. This section reviews some of the basics of daily care for your child.

Bathing and Skin Care

Many parents bathe their children daily, but this may not be necessary as long as you keep your child's face, mouth, hands, and diaper area clean. While your child is a newborn, you can give her sponge baths using a soft cloth. After her umbilical cord stump falls off, you can bathe her in a washbowl, sink, or baby bathtub. When she is older and you feel more secure, she can be bathed in a tub with just an inch of water and under *constant* supervision.

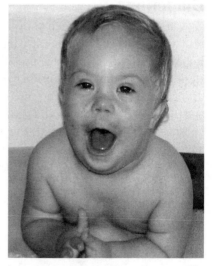

There are many safety devices available commercially for use when bathing your baby. None of these is essential and some devices can be dangerous because they can provide false confidence that your baby is safe in the bathtub. Nothing replaces the safety of keeping your hands and eyes on your baby during bath time. One necessary item is a non-slip mat to provide traction for sitting or standing in the tub.

Children with Down syndrome have a tendency to develop dry skin, with areas of rough, red, flaky, or irritated patches on the legs, buttocks, arms, hands, and feet. To prevent and control this, it is important to develop a good skin care routine. You should use moisturizing soaps (Basis, Dove, Caress, Tone), and apply lotion (Eucerin, Nivea, Aquaphor) immediately after bathing, while the skin is still moist. Lotion helps to lock in the moisture the skin absorbed during bathing. Applying lotion to dry skin is not very effective. Apply lotion more than once a day, particularly on the hands and face after mealtime washing. If the problem persists, consult your healthcare provider. He or she can prescribe more potent skin lotions or suggest other ways to treat dry skin.

Parents often ask about their infant's scalp, which can become crusted and flaky. This "cradle cap" is quite common in the early months of your baby's life and is part of the scalp's normal way of shedding dead skin cells. The best treatment is to rub a thin layer of petroleum jelly into the scalp to soften crusts twenty to thirty minutes prior to shampooing. Shampoo your baby's hair daily with baby shampoo, keeping the shampoo out of her eyes. Gently brush the scalp with a soft brush during bathing to remove the dead skin. It is all right to gently wash over "soft spots." Continue daily shampooing for several days after the cradle cap disappears. Then shampoo at least weekly thereafter.

Diapering

It is important to keep your baby's diaper area clean. Wash the skin with plain water during each diaper change to prevent diaper rash. It may be helpful to routinely use a lubricant such as petroleum jelly, Desitin, or other baby diaper skin care product to protect the skin from dryness and irritation. Do not use cornstarch because it can encourage the growth of bacteria and yeast. Do not use baby powder, either, because your baby might inhale the powder particles, which can cause a breathing problem for some infants.

Your child's skin may be sensitive to the brand of diaper you are using. If you suspect sensitivity, switch to another brand. Always fold the plastic top of the diaper away from the body. The best treatment for diaper rash is prevention, by keeping the skin clean and dry. If your baby develops a rash that is not clearing up with these prevention techniques, consult your healthcare provider.

Diapering can be an excellent time to incorporate developmental activities into your baby's routine. It is an opportunity for talking to your baby and making eye contact. Playful talking, touching, and movement during diapering can provide her with helpful stimulation. At the very least, diapering is a good time to be sociable, to talk to your baby, to stroke her body, and to help her move her arms and legs. Your baby's teacher or therapist may also have some good ideas on positions and movements during diapering.

Eyes

Like other children, babies with Down Syndrome sometimes develop blockages in a tear duct, resulting in increased tearing or crusting of eye drainage. In some children this corrects itself, while in others it may require medical treatment. To help avoid blocked tear ducts, you can clean your baby's eyelids by wiping gently from the inner corner toward the ear. This can be done with a clean, moist washcloth or cotton ball.

Ears

Although children with Down syndrome are often more prone to ear infections (discussed in Chapter 3), your baby's ears can receive typical care. Ear wax builds up naturally in the ears and works its way out. Some children with Down syndrome have drier ear wax and eliminating it may require treatment from your child's healthcare provider. He or she can look in your child's ears to determine whether excessive wax is a problem for your child. Parents should never put any object—including a Q-tip—into their child's ear. At bath time, simply wash the outer ear and the area behind the ear gently with a soft cloth and then dry it.

Nose

Some children with Down syndrome experience more frequent runny noses and thickened secretions due to their smaller nasal passages and flattened nasal bridge. Usually, using a cool mist humidifier in your baby's room is recommended. This will help loosen secretions and make it easier for your baby to breathe. A cool mist humidifier can be especially helpful if your home has a dry forced-air heating system. When using a cool mist humidifier, be sure to follow manufacturer's directions for cleaning the humidifier.

To clean the outside of the nose, wipe it with a warm, moistened cloth such as a clean cloth diaper or soft cotton washcloth. Occasionally, nose secretions become dry and crusted around the outside of the nose. You can remove these gently with the use of a lotion or a cream. Try not to irritate the nose further by frequent wiping. Many tissue manufacturers now make tissues that contain lotion. These can reduce the irritation of frequent nose wiping. Petroleum jelly or lip balm will also ease the irritation. If the inside of your baby's nose becomes dry and crusty, ask your doctor about saline nose drops. Nasal aspirators do not work well and may cause irritation.

Teeth

As with any child, it is important to teach good habits of dental care at an early age. This benefits your child in a number of ways. First, if your baby breathes with her mouth open much of the time, there can be an extra buildup of tartar in her mouth. Tartar is a sticky coating on the teeth that can cause cavities. Second, brushing helps stimulate a number of developmental skills—from getting used to sensory stimulation all around the mouth, to practicing sound production in the mirror, to learning how to handle the toothbrush by herself. To avoid dental problems later, good oral hygiene is essential now.

The care of your child's teeth is no different than for other children. Teeth cleaning should begin as soon as teeth erupt. Wipe your baby's first teeth with a clean, moist washcloth or gauze before bedtime each night. A soft toothbrush can be used as early as your child can tolerate it in her mouth. Some dentists recommend battery operated toothbrushes for young children. Many electric brushes have a feature that beeps every thirty seconds to prompt you to clean a different area, and shuts off automatically after two minutes. Oral-health experts say we should brush twice a day for two minutes, and there's evidence that people brush longer with an electric toothbrush than with a manual brush. Check with your child's dentist about what is best for your child.

Once your child is two to three years old, she should brush her own teeth two to three times each day to encourage good hygiene habits, but at bedtime you should complete the tooth brushing. Parents will need to finish the tooth brushing until the child has the motor skills to perform a thorough cleaning. This can be at six years of age or older.

The Academy of Pediatric Dentistry recommends that a child's first dental visit occur at approximately two years of age. This first examination will reveal your child's tooth eruption pattern and will provide an opportunity for oral hygiene instruction. By the time your child is three years of age, she will be familiar with the dental office and staff, and will be able to participate in the dental exam, cleaning, and fluoride treatment.

Don't let your baby fall asleep with a bottle in her mouth. Never put her to bed with a bottle of formula or juice, since the sugar in these fluids pools in the mouth and sticks to the teeth, causing cavities. This is important even if your baby's teeth have not emerged yet. If your baby has developed the habit of taking a bottle to bed, slowly wean her to a bottle of water by diluting the bottle contents with water, gradually increasing the water and decreasing the juice or formula until it is 100 percent water.

∷ Eating

From birth, mealtime is one of the most important times parents spend with their child. Babies are usually alert and attentive while they are eating, and mealtime can be an enjoyable time for all family members to get together. As your child grows, she will enjoy being at the table with the rest of her family, participating in the discussion about everyone's daily activities.

For your newborn baby, eating is the single activity that requires the most energy and work for her physically. Babies who are born with heart problems can sometimes have difficulty eating. The work of eating is so great that they require more frequent, smaller feedings. Some issues to discuss with your child's healthcare provider include the volume of the bottle your child drinks or length of time at the breast and the frequency of feeding. Signs that the work of feeding is greater than usual for your child can be:

- excessive yawning,
- paleness of the skin around the mouth or on the lips and tongue,
- bluish skin color,
- poor appetite,
- difficulty breathing or noisy breathing,
- sweating while feeding, or
- failure to gain weight.

As with all children, children with Down syndrome have to learn feeding skills, and this process requires time and patience. It takes practice for your baby to learn to feed herself, and, as with other children, there will be plenty of messes. You have to be ready to wipe up spills and clean up faces and hands. But rest assured, all children with Down syndrome learn to feed themselves.

Breast or Bottle Feeding

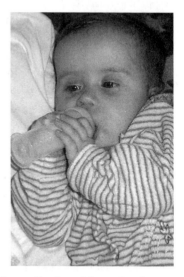

Babies with Down syndrome can breast or bottle feed like other children, but may need some extra help. It may be harder at first for them to feed in a coordinated way, but most learn with consistent effort. If you understand your baby's potential feeding problems and how to overcome them, feeding can become a special time for both of you.

Whether you are breastfeeding or bottle feeding your baby, regular checkups with her healthcare provider are essential to monitor her growth and nutritional health. This can be particularly important because possible medical problems (such as a congenital heart defect) and low muscle tone associated with Down syndrome can result in a weak suck.

The following information is important whether you choose to breast or bottle feed your baby. Babies and children with Down syndrome often have physical characteristics that affect how they eat. In particular, their low muscle tone makes the work of eating a challenge for some babies. The muscles of their lips, tongue, and cheeks may not move in a coordinated way due to low muscle tone. Consequently, your baby with Down syndrome may have more difficulty getting a tight seal on the nipple of the breast or bottle. She may also have a weaker suck, and later may have more difficulty moving food around in her mouth, which is necessary for chewing and swallowing. As you work with your baby's teacher, therapist, and healthcare provider you will be amazed to learn how complex the act of eating can be and how it is affected by your baby's development.

Overcoming Common Obstacles

Some babies require special techniques to strengthen their *oral motor skills*—the ability to use the muscles of the mouth to suck, chew, and swallow. Oral motor muscle skills can be reduced due to your baby's overall low muscle tone. Oral motor exercises are used to enhance the natural patterns your child has for sucking and swallowing. Frequently, parents need instruction from someone familiar with these techniques—such as their child's speech or occupational therapist, nutritionist, or teacher. In general, it is a good idea to have a therapist check your baby's eating patterns to help you provide the best feeding stimulation. Remember, these techniques require time and practice.

Pacifiers are controversial but some believe the use of a pacifier can strengthen your baby's mouth muscles and can help soothe her when she is upset. You can choose from a wide variety of shapes, sizes, and materials. Your baby may respond more positively to one than another, so be ready for some experimenting. But remember that, just like other babies, your child may not want or need to use a pacifier.

You can also use the nipple of the breast or the bottle nipple to stimulate your baby's rooting and sucking reflexes. Gentle pressure on her cheek or lips will get her to turn her head toward the nipple. Gently rub the cheek towards the baby's mouth on the side closest to the nipple and she will then turn in that direction. Your baby will need good lip closure on the nipple, and you can help her by holding her in a flexed position. This position is tight in your arms with your baby's knees and arms held snug into her trunk.

Good lip closure can also be promoted by rubbing your baby's cheeks toward her lips, and rubbing upward from her chin and downward from her nose toward her lips. Use the back of your pointer finger to provide gentle pressure. This oral motor stimulation will help your baby to be organized and more focused on her feeding.

Breastfeeding. If you breastfeed, consult your healthcare provider for the name and phone number of a breastfeeding (lactation) consultant who can provide expert guidance as you and your baby both learn the mechanics of breastfeeding. Some communities have organizations where women volunteer to provide support and guidance about breastfeeding to new mothers, based on their personal experiences.

Breastfeeding is recommended whenever possible, as it provides your baby with essential nutrients, and natural immunity from illnesses such as ear infections, colds, and diarrhea. However, be aware that breastfeeding is not always possible for all mothers and babies. It is also a personal choice that mothers need to make in consultation with their doctor.

Bottle Feeding. If you choose to bottle feed your baby, there are a wide variety of commercial nipples available. Your baby may prefer one commercial nipple to another. When choosing a commercial nipple, check to make sure that there is a nice, even flow of milk. There are a wide variety of bottles on the market. For a child with a weak suck, it may be helpful to use a soft plastic bottle or bottles that have a disposable plastic bag. Either of these will allow you to apply gentle pressure on the bottle or bag to help milk flow out evenly. Once you choose a particular nipple, use only that same style for all bottle feeding. Avoid switching nipple styles. Each different nipple style requires a slightly different suck. Changing nipple styles will make it more difficult for your baby to learn and master a particular suck pattern and will frustrate and confuse her.

Babies need good support to drink from a bottle comfortably and efficiently. Low muscle tone makes it more difficult for your baby to hold herself in a position that promotes proper sucking and swallowing. At first, mother or father must provide good support for their baby while she is feeding. Obviously, the type of support depends on your baby's age and developmental level. When they are tiny, babies should be held in a semi-upright position with good head support, with the head tilted slightly forward. A newborn should be cradled snugly and securely in your arms with her legs supported in your lap.

Scheduled Feeding vs. Feeding on Demand. There are two ways to structure your baby's mealtime: you can establish a schedule or you can feed her on demand. With demand feeding you offer your baby food when she shows she is hungry and ready to eat. Scheduled feeding means that you set a routine, usually feeding your baby at three- to four-hour intervals.

Babies with Down syndrome generally do best when they are fed on demand. Learn to recognize your baby's signs that she is hungry. Many babies whine or get fidgety before they cry to express hunger. If your baby has difficulty eating, mealtime will go more smoothly when she is hungry and ready to eat. Any baby will concentrate better when awake, alert, and giving signs that she is hungry. These signs include lip-smacking, hand-to-mouth activity, restlessness, fussing, rooting, sticking out her tongue, or crying.

Some babies with Down syndrome tend to sleep through what should be their mealtime. Feeding your baby only on demand may not meet her nutritional needs. Your healthcare provider may suggest you wake up your baby on a schedule of every two to three hours in order to give her adequate feedings. Monitor your baby's feeding to make sure she is getting enough nutrition and consult with her healthcare provider. Well-hydrated babies have six or more wet diapers a day, and the urine is clear or very pale.

Introducing Solid Foods

Your baby can be introduced to solid foods at the same age as other children. This is usually from four to six months of age, but some parents wait as long as a year. It is generally recommended that babies with Down syndrome be introduced to solid foods by six months of age.

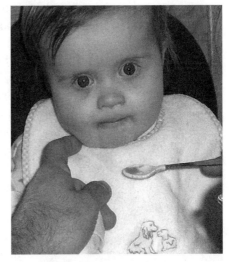

Eating solid foods helps develop a number of important skills, including fine motor skills, sensory awareness in the mouth, and making sounds. Fine motor skills are the movements that use your baby's small muscles. An example is the ability to pick up small pieces of food using the thumb and pointer finger in a pinching motion.

More importantly, introducing your baby to solid foods helps her to tolerate different food textures. Babies with Down syndrome can be especially sensitive to differing textures; if this happens, they may refuse to try different foods.

Some babies with Down syndrome gag or swallow too much food at one time. This can result from being offered too much food or from food collecting in the mouth. Check with your baby's doctor or teacher to determine when she is ready to start eating solid food. Remember that the introduction of solid foods does not substitute for the nutrition received through breast or formula feedings during the first year of life.

When you do introduce new foods, give your baby a choice of either commercially prepared, pureed baby foods, or foods you puree at home. Both options are fine. Commercial baby food companies now emphasize nutrition in the preparation of their foods by limiting the amount of added salt and sugar. The order in which foods are introduced varies, but many people first offer infant rice cereal, then yellow vegetables, green vegetables, and fruit, with meats and fish offered last. Your baby may not like all these foods, but what baby does? Just strive for a balanced diet. Consult your healthcare provider to establish nutritional guidelines for your baby.

Give your baby small amounts of the new food each day for several days to see whether she can tolerate it. Babies will often push food out of their mouths with their tongues. When this happens, you can try putting a small amount of food onto the middle part of her tongue as you apply some downward pressure from the bowl of the spoon. You can also try applying some gentle pressure on her upper and lower lips to keep her mouth closed around the food.

Letting Your Baby Feed Herself

As babies gain control over eating solids, they start finger feeding, a very important and enjoyable activity for them. Finger feeding provides

babies with independence and gives them another way to explore their environment. In addition, finger feeding develops sensory awareness and fine motor control.

Finger feeding is an extension of the hand-to-mouth activity begun at a very early age. You should offer your baby a large variety of finger foods. Sticky foods are good for children who have not yet developed a good grasp with their fingers. Try cottage cheese, yogurt, or pudding so your baby can dip her fingers into the food and bring it to her mouth. Later on, when your baby develops a better grasp, she can start reaching for small bits of food such as dry cereal, cooked pasta, cooked vegetables, and fruits.

When your baby starts to use her own spoon, you will have to try some of the different sizes and shapes available. Use a baby spoon with a narrow bowl first and then progress to a toddler spoon with an easy-to-hold handle. Your baby will have more success if the spoon is easier to hold and place in her mouth. You can buy baby spoons with flatter bowls and wider grips. Some have small holes in the bowl that help keep the food sitting on the spoon until your baby places it in her mouth. Again, it is a good idea to have a therapist check the way your baby takes the food from the spoon into her mouth and the way she holds and moves the spoon.

Proper posture and support are as crucial for eating solid foods as they are for breast or bottle feeding. How your baby sits affects how well she can manipulate food and hold a spoon. Your child should be fed in a highchair with her feet well supported, her trunk secure and upright, and the height of the tray at her elbow level. Some children benefit from foam supports in their highchairs to keep them in a proper position before they can easily do it themselves. You should ask your child's teacher or therapist whether your child needs the extra support and where she needs it.

Mealtimes with your child will be noisy and hectic; they can also be wonderfully enjoyable. Like all children, your child may often wear more food than she eats. What can you do to prevent mealtimes from becoming too chaotic? First, consistent discipline is essential. Set mealtime rules for all your children and enforce them. But remember, mealtimes are excellent opportunities to work on development, language, and self-help skills. Strike a balance and strive for enjoyable mealtimes, knowing that they can be both rewarding and frustrating.

Drinking from a Cup

How soon your child makes the transition from breast or bottle feeding to cup drinking depends on her ability to reach, grasp, and con-trol a cup. By the time your baby is ready to drink from a cup she already has taken an active role in holding her bottle or the breast and can bring it to her mouth.

For good cup drinking, your baby should be able to sip from the cup rather than suck. This sipping skill can be encouraged initially by having your baby take liquids from a cup that has a wide lip or a lid that allows small amounts of liquid to pass

through holes in the lid. Cups with spouts should be avoided because they promote sucking, not sipping.

While your baby drinks, pay close attention to make sure she is not resting the cup on her tongue instead of on her lower lip. Babies are tempted to do this because it is easier to hold the cup still with the tongue than with the lower lip. This is particularly true if your child is in the habit of sticking her tongue out. This habit is difficult to break when your child is older, so it is a good idea to discourage it early. Giving gentle support under the chin can enable your child to hold the cup in the correct position without using her tongue. Your teacher or therapist can be very helpful in teaching your child to drink correctly from a cup.

Weight Gain

Some babies with Down syndrome have difficulty gaining weight. This is generally a problem among children who have a congenital heart defect. It is usually a concern during the first year of life. These babies should be monitored by their cardiologist and doctor. Special diets and other medical treatment can be prescribed to improve weight gain.

Your child should have her growth monitored, using a special growth chart for children with Down syndrome. (See the growth charts on pages 132-139 at the end of this chapter for an idea of the range of height and weight for girls and boys with Down syndrome.) Children with Down syndrome usually have a slower rate of growth than other children. The important thing is to maintain balance between weight gain and growth in height.

As parents, you want to guide your child's food choices to help her form lifetime habits of good eating. In the United States, we have an obesity epidemic. Studies of children with Down Syndrome have found that many develop obesity. This obesity is usually caused by a combination of overeating and inactivity. In addition, basal metabolic rate (the amount of energy you use at rest) is about 15 percent lower in people with Down syndrome, so they burn fewer calories. An additional factor is that children are frequently rewarded for activities with sweets and high calorie foods.

Early exposure to the taste of salty and high fat foods can lead to a long-term desire for such foods. It is far easier to not develop this desire than to stop it later. Be aware than convenience food that is bought packaged at the grocery store and "fast food" are often very high in salt and fat, and should be avoided.

Remember that early dietary habits and preferences can influence lifelong nutrition. Consult your child's healthcare provider about your concerns and questions about her weight gain. As your baby grows, continue to have periodic discussions about your child's unique nutritional needs in order to prevent obesity.

∷ Sleep and Rest

Newborns do not have predictable sleep patterns. They often sleep most of the time and wake primarily to eat. Of course, each child is different, but generally newborns with Down syndrome have typical sleep patterns. As your child grows, the periods of wakefulness and sleep increase. By two to three months of age, your baby's sleep becomes more organized, and a regular pattern develops.

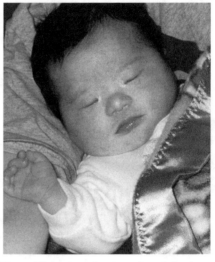

Parents learn early to interpret their baby's cues for sleep as well as for hunger and attention. Your baby will express her needs for each of these with different cries, movements, and vocalizations. You will come to know when it is time for her to sleep—hopefully when you want to sleep—and when it is time to be awake.

Always place your child to sleep on her back. Back sleeping has been shown to decrease the occurrence of Sudden Infant Death Syndrome (SIDS). Never use a comforter, pillow, or soft mattress. If you leave your baby in the care of another adult (daycare provider, babysitter, a relative), make sure that he or she also follows these safety rules. The crib should be free of toys and stuffed animals. Consult your child's healthcare provider about crib safety.

Once asleep, your baby's level of sleep varies, and she frequently will make noises, twitch, and move. These are all normal signs of sleep. Excessive snoring, thrashing around, or sleeping in unusual positions *may* be normal for a baby with Down syndrome. But it may also be a sign of sleep apnea (see Chapter 3). Report your observations to your baby's doctor.

As in all daily care activities, routine is important. Many parents complain that their children won't sleep through the night, or won't settle down without being held or being allowed to sleep in the parent's bed. Don't assume your child needs comforting any more or less because she has Down syndrome. She will be just as quick as any other child to manipulate you in your attempts to settle her down for the night. A regular sleep and bedtime routine that is consistently enforced may help to avoid these problems. For example, if your child gets into the pattern of listening to soothing music or a story at bedtime, she will learn to associate these activities with going to bed.

Parents typically keep their child in a crib until it becomes unsafe to do so because of the child's size and ability to climb out and hurt herself. Because of low muscle tone, your child's climbing skills may be slower to develop and she may be able to stay in her crib longer. Your child may be ready to make the transition to a bed sometime between the ages of two and four. Discuss safety issues with your child's healthcare provider when she seems ready for the transition.

■■ Constipation

Many children with Down Syndrome experience difficulty with constipation, when bowel movements are hard and dry. Parents have differing expectations about their babies' bowel movements. What your infant eats influences the color, frequency, and consistency of her bowel movements. For example, breastfed babies may have four to six bowel movements per day, while bottle-fed babies may have one to three bowel movements per day. The frequency and consistency of your baby's bowel movements and any concerns should be discussed with your healthcare provider.

If your child with Down syndrome has problems with constipation, it may be due to low muscle tone, which makes it more difficult for her to develop a strong push to have a bowel movement. There are several things you can do for constipation.

First, control your child's diet. Constipation can trouble children who eat a typical fast food diet that is rich in fats (burgers, fries, milkshakes) and processed sugars (candy, cookies, sugary soft drinks). These children may have bowel movements that are hard, dry, and painful.

Their time between bowel movements may be four days or more. It is important to have a good balance of whole grain cereals, vegetables, and fruits. This helps digestion and minimizes constipation.

Second, make sure your child is drinking enough fluids, especially water. Increasing fluid intake can reduce constipation. Constipation often becomes a problem for toddlers when their fluid intake decreases as they begin to eat more solid foods.

Third, if you notice your child struggling to have a bowel movement prior to being toilet trained, try flexing her legs up to her abdomen. This puts pressure on the belly and helps your child to push. Once she is able to use the toilet or potty chair, be sure your child's feet have support to help with bowel movements. If you are using a potty chair, your child's feet should be on the floor. If using the bathroom toilet, place a stepstool to support your child's feet.

Fourth, ensure that your child is getting plenty of exercise, because physical activity helps get the bowels moving. Encourage dancing, pushing cars, taking walks, and other fun activities that give your child some physical activity.

Finally, setting a regular meal schedule can help some children develop regular bowel habits, since eating is another natural stimulant for bowel activity. If necessary, schedule breakfast a little earlier to give your child a chance for a relaxed visit to the bathroom before school.

Some children become constipated because they ignore the natural urge to empty their bowels. They may not want to use a restroom away from home, or they may feel embarrassed to ask a teacher to be excused from class. When this happens, simple reassurance from you and your child's teacher may be the only treatment necessary. However, if your child has painful constipation, be sure to consult a doctor.

Most childhood constipation problems can be helped by sensible changes in lifestyle or diet. Laxatives are not usually needed. In fact, using laxatives unnecessarily can actually *cause* constipation. There are numerous over-the-counter remedies for constipation, which should never be given to your child without the advice of your child's health care provider. Some of these products could be dangerous for infants and young children.

Always ask your child's healthcare provider before giving your child any medicine for constipation. Be aware that changes in bowel movements can be a sign of other medical problems, so keep your child's healthcare provider informed if your child continues to have bowel problems.

The treatment of constipation must be tailored to each individual child. Your child's healthcare provider can provide treatment and monitor this problem to meet your child's individual needs.

:: Toilet Training

Children with Down syndrome, like all children, experience success at toilet training at different ages. Some are toilet trained relatively early, while some do not become toilet trained until well

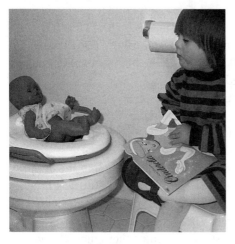

after the age of three. Toilet training can require considerable time and effort, but rest assured your child will become toilet trained.

Toilet training can be a challenge for your child with Down syndrome because of the need for many areas of development to come together at once for this new skill to be achieved. Some of these areas, including communication, muscle control, and the awareness of the need to urinate and have a bowel movement, are often delayed in children with Down syndrome.

As your child grows, she will start to become aware of her need to urinate and have a bowel movement. At that point, she will need to know how to let you know she needs to go to the bathroom.

Look for signs or cues that your child is aware that she has a wet diaper or has had a bowel movement, such as showing discomfort and asking to have her diaper changed. These signs let you know that your child is aware of her toileting needs. Other cues that indicate readiness for toilet training may be squatting, grunting, pulling at the pants, jumping up and down, or even whimpering. You may also notice that your child is able to stay dry for longer periods of time. Once you sense your child has developed this awareness, there are several specific steps you can take to initiate toilet training. (See box on the next page.)

Some authorities on toilet training advocate gradually guiding a child to use the toilet, perhaps observing her to see when she most

:: Steps in Toilet Training

1. Get a potty chair.
2. Allow the child to become familiar with the potty chair.
3. Place the potty chair in a convenient place for the child.
4. Do not pressure the child to use the potty chair if he or she is afraid of it.
5. Let the child sit on the potty chair fully clothed once a day as a routine, then try it with clothes off.
6. Take the feces from the diaper and put it into the child's potty chair so he/she can see it where it should go.

Adapted from American Academy of Pediatrics Toilet Training Guidelines.

often wets or soils her diaper. Other authorities suggest waiting for the child to show readiness or awareness of her own toileting needs. Be careful not to place pressure on your child to toilet train. Avoid overly praising her for success on the toilet; praise should be consistent with the praise given for her other accomplishments. It is important to remember that this is only one of the many tasks your child is attempting to master simultaneously. Appreciate that, and understand her frequent lapses.

Toilet training is a multistep process. Setbacks are common and should be anticipated, not regarded as failures. Setbacks or regression typically occur during periods of stress or changes in routine, such as illness or hospitalization. Some useful resources to aid you as you work with your child on toilet training are listed in the Reading List at the back of this book. After implementing a toilet training program be sure to pay attention to your child's toileting behaviors in order to maintain healthy habits and good hygiene. Also, be sure to watch for and not allow inappropriate behaviors such as playing with feces.

:: Exercise

Exercise is critical to children with Down syndrome. It can break the vicious cycle of low muscle tone leading to inactivity and obesity. Because low muscle tone requires your baby to work harder to move, you need to take an active role in monitoring her movements, designing a good exercise program, and motivating her to move around.

A physical therapist, teacher, and selected books can get you and your baby started on an exercise program. They can also make sure that your baby's exercise promotes development and does not cause problems. Strengthening muscles, improving coordination, and learning balance all can help tremendously in many areas of development.

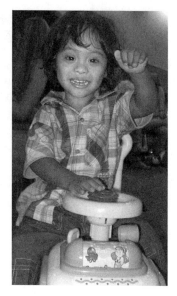

If your child has a medical condition such as a congenital heart defect, consult your child's cardiologist or healthcare provider for recommendations on appropriate activity level.

■■ Child Care

If your baby has seizures or other serious medical problems, a babysitter with special training should be used. Otherwise, no special training is required. Any caring, careful, and mature person with whom you feel comfortable can baby-sit your baby. Of course, you will need to spend some time showing the babysitter how your baby eats, sleeps, or plays, as you would do for any child. The important thing to remember is that it is good for everyone if you get a babysitter once in a while. You need to take some time for yourself, and your baby needs to learn to interact with people other than immediate family members.

It is often difficult for new parents to leave their baby with Down syndrome with a babysitter. This is especially true if your child has medical problems. The constant fear that an emergency will arise while you are out can trap you at home unnecessarily, depriving you of valuable opportunities for enjoyment and stress reduction. With a competent babysitter, however, this problem can be easily avoided.

If you prefer a trained babysitter, send your babysitter to a local course on child care safety. Many community hospitals provide such courses for a small fee. To find child care, use community resources such as your local Down syndrome parents support group (often called PODS for Parents of Down Syndrome), ARC, or the special education or nursing education department of your local college or university. They may have a list of sitters in your area who specialize in child care for children with special needs. Another idea is to start a pool of parents (especially other parents of children with Down syndrome) who are willing to trade babysitting with you. Many jurisdictions have funds available for family respite care and trained providers. Contact your local ARC for information.

If you are planning to return to work either full-time or part-time, you will need to find child care for your baby. Many parents find successful day care for their child while they work. Because your child's needs are more typical than different, most day care centers welcome children with Down syndrome. Think about your family's needs and consider center-based day care, licensed family day care (multiple children cared for in the home of the child-care provider), and home child care in your own home.

▪▪ Conclusion

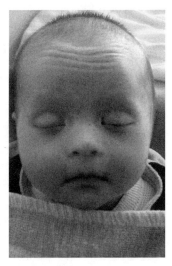

Caring for a baby—any baby—is quite an imposing challenge. When that baby has Down syndrome and special needs, the task becomes more complicated. Though your baby is special, her daily care will be very much like that of other children. She can adjust to your life and fit in like other children. Information, patience, and persistence will help ease your new baby into a routine that is good for everyone. Consult the books in the Reading List and seek the help of healthcare providers, teachers, and therapists. And always remember: your baby with Down syndrome, like every other baby, needs love, attention, and care.

▪▪ Parent Statements

I couldn't get Abby to latch on in the hospital when she was first born, but I think part of that was I couldn't get relaxed due to lack of privacy. Once we got her home, she took to breastfeeding like a champ.

❧❧❧

For the first couple of months, our baby always fell asleep before she was done feeding. We'd have to jostle her around and unwrap her to make her cooler to get her to wake up and finish.

❧❧❧

We had to experiment with a lot of different nipples to find one that worked for Jayden. People kept suggesting we use the kind with the plastic bag inside so we could squeeze it and help squirt milk into his mouth, but he didn't like that. When we found a brand he liked, we went out and bought a couple dozen of the nipples just to make sure we always had the right kind.

❧❧❧

Our baby has been nursed from when he was an infant so that's very lucky. He always nursed properly and started on solids at four months. He's twenty months now, and he feeds himself with a spoon. My husband is the best person to teach him how to eat because he really can give us the run-around if he wants to. We try not to let mealtimes become a battleground, but he likes testing. He's going through a testing phase, so we find him deliberately holding things over the side of his high chair and watching to see if we're going to say anything before he flings it over. But he can eat properly if he wants to.

❧❧❧

I did not have any luck with breastfeeding my daughter. She had a very difficult time latching on, and when she would latch on, she would fall asleep so quickly she did not suck very long. She lost weight very quickly as a newborn, so I ended up pumping and bottle-feeding the expressed breast milk for six weeks, until my milk dried up. She regained her weight quickly once she was being bottle-fed breast milk and supplemented with formula.

❧❧❧

One night I went in to give Ben his final goodnight kiss and there he sat in the middle of his crib, a sodden mess, hair sticking out in all directions, pajamas and crib sheet soaked with milk. His dexterous little fingers had unscrewed the bottle cap and he had poured the whole bottle of milk over his head! I took the hint—he was off the bottle for good.

❧❧❧

When she was a toddler, our daughter was very resistant to holding her own bottle. It wasn't a matter of strength, she just preferred someone there, holding it for her! Finally, I found a tiny two-ounce bottle that she would hold for herself.

⚜

We had a hard time teaching Abby to use a cup. We'd heard you shouldn't use a Sippy Cup because that encourages using the wrong muscles to drink, so we invested in every other kind of "training" cup known to man. It seemed like she'd always get too much liquid in her mouth at once, though, and then she wouldn't want to try any more.

⚜

When Sam was an infant, I used to always nurse him to sleep. We knew you weren't "supposed" to do that, but it was just the easiest way. Then we'd pick him up ever so gently and put him in his crib. Sometimes he'd wake up and start howling, so we'd have to start all over again.

⚜

Our daughter cried so softly when she'd wake up at night, hungry. She sounded like a hungry little cat. A baby monitor was essential, even though her room was right next door to ours.

⚜

Until about three years of age, our daughter was unable to put herself to sleep. If she was not rocked to sleep, she would lie in her crib and cry. So, for every nap and at bedtime we fed her a bottle, rocked her to sleep, and held her for at least fifteen minutes before putting her in her crib. I'm sure some thought I was spoiling her, but it was the only method that worked. Then at a Down syndrome convention I attended, I learned that many babies and children with Down syndrome have trouble putting themselves to sleep and staying there. It made me feel better that I was not alone in this. And of course, I did not mind the extra cuddle time with my baby!

⚜

It can be hard to get a spoonful of cereal into our baby's mouth. Her tongue just seems to want to push it out. She loves eating, though, so I'm sure she'll get better at eating from a spoon soon.

⚜

When our daughter was about three, she became very interested in picking out her own clothes (and putting them on herself, if possible). She would come up with the most clashing combinations. Since I didn't want to discourage her independence, I decided just to get her solid-color pants and shorts. That way she could pick out her own clothes without coming up with any combinations that were too outrageous.

❦

Labels in clothes really bother our son. We always cut them out.

❦

In early intervention, they've been encouraging Sam to take off his own socks when he's lying on his back with his knees flexed up toward his chin. We work on this with him when he's on the changing table. He's starting to get the hang of it, which is really pretty exciting.

❦

Ravi is sixteen months old and still doesn't have any teeth. He mushes food pretty well with his gums, though. I don't think it's slowed him down with progressing through the food stages.

❦

Our daughter just doesn't like the taste of most toothpastes. We've tried most of the children's flavors, and I think they're too intense for her or something. There's a brand that they sell in health food stores that just has a hint of strawberry flavor that she tolerates, though.

❦

Marissa put up a fight every time we tried to brush her teeth with a normal toothbrush. She would clamp her mouth tightly shut and shake her head. Her speech therapist suggested a battery-operated vibrating toothbrush with a fun character on it. Marissa and I went to the store and she picked out a toothbrush that looked like an ice cream cone. She now lets me brush her teeth without a fight and even reminds me in the morning before she goes to preschool. She opens her mouth wide and points to it until I brush.

❦

I think we waited too long to start toilet training. By the time we started, our daughter was very much into the "terrible twos" (although chrono-

logically older) and everything was a big power struggle with her. If I had it to do over again, I think I'd start shortly after she started walking.

❧

Our kid has an iron bladder. When we were toilet training, she'd hold it in all day and then not go until we finally put a "pull-up" on her at night.

❧

Having a wet or messy diaper never seemed to bother our son. I wonder if it's common for kids with Down syndrome to have that kind of under-sensitivity?

❧

At preschool, our daughter saw the other kids using the toilet and wearing real underwear, and that was the best motivation for her. We brought in a special squishy potty seat for her to use on the toilet and the teachers ended up doing most of the training for us.

❧

Toilet training Michael was no big deal. He took to it a little later than some other children, but he really had no more problems learning toileting than other kids.

❧

Marissa (who is three and a half) has been using the potty since she was almost two, in addition to wearing "pull-ups." There will be days she signs to me she has to use the potty, and keeps her pull-up dry for hours. And then there are days where she does not tell me at all. I think the biggest obstacle we have is with communication. She has made up her own sign for potty. But, if we are not in the room with her and miss seeing it, she goes in her pull-up. I am hoping that when she becomes verbal she will communicate her need to use the potty more consistently.

❧

I think I've bought every book on toilet training ever published and our daughter still isn't trained. We take 2 steps forward and then one and a half steps back. I wonder why she's taking so long with this when she has learned a lot of other things without too much delay.

❧

Abby needs the bath water to be pretty cool. It's as if she feels that water that is the least bit warm is burning her. We have to ease her down into the bath, little by little, or she draws up her legs and won't sit down.

❧

It can be hard to give your kid a bath if he has ear tubes in his ears. You have to pour the water carefully over his head so you don't get any soapy water in his ears. The ENT told us to try using ear plugs, but Jayden just pulls them out.

❧

We feel it's very important to treat Chloe normally. It's having normal expectations for behavior. For example, we put a lot of emphasis on eating properly, using her utensils properly, chewing properly, and things like that. We've had high expectations for her here at home, and her eating has been very good. Expecting normal behavior all the way around, even if you have to work harder at it, is the trick.

❧

As far as little things go, I don't do too much differently with her except just pay more attention to her skin care. Other than that, I treat her like a normal baby; she didn't have any problems that I had to be careful about.

❧

When our daughter was two, she was a very plump little child. I think the Down syndrome makes her look heavier than she probably would otherwise. Her muscle tone has improved in the past few months, and she's getting good rotation in her trunk. So, that is helping her look slimmer.

❧

Before the heart surgery, we were pushing calories on our daughter. It's really hard when you have to switch gears after something like heart surgery. Before the surgery it was give, give, give, fortify, fortify—anything she wanted she got. It's hard for the child—and parents—to get out of that pattern!

❧

We have a hard time leaving her with a sitter. We just haven't felt comfortable doing that. I guess we just feel kind of protective. We didn't even go out for almost two years. Lately we have felt differently. We've left her with more people and she just gets along fine.

❧

We hardly ever left Abby with a sitter when she was a baby. Once she started preschool, though, we started going out more. One of her pre-school teachers did babysitting on the side, and we felt very comfortable leaving Abby with her.

❧

Our son was in daycare from the age of three months, so we got used to other people taking care of him. Of course, we worried about leaving him with relative strangers to begin with, but he always did great. He doesn't have any special healthcare needs, though, so taking care of him is pretty much like taking care of any other kid.

Growth Chart for Boys with Down Syndrome (0-3 years)
LENGTH

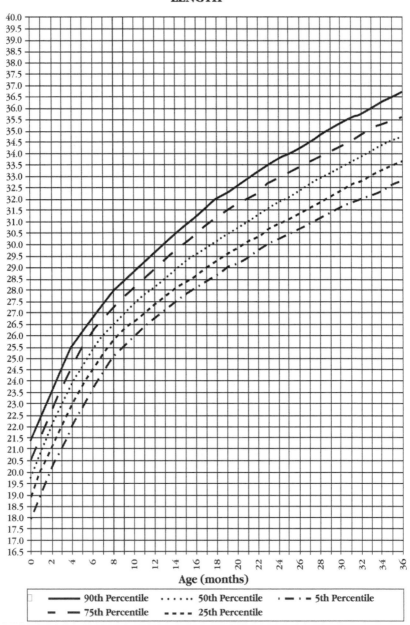

Recreated with permission from www.growthcharts.com
Reprinted with permission from National Down Syndrome Society ▪ 800-221-4602 ▪ www.ndss.org ▪ info@ndss.org

Growth Chart for Boys with Down Syndrome (0-3 years)
WEIGHT

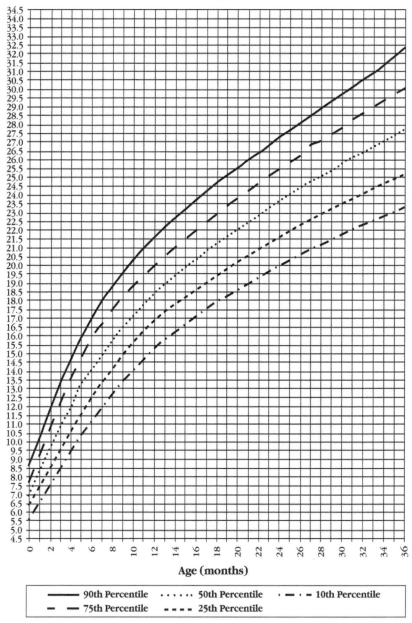

Age (months)

| —— 90th Percentile | ····· 50th Percentile | · — · — 10th Percentile |
| — — 75th Percentile | – – – – 25th Percentile | |

Recreated with permission from www.growthcharts.com
Reprinted with permission from National Down Syndrome Society ▪ 800-221-4602 ▪ www.ndss.org ▪ info@ndss.org

Growth Chart for Boys with Down Syndrome (2-18 years)
HEIGHT

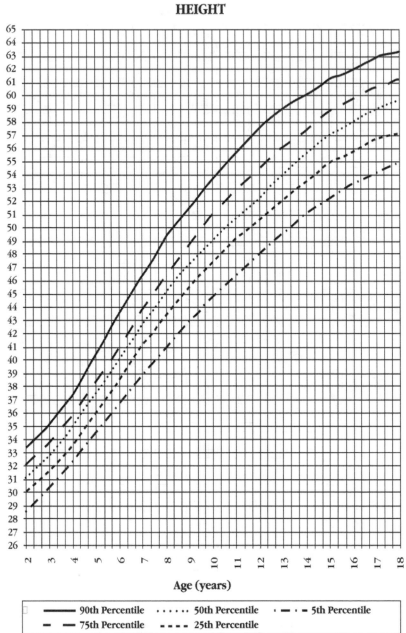

Legend:
——— 90th Percentile   • • • • • 50th Percentile   • — • — 5th Percentile
— — 75th Percentile   – – – 25th Percentile

Recreated with permission from www.growthcharts.com
Reprinted with permission from National Down Syndrome Society ■ 800-221-4602 ■ www.ndss.org ■ info@ndss.org

Growth Chart for Boys with Down Syndrome (2-18 years)
WEIGHT

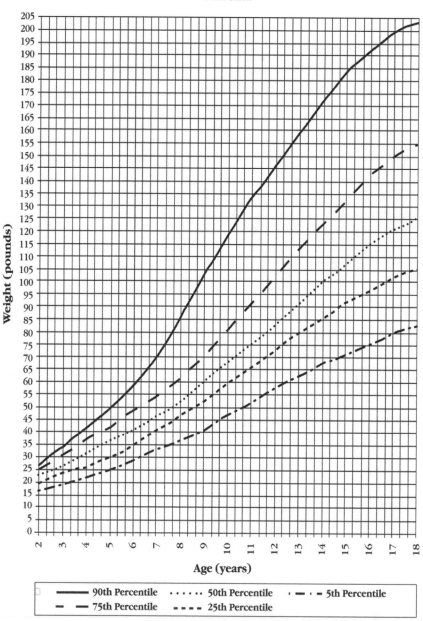

Growth Chart for Girls with Down Syndrome (0-3 years)
LENGTH

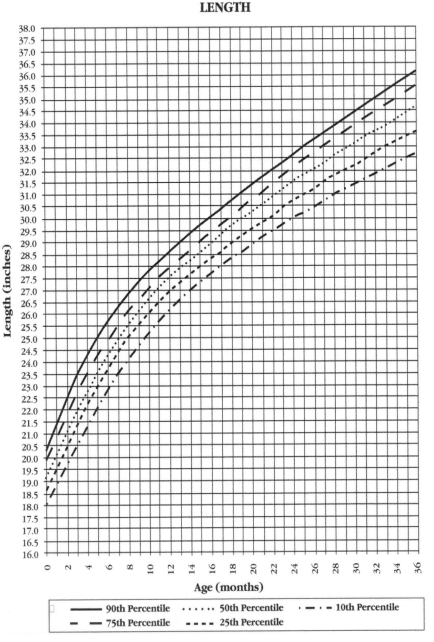

Age (months)

| —— 90th Percentile | · · · · · · 50th Percentile | · — · — 10th Percentile |
| — — 75th Percentile | – – – 25th Percentile | |

Growth Chart for Girls with Down Syndrome (0-3 years)

WEIGHT

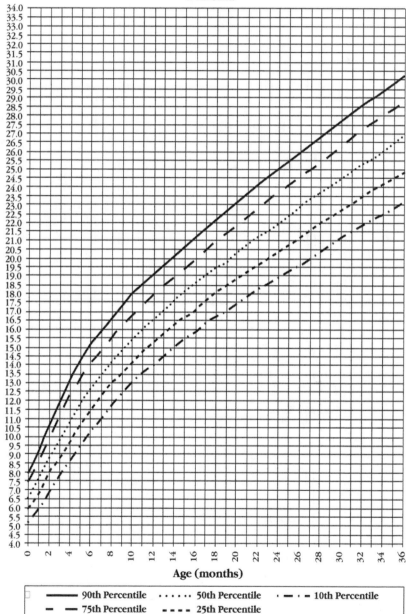

Growth Chart for Girls with Down Syndrome (2-18 years)
HEIGHT

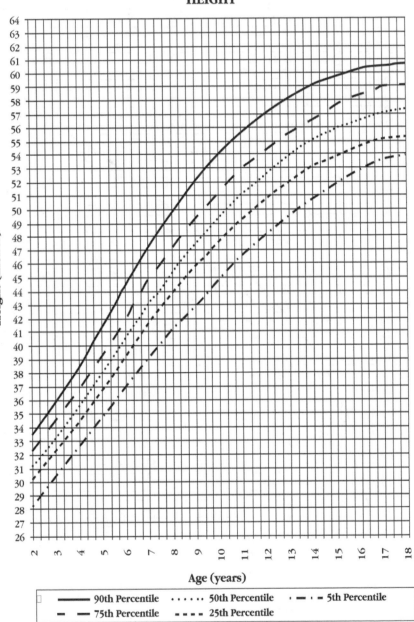

Age (years)

———— 90th Percentile	······ 50th Percentile	· — · — 5th Percentile
— — 75th Percentile	- - - - 25th Percentile	

Growth Chart for Girls with Down Syndrome (2-18 years)
WEIGHT

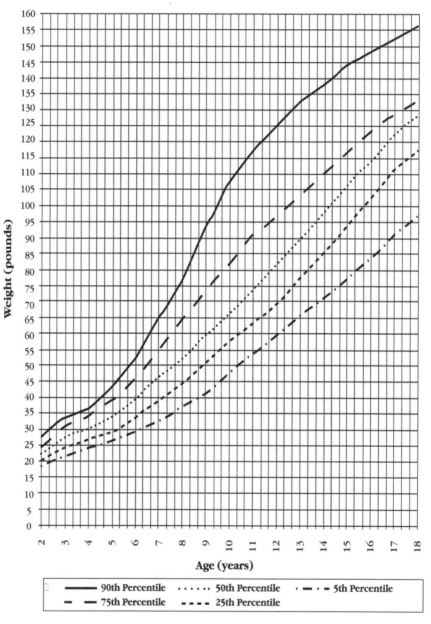

5

FAMILY LIFE WITH YOUR BABY

Marian H. Jarrett, Ed.D.

You have undoubtedly thought about the changes in your life that the birth of your baby will bring. Many of these thoughts are happy ones, and rightfully so, because your baby will bring you great joy. But the arrival of a baby with Down syndrome may also bring stress and strain on family members and on family relationships. Having a child with Down syndrome requires

coping by the whole family. You will face the challenge of adjusting in your own way, but right from the start you should know that it can be done. Thousands of families can testify to that.

Today the future is bright for families of children with Down syndrome. So much has been learned to help families successfully raise their child. With early intervention for infants, special education programs, inclusion, better social acceptance, support groups, and vastly improved medical care, family life is dramatically better than it was even a generation ago. Families now have many sources of information and support.

Most parents worry about what having a child with Down syndrome will do to their families. One of the most common concerns is how well the child will fit into the family. Parents ask, "Will our child have so many needs that everyday family life will be disrupted? Will I or my children be embarrassed by our child with Down syndrome? Will normal family fun come to an end?" These questions reflect the common concerns of new parents of babies with Down syndrome.

Parents also worry about how they can meet the challenge posed by a child with special needs. There is a great deal of work involved in raising any child with a disability, and raising a child with Down syndrome is no different. The challenge of fostering development, independence, and social ability is considerable, and parents naturally wonder how they can do all the work that is required. How can they give their child with Down syndrome all he needs and still meet their other responsibilities: to their other children, to their spouse, to their jobs, to themselves?

A major part of the worry that parents feel is fear of the unknown. But remember, other parents have faced the same fears and worries. They will tell you that raising a child with Down syndrome forced changes in their lives that involved hard work and considerable adjustment. They will also tell you that their child was a positive addition to the family and that they cannot imagine life without him or her.

Parents are the key to how well a family adjusts to having a family member with Down syndrome. Children, other family members, and friends follow the parents' cues. How you act toward your child sets the pattern for the whole family from the moment your baby is born.

** Being the Parent of a Baby with Down Syndrome

Before the birth of your baby, you may have imagined that child-rearing would come naturally. But the parent of a baby with Down syndrome faces unique challenges, and you may now doubt your ability to meet your child's "special" needs. You may ask yourself, "How can I feed this baby who struggles so much when he is being fed? Will I have to do special exercises to teach him to walk? Will he ever talk and will we understand what he says?" You may wonder how this baby can ever be a part of your family if you are coping with these kinds of worries about the future.

All parents face worries and conflicting emotions in the early stages of their baby's life. Like parents of babies with Down syndrome, they worry about colic, feeding schedules, rashes, colds, and count-less other details of child care. They soon learn to depend on love, acceptance, and discipline as the staples of good parenting. You will undoubtedly depend on these also in raising your child. Although this section focuses on those areas of family life that are *different* because your child has Down syndrome, the goal for you is the same as for all families: integrating your child into your growing family as a valued, contributing member.

You may turn to your family and friends for help in meeting the challenge of bringing up your child. Also remember that your child's teacher and other professionals can be a tremendous source of support for you. The parent-professional partnership, which is discussed in Chapter 7, can be a great source of practical information on coping. Just having someone you can ask about problems or questions makes your daily work easier. Nagging uncertainties, worries, and questions can be dealt with quickly. More importantly, the advice of teachers and other professionals is based on the collective experience of many children and families. As a result, this advice can be very useful in offering you options for dealing with your own problems and worries.

Becoming Part of the Family

Right from the start, you should expect that your baby with Down syndrome will be a part of your family, not the center of it. Just because your child has a disability does not mean he should dominate family life. This is not good for your baby nor for the rest of the family. Your baby does have special needs and he will demand emotional and physical resources that other children might not demand. But remember, your goal is to balance all the competing demands so that everyone in the family can be an equal and contributing member. This is the same challenge that all parents face, whether they have a child with disabilities or not.

The relationship of each family member with the child with Down syndrome will be a reflection of your attitudes as parents. If you hold and cuddle and love your baby, if you voice your feelings of affection, if you face challenges in a positive manner, then other family members will too.

As you begin the task of integrating your baby and his disability into your lives, you and all of your family will grow to love your baby more and more. That love will be your strongest ally, your strongest bond. Through patience and understanding, your child can be a loved and loving member of your family.

In addition to a supportive environment, it is essential that your children have information. Leaving things unsaid will only send a confused and troubling message to your children. Tell them that their sibling has Down syndrome as soon as you think they are ready. Explain it on a level they can understand, and give them more information as they get older. Children have the ability to love their brother or sister unconditionally. You will be surprised at how much they understand and how easily they accept what many adults receive with shock and sadness.

If you accept your child with Down syndrome and are comfortable with him, he will fit into your family and your lifestyle. Your child will enjoy family mealtimes, outings, and going to school with other children. Your child will probably be able to receive some, if not most of his education in a school where he is included in a regular classroom with typically developing children. This can allow your child to learn from the example of the children in his regular classes. Working to make your child as much a part of the "normal" world in his school and in your family life will help him tremendously. And the benefits of this are twofold. Not only will it help your child, but it will also help others in your child's world become more familiar and more comfortable with people with Down syndrome.

Take your child to the swimming pool, to the grocery store, to restaurants. Often the promise of "going out for spaghetti" can make a day go better, and the meal can be a special time for the entire family. Make sure your child participates in a variety of community activities, such as sports, scouts, and art classes. Find things that he likes and can participate in with other children.

The medical problems that some babies with Down syndrome have can add to the stress a family experiences. Although the goal is to make your child an integral part of your family, medical needs may make this difficult at times. Parents sometimes need to focus their attention just on their child with Down syndrome. This is not unreasonable. It can happen in any family when a child is sick or has a special problem. Remember to let your other children be involved with their sibling. Encourage them to make hospital visits and to express their feelings. Above all, keep them informed. They will be concerned and will want to help.

Love and Acceptance

The birth of a baby with Down syndrome comes as a shock to most parents. In addition to the feelings of love and protection they have for their new baby, many parents also feel sad and disappointed. These mixed feelings toward the baby often continue as the child grows. Do not hesitate to recognize these feelings within yourself and accept them without feeling guilty about them. No parent feels good about their child all the time.

Get to know your baby. Learn more about Down syndrome. Initially, you may be afraid to love your baby because you know so little about him and his condition. The closer you get to him, the more at ease you will become.

Today you can develop a relationship with your baby with confidence. Bolstered by the guidance and support of informed professionals, community support groups, and family and friends, you can provide an environment in which your child can grow to be a unique individual supported by your love.

Some parents feel that they cannot keep their baby with Down syndrome at home. One alternative is to place the child for adoption. There are agencies with waiting lists of people who specifically want to adopt a baby with Down syndrome. The Down Syndrome Association of Greater

Cincinnati also operates an Adoption Awareness program that can help prospective adoptive parents locate a child with Down syndrome (see the Resource Guide). Foster homes are also a viable alternative because children with Down syndrome benefit most from family life.

Expectations

Babies with Down syndrome are born with a variety of physical and intellectual abilities. As Chapter 6 discusses, these abilities are often different from those of other children, but it is not possible to predict any child's full potential at an early age. At this point in your baby's

life, do not set limits on what he will or will not be able to do. Strive for that delicate balance between a realistic assessment of your child's development and the self-fulfilling prophecy of low achievement. Most of all, ensure that your child will lead a happy and useful life by providing appropriate support and training from an early age.

Parents spend more time with their young children than anyone else does, and their expectations can affect their children in tangible ways. For example, if you do not expect your child with Down syndrome to dress himself, he may not. Perhaps you unwittingly have not given him the chance. You may dress and undress him or simply help him too much because your expectations are too low.

Do not form your expectations in a vacuum and do not base them on stereotypes. Talk to doctors, teachers, therapists, and other parents of children with Down syndrome. Read current books and journals and attend seminars and conferences to keep abreast of the latest research. It takes information and exposure to realistically set your expectations. More importantly, try not to look too far into the future. Focus on the next developmental skill; set short-term goals. After all, the future is made up of what your child learns along the way.

Limit Setting

Discipline is the parents' responsibility. Having a child with Down syndrome does not change that. You do not do your child a favor by failing to demand appropriate behavior because you feel sorry for him or because you think he cannot understand how to behave. If you allow your child to misbehave, you can be assured he will continue to misbehave. Your child's safety, social integration, and education depend on appropriate behavior. You owe it to your child to demand acceptable behavior.

Disciplining your child may be difficult for you to do. You may feel sorry for him because he has Down syndrome. You may not be sure he understands what is expected of him. And, after giving him the same direction over and over, you may lose your patience and do it yourself. In public and with friends it is even harder. Not only do you not want to cause a scene, but you may not want to call attention to your child or to how difficult it appears to be to deal with him. However, the experience of many families is clear: discipline needs to be applied consistently. Children need to know what is, and what is not, acceptable conduct in all situations. Firmness and consistency work best; don't take the easy way out for reasons of convenience, embarrassment, or frustration. Unless you can teach your child safe and acceptable behavior, he may always be dependent on you.

The social development of children and adults with Down syndrome is often more advanced than their level of mental development. Give your child every chance to succeed in life by teaching him to behave the way you expect his brothers and sisters to behave. Set limits and be consistent in enforcing them. And remember, emphasize the positive. Praise and affection are the most powerful motivators for good behavior.

If your child can make the connection between his behavior and the consequences you might impose, removing him from the scene, placing him in a "time out" or "time away" chair for a few minutes, or denying him a later pleasure are good tactics to try. Be sure that you clearly state your expectations for his behavior. "No hitting. Tell Ben 'My turn.'" This lets your child know what not to do and gives him an acceptable alternative. Once he understands, you can explain briefly and unemotionally that if he misbehaves, then something will happen.

An extremely effective method of discipline is positive reward. For a young child, a big hug and "I like the way you play!" can go a long way in achieving acceptable behavior. For older children, you might try a reward chart with a star for each time he plays in the yard without throwing the ball over the fence or takes a bath without soaking the bathroom. Distraction can be effective also. If your child is doing something inappropriate, you might try suggesting something else you know will interest him.

For some children, the positive approach is the only one that consistently gets results. Your child may not understand why he is be-ing punished. He may "dig in his heels" when you get angry. You may find that he responds better when you change your expression to a pleasant one, make your voice encouraging, and explain with excitement what he needs to do. This can move him in the direction you want to go without a prolonged battle, which you might win, but which will leave both you and your child in no mood to enjoy an activity.

An important consideration in disciplining your child is how others will handle him. With babysitters, grandparents, relatives, and friends, there is often the opportunity for your discipline to be undermined. It will be necessary for you to politely yet firmly let others know that discipline is important to you and to your child. Explain to them what conduct is acceptable and what is not. Help them understand and enlist their help. Firmness and consistency are not always easy to maintain, but they will pay off.

When setting expectations for your child's behavior, you must learn to give him enough time to process information. Do not expect instant responses or fast transitions from one activity to another. It is possible that he needs a little extra time to understand your wishes and to decide on his own response. What may appear to be resistance or stubbornness may simply be an inability to cope with your verbal demands or to deal with a transition.

Some children find a change in routine a difficult emotional step and feel anxiety in moving from one activity to another. What you encounter may result less from "I don't want to do it" stubbornness and more from your child enjoying what he is doing and feeling anxious about being asked to do something else. He also might not understand or remember what is going to happen next. Many children with Down syndrome benefit from visual prompts to let them know what is coming next. For example, if you are heading for the playground, you could show your child a picture of the playground or hand him the sand shovel that he uses at the playground. Older children with Down syndrome frequently benefit from picture schedules that show—with photographs or drawings—the series of events that they will encounter during the course of their day.

If you are faced with a pattern of resistance, you can often break through it by offering a more interesting and exciting alternative. For example, suggest your child kick a ball into an overturned garbage can instead of toward the street or wonder aloud if all his bath toys will fit in the tub at once. You will have to observe your child and consider his developmental level and his ability to understand in order to distinguish between his resistance to reasonable expectations and his inability to process your demands. You as his parent will be in the best position to judge.

One further consideration is that sometimes what looks like misbehavior to you may actually be your child's attempt at communication. Especially when children have difficulty expressing themselves with words, they may use behavior to get their message across. For example, a child who is terrified of walking past a house where a large, rambunctious dog lives may flop down on the sidewalk or throw a tantrum to communicate that he does not want to walk in that direction. Or, a child who cannot figure out how to get a playmate's attention any other way may hit or bite him.

If you notice patterns in your child's behavior—especially if he is not speaking or using sign language yet—a speech and language pathologist can help figure out more appropriate ways for your child to communicate. You also might ask your child's early intervention program or school to do a "functional behavior assessment," which is a systematic way of determining what somebody is trying to communicate with his behavior.

Independence

It is natural to feel that your child is particularly vulnerable because he has Down syndrome. It is a natural reaction to think he needs extra help and to want to protect him. But for the sake of his future, you must treat him as normally as possible. Your child needs to learn independence and responsibility. He needs to feel good about himself and what he can do.

Your job begins early in teaching your child self-help skills such as dressing and feeding himself. Give your child the opportunity to do things for himself. Don't rush to help him before you give him the chance to try something on his own. Encourage and praise him along the way and reward him with a big hug for a job well done.

Your child will likely be involved in an education or therapy program at an early age and will need to be "on his own" in many of these

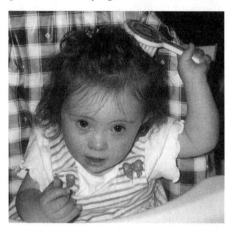

situations. Don't let your child's crying tempt you to give up on a new school or program that may be strange to him. Give him time to adjust. Children usually adjust well and enjoy school.

Expose your child to new situations whenever possible. Provide him with a variety of experiences and help him adjust to what is new and different. Take him to the zoo, introduce him to a sandbox, let him explore the local shopping mall. Give him responsibilities and chores within the family. When he is a preschooler, insist that he pick up his toys, but help him put them in the toy box or on the shelf. As he gets older, build on the things he enjoys. Maybe he can dust the furniture, take out the newspapers for recycling, help you work in the yard. Take the time to teach him and make sure that he can be successful at whatever task you ask him to do. When all the family works together, include your child with Down syndrome. Like all of us, he needs to feel like a valued member of the family. Think positively about what your child can do. Feel positive about his capabilities. Increase your child's self-esteem by giving him the opportunity to succeed within the secure confines of the family. This will help prepare him to move out into the larger world of friends, school, work, and community.

If your baby has a congenital heart defect, you may not be able to treat him as you would any other baby. Frequent trips to the hospital for cardiac studies, the risk of respiratory infection, and difficulty in feeding will necessitate extra care and caution on your part. Provide this care and protect your baby wisely, but be ready to allow him to move out into the world as soon as he is able. To be sure, this is not easy. Conflicting emotions and real medical concerns intensify the natural urge to protect your child and complicate the necessary process of letting go. If in doubt about what health-related precautions you should take, ask your doctor.

■■ Brothers and Sisters of Children with Down Syndrome

Being the brother or sister of a child with Down syndrome is special. In many subtle and not-so-subtle ways your other children's lives will be different because they have a sibling with a disability. But do not assume that this difference is all bad. Far from it. Having a sibling with Down syndrome is stressful and enriching, frustrating and fun, worrisome and rewarding. Most of all, it is very much like being the sibling of any other child, complete with all the annoyances and joys. This section reviews the effects that children with Down syndrome can have on their siblings, and focuses on what you, the parent, can do to help all your children build healthy relationships with one another.

Children's Feelings

From the time they are old enough to understand, your other children will have thoughts and feelings about their sibling with Down syndrome. At first, they may perceive only that it takes their brother

or sister longer to do things like walk or talk. Later, they will begin to understand that their brother or sister has a disability. What follows is a summary of the thoughts and feelings typically experienced by siblings of children with Down syndrome.

Ages Two to Four. Children are very perceptive, so it is possible for your other children to react to the anxiety you feel about your baby with Down syndrome. At this age they are unlikely to recognize any difference in their sibling or understand what Down syndrome is, but preschoolers may perceive developmental differences and try in their own way to help teach skills. They want to help. Mostly this is an age when children fall in love with their sibling and want to help take care of him.

Ages Four to Six. As children become more sophisticated, they often begin to wonder what is "wrong" with their sibling. They may worry about catching Down syndrome or worry that something is different about them as well. Additionally, they often feel guilty about any negative thoughts they may have toward their sibling. For example, anger caused by frustration—a perfectly normal response for young children at times—can cause feelings of guilt. Sometimes children try to compensate for their special sibling's problems by trying to be especially exemplary themselves. They become excessively helpful and obedient beyond limits that are good for them, for your family, or for your child with Down syndrome.

Ages Six to Twelve. Children at these ages often have conflicting emotions. On the one hand, they can feel good about being needed by their sibling with Down syndrome, and on the other hand, they can consider their sibling a nuisance. They may respond to teasing of their sibling by becoming hostile toward the culprit or by being protective. At the same time, they may be resentful of any extra work imposed on them as a result of their sibling's special needs.

Children at these ages may also have a tendency to "correct" their sibling's behavior. For instance, they may feel it is their job to remind their brother to use his napkin or to tell their sister to talk more quietly in the library. This pseudo-parental behavior can rub your child with Down syndrome the wrong way, especially if he is older than his brother or sister. Also during this stage, if you appear preoccupied with your child with Down syndrome, your other children can view this as "babying," which they may consider unfair. But be aware that children of this age perceive many things as unfair, whether or not they are connected with Down syndrome. When one sibling gets to go on a field trip and another doesn't, or one misses school due to a dental appointment and the other doesn't, this is likely to be considered unfair, too.

Ages Twelve to Sixteen. During this important period of adolescent development, your child's social life often causes some very normal problems. Teenagers can feel embarrassed by their families. When friends and dates come to your house, your teenager may feel embarrassed by your child with Down syndrome. Your teenager will love his or her sibling and care about him, but just as certainly will want to exercise freedom and independence. This is a time when responsibilities imposed on your children—including responsibility for your child with Down syndrome—may be resented. Concerns over the future also can arise. Your other children may worry whether they

will have to take responsibility for their special sibling in later years and whether their own children will have Down syndrome.

These are just some of the feelings your child with Down syndrome may trigger in your other children. Emotions come in every shape and size, and each child's feelings are unique. But some feelings seem universal. Love, fear, jealousy, resentment, anger, pride, and frustration are present at some time in children, just as they are in adults. The central challenge for a caring parent is to deal with these many genuine—and conflicting—human emotions.

Dealing with Your Children's Emotions

Just as you experience stress as the parent of a child with Down syndrome, your other children may find it stressful to be the sibling of a child with disabilities. But the strongest factor in their adjustment will be your reaction. They will follow your lead in interacting with their brother or sister. Keep in mind, however, that, like you, they will have conflicting emotions about their sibling. It would be easier if children clearly showed their feelings, but often children do not, or cannot, express how they are feeling about life with their sibling. Parents must be emotional detectives, deciphering their children's emotions from clues in their behavior. First and foremost, dealing effectively with emotions requires observation and listening.

Information. Children can deal better with their sibling with Down syndrome if they have information. You should be the main source of this information. Even if they do not ask, give them information. As with other subjects, give them information appropriate to their age level and expand it as they grow. There are many fine books written specifically for siblings of children with Down syndrome and other disabilities. The reading list at the back of this book includes some of these books. Capitalizing on "teachable moments" is also a good strategy. If your other children notice another child with Down syndrome on the playground or in a movie, try using that as a springboard for discussion.

Even with an explanation of what Down syndrome is and what it means to have an intellectual disability or developmental delay, your children may still have an imperfect understanding. They may worry about catching Down syndrome, about having children of their own, and about caring for their sibling in the future. Then again, they may think that Down syndrome is something your child will "grow out of." Continue to provide information and to reassure your children. Be ready to debunk the myths they may hear by giving them the facts.

Even if you think you have already explained Down syndrome perfectly to your other children, be sure to check their understanding from time to time. You may be surprised to find that the differences they notice and care about are not the ones you assume they notice. For example, a younger child may wonder why his sibling with Down syndrome cannot whistle or ride a two-wheeler without training wheels, but may not even be aware of delays in cognitive skills.

Communication. It is important that you encourage and even prod your children to talk about the feelings they have for their sibling. Let them know it is normal to feel as they do and that it is healthy to express themselves. If possible, let them join with other siblings of children with disabilities to work through their feelings. Sibling groups are sponsored by a variety of organizations, and are listed in the book's Resource Guide. Urge your children to take advantage of the opportunity to sort out what they are feeling and experiencing.

Children get angry, annoyed, frustrated—as we all do. Sometimes they fight. But when a sibling with Down syndrome is the cause of that anger, young children can experience great difficulty. Sometimes out of sympathy for their parents or their sibling, children feel guilty about their anger. They may

avoid interacting with their brother or sister with Down syndrome or may let him get away with behavior they wouldn't accept from another child. As a parent, it is vital for you to let your children know that it is sometimes reasonable to get angry with their sibling and to vent that anger. All of your children need to communicate their anger over things like broken toys or misplaced keepsakes. Protecting your child with Down syndrome from the well-deserved wrath of his siblings cuts off communication and forces feelings underground. Anger is a natural part of family life. Every member is a target from time to time. Having a child with Down syndrome should not change that.

Balance. It is important that you balance the needs of all of your children. Encourage all of them to succeed and to fulfill themselves. Do not give all of your attention to your child with Down syndrome. It is not healthy for one child to dominate parental attention. Instead, you need to skillfully juggle the many demands on your time and attention.

Do not allow your child with Down syndrome to become overly dependent on his siblings. Rather, encourage your children to take an active part in their sibling's educational and therapeutic programs. They, too, will become emotionally attached to their sibling and will rejoice in each independent step he takes. And, remember to allow them to do this as a brother or sister. Do not press them into the role of parent, even if they seem willing to assume it. Do not expect that an older child will feed, bathe, and dress his brother every day. Do not insist that his brother always go along to the grocery store or the drugstore when you send your teenager on an errand. And do not insist that your child change his plans in order to babysit his brother. This can breed long-standing resentment. Better to sit down with all family members and work out how you will share responsibilities for your child with Down syndrome so that each person's needs are met.

Organization. With all that is urged upon parents of babies with Down syndrome—early intervention, monitoring for medical problems, all the normal baby-care responsibilities—it is easy to unintentionally overlook your other children's needs. There is only so much of you and only so many hours in a day. Try to organize your time. With a child with special needs, the challenge is a little greater, but it can be done.

Children do not conveniently schedule their crises. They get hurt, upset, or excited on their own time, and when they do, they demand your immediate and full attention. Parents often cannot control their own schedules, but there are a few things you can do to keep things running reasonably smoothly. Here is a short list of ideas:

- Try to spend some individual time with each child and with your spouse. And leave some time for yourself.
- Whenever possible, schedule the time that must be spent exclusively with your child with Down syndrome at times when your other children are not at home or are otherwise occupied.
- When your children are at home, organize group play that includes all your children. Let your older children lead and your younger children follow.
- Keep your children busy. Schedule play times, visits to friends' houses, and outings to the park. But avoid overdoing it—avoid the syndrome of rushing around all the time, trying to cram too much into each day. Give everyone the opportunity just to "hang out" sometimes.
- Don't try to do it all yourself. Participate in car pools and play groups. Pay a babysitter or trade with another parent.

Individuality. Just as this book encourages you to treat your child with Down syndrome as an individual, it is equally important to do the same for your other children. They need lives outside their family. They need to experience peer friendship, social acceptance, and nonfamily responsibilities. Their identity cannot be limited to being the sibling of a brother or sister with Down syndrome. Provide them with activities away from home, with their own friends. Encourage them to pursue their own interests and talents and to exercise their independence. Make sure you attend their concerts, games, and other events that are important to them. Build their self-esteem just as you would with your child with Down syndrome. Children with balanced lives will be far better adjusted to their family, as well as more supportive of both you and their sibling.

Your expectations of your children can make a difference. Expect, demand, and work to build and maintain normal family relationships. Allow your other children to act like children. And let them know that you expect your child with Down syndrome to behave appropriately. Siblings resent favored treatment accorded to others. It is important to both your children and your child with Down syndrome that you require him to help take care of himself and to contribute in helping with the family chores. Don't settle for less.

Specialness. In addition to encouraging your other children to lead their own lives, it is also very important to give them a sense of their own specialness. One way is to encourage their individuality, as described above. You can also let them know how much you appreciate their help around the house. Most siblings naturally feel good about being needed by their sibling with Down syndrome. As parents you can reinforce those feelings. Praise their compassion, the extra work they do around the house, and the extra coping required of them. Make them feel that their efforts are recognized and appreciated.

Dealing with Problems

Although society has become far more sensitive and compassionate toward people with disabilities, there is no guarantee that your children will not occasionally be wounded by teasing or cruel remarks. Siblings of children with Down syndrome know their brother or sister is different, and they often are quite protective. When feelings are hurt, parents usually get the job of soothing. Good family communication is a must in these situations.

When adults say insensitive things, siblings of special children can have surprising responses. They may think the adult is ignorant or mean. But if the adult is someone they know and trust, confusion and uncertainty can arise. Parents need to confront these incidents head-on, with facts. Reassure and support your children with information and understanding.

Dealing with the cruel remarks and teasing of children can be more difficult than dealing with those of adults. As children grow, peer acceptance and social interaction increase in importance. Children with Down syndrome can sometimes embarrass their siblings, who in turn may alienate their own friends in defense of their special sibling or perhaps turn on their sibling with Down syndrome. In addition to encouraging them to express their feelings and offering them reassurance, parents should make sure that their other children have time to be on their own, with their own friends.

Children sometimes repeat the comments and teasing they hear and see at school. When parents overhear teasing or get a report from their children, they sometimes get angry and want to set things right. Children, however, need to learn to cope with life on their own. Unless there is a risk that your children may be emotionally or physically harmed, fight the urge to rescue. If one of your children is truly in danger, then, by all means, get involved. Contact school authorities if the incident occurred at school, or the parents of the children involved, if you think that will be more helpful.

Children can develop their own effective ways of coping and they can do it without losing their love for their special sibling or the friendship of their peers. Talk to your children. Urge them to talk about how they felt when they were teased. Talk with them about reasons why someone might make such comments. Help them think of ways they might respond and choose how they will react in the future. Help them to think of ways to talk about their sibling to help explain his differences to their friends and playmates. Often a simple explanation that it is harder for him to talk or that it takes him longer to learn something is all it takes. Your children will have to deal with others' reactions to their sibling for a long time, so avoid fighting their battles for them. All of you will feel better when they find the way that is comfortable for them.

Counseling can help children who experience trouble in coping with their sibling. Talking to someone outside the family, such as an objective, caring professional, can help a great deal. Not all problems need to be solved within the family. Sometimes giving your child room to adjust with the help of a counselor can accomplish what you cannot. Do not be afraid—or too proud—to seek help. Pediatricians, therapists, special educators, and school counselors are frequently asked by parents for names of counselors who are especially good in working with children. Also remember that you have the experience of other parents and of the organizations listed in this book to guide you in finding someone who can help.

The Future

As your other children grow and mature they will begin to think about their future with their special sibling. Questions about responsibility and care will be asked. Again, you need to provide facts. Let your children know that they will not need to be responsible for their adult sibling with Down syndrome unless they choose to be. With careful estate planning and access to government benefits and programs, it is usually possible to ensure that siblings will not have to support their brother or sister with Down syndrome.

Your children and their future will likely be affected by their sibling with Down syndrome. Being the sibling of a child with Down syndrome can cause problems and frustrations, but at the same time it can warm the hearts of your children for a lifetime. Many siblings develop a strong capacity for love and acceptance of someone who is different. They may develop a sense not only of social understanding, but also of social responsibility. They may choose a career in one of the helping professions in an effort to make things better for those who are different. Your children may also develop a sense of specialness about your family and the special ties that bind you together.

This section has emphasized the importance of communication between parents and their children. Remember, parents are not infallible and do not always have all the answers: they hurt, they worry, they feel frustrated. It is not always necessary to put up a cheerful front for the sake of your kids. Let your children know that you do not have all the answers, that you need their support, and that you are all in this together. Children usually surprise parents with how much they understand and how much they care. Make sure all your children have the information and support they need to be fully participating members of your family.

∷ Your Relationship with Your Partner or Spouse

Often the greatest source of support you have as parents of a child with Down syndrome is each other. Although Down syndrome may be a source of stress and strain for each of you and for your relationship, you

can help one another in dealing with this unexpected event in your lives. The starting place is to identify ways in which you have coped with other difficult situations in your lives. Use these same strategies in dealing with the needs of your child with Down syndrome.

If your relationship with your spouse is strong, your marriage can probably withstand the additional stress imposed on it by the birth of your child. In fact, some parents feel that their baby has drawn them closer together. They speak of their awareness of their parental roles and of their responsibility to their child: "we feel we must stick together and support each other in each new crisis related to him."

One of the best ways to support one another is to openly share your feelings about your child with Down syndrome. Remember that you will feel love, hate, anger, fear, guilt—a full spectrum of conflicting emotions. It is perfectly normal to have these feelings, and you should let your spouse know that it is okay for him or her to have them too. If you share and acknowledge these feelings, you can work through them together, or together you can seek the help of others to aid you in this important process. You may find it helpful to talk to a friend, another parent, a priest, rabbi, or minister, a psychologist, or a counselor.

When your baby is young, he may be like any other baby in terms of the amount of care and attention needed. But as a toddler, his physical and educational needs will increasingly infringe on the time and energy you can devote to one another. Remember, however, this is true of any toddler! One parent of an infant with Down syndrome spoke about the influence of the infant on his relationship with his wife:

The most difficult thing has been finding the time to be alone together to work on our relationship. We have so many extra doctor appointments. Also, we must work much harder to stimulate our baby. We really don't spend more time playing with her, but more energy. It takes more psychological energy to get her to respond.

Like all parents, you worry about your child's future. You think about his education, his ability to participate in sports and other peer activities, his prospects for employment, and his ability to live independently. Although you will want to find more information about each of these subjects at the appropriate time, you must also learn to live one day a time. Learn to focus on small steps in your child's development. He now rolls to get what he wants, he stays dry all night, he sits through a whole story at circle time, he plays soccer with the kids at recess. Learn to enjoy today with your child. Celebrate life's small triumphs.

Earlier in this chapter the statement was made that your child with Down syndrome should not be the center of your family. If you allow that to happen, anger and resentment can build up in you and in other family members. Likewise, your child should not be the center of one parent's or partner's life or the sole responsibility of one parent or partner. Each of you should share in the care, stimulation, education, and the pleasure of loving your child. You need to decide what arrangement works best for you. Even though you are tired at the end of the day, a short play session with your child or a fun time in the bathtub can be a great stress reliever. When your child is unable to enjoy activities that his siblings like, Mom may want to go off to the museum with the other children while Dad stays home and takes him to the grocery store.

Your child will probably require extra time and attention at some, but not necessarily all, ages and you may feel you need to be a "super" parent. You and your partner may have radically different expectations or may not be able to support one another in dealing with your child's special needs. Perhaps your feelings of anger or guilt will cause you to do everything for your child to make his life easier. This will likely leave you exhausted and frustrated—and not available to other family members. Don't try to do it all. It's okay to let things slip once in awhile. Take time for yourself. Take a good look at what you are doing and why. Talk to your spouse or partner; nothing replaces open, honest communication. Get help if you need it. Talk to your minister or a family counselor. Read books about parenting and relationships and find ways to strengthen your marriage and your family.

■■ Conclusion

In many ways, having a child with Down syndrome in the family is richly rewarding, but it can also be stressful—on children, on parents, and on the whole family.

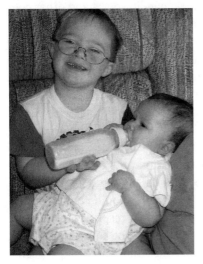

There is no formula for coping perfectly with Down syndrome. Love, communication, acceptance, and the steadfast belief that your family will in the end thrive are your best bets to ensure a healthy and rewarding family life.

There are many books on families that have children with special needs. As you begin the task of integrating your child with Down syndrome into your family, reading about the experiences of others can help a great deal. So can talking to other parents of children with Down syndrome. Their advice, based on what has worked best for them, can be very helpful. Just sharing similar problems and triumphs can help put your life in perspective. Most importantly, remember that you, your spouse, and your whole family are all in this together.

■■ Parent Statements

My relatives were all very good. They were amazing, actually. All my brothers and my sister just concentrated on our son; they just responded to him completely. And my mother acted as if there was nothing different about him at all.

✤✤✤

Our relatives' reactions have varied. One relative was a little bit condescending about it. He said, "Oh, he's one of God's children; it's okay." He was trying to comfort us, but I think he took the wrong approach.

❧

Christopher has made us a family. He's a little child, and you know, it doesn't really matter that he has Down syndrome. Mothers and fathers and children make families and he's been in every way affectionate and childlike and all the things that children are. That's what makes a family.

❧

We decided that any child would have to fit into our lives. For example, Laurie has so many appointments and needs, but I had originally decided to go back to work. I adjusted my plans a little and went back part time. I decided I needed that for myself. We still had to go out at night. We still had to have time alone.

❧

I think every child with Down syndrome needs someone to energize him, and I don't think it should be a parent. A sibling, an aunt, a next-door neighbor. I know three kids who have a person like that in their lives, and all three kids seem to have a spirit to them.

❧

Our family has been somewhat varied in their reaction. I think there was a lot of sorrow. But I think our own attitude helped most of our relatives work it out. Our attitude of "We're just crazy about this baby" helped everyone a lot.

❧

We treat Sam generally just like another kid. If we want to go out shopping, okay, he's going to go shopping. He eats what we eat. We don't try to shield him. He has to live in the world. The world's not going to change to accommodate him. The more he is out in the world, the more he will be able to adjust to it.

❧

An old friend has a son who is five. Recently, we went to visit them for the first time in about two years. They decided not to say anything to their son about Josh having Down syndrome, and to just see what happened. Their son treated him just like a regular kid; it didn't bother him that Josh didn't talk much. They got along great. Maybe if you don't prejudice them, kids accept each other as they are.

❧❀❧

We have two kids, one with extremely high intelligence, and the other with Down syndrome. It's tough to switch gears sometimes. It takes a lot of patience, and I don't think I have as much as I'd like to have.

❧❀❧

I didn't really feel a sense of mourning or disappointment until recently. It all evolved around getting our son placed in school and integrated into the neighborhood. I realized that I was working so much harder to make things easier for this child than with our other two children. I sometimes find myself wishing that it were a little easier.

❧❀❧

We like to keep strict tabs on her behavior. We find ourselves saying, "That's cute at four but it's not going to be so cute at eight."

❧❀❧

We use discipline with a lot of consistency and a lot of patience, and we never expect more than she's able to comprehend at the moment.

❧❀❧

Sometimes I worry about Ethan because he gets so much attention from adults. He has teachers and therapists coming to the house and fawning on him for an hour at a time. I'm afraid he'll get away with things just by being cute.

❧❀❧

We've tried different things for discipline. Our infant educator told us to try modeling what he should do. It worked instantly. We picked up all the food he threw down and put it in his hand and told him to put it back on the table. He did it and he was so pleased with himself that he started doing it normally.

❧❀❧

I'm kind of a strong disciplinarian and I try to keep the same standards of discipline for all three kids. But with Julie you can't let too much time elapse between the event and saying, "No, this is something we don't do."

❧❀❧

We feel strongly that our children need clear boundaries and to be held to a high standard of age-appropriate behavior. We communicate in simple terms with both of our children, lead by example, and have high expectations that they will be respectful and well-mannered, and we have not had any significant behavioral issues. Although it's not always easy or convenient, we try to always follow-through on punishments, and have had success with using time outs, a "3 strikes" system, and redirection to reinforce our rules. We are extremely careful not to make excuses for our son with Down syndrome, or to expect less of him because of his disability. After all, if he doesn't learn to abide by society's rules, he will never have the opportunity to be fully included.

❧❦☙

We have to be careful about how we discipline our three-year-old daughter, since she is a very sensitive child. We use time outs as our main source of discipline, along with explanations as to why Mommy or Daddy did not like that behavior. If she is just told "no" without an explanation, she seems to repeat the unwanted behavior. But, if we explain in simple terms, that behavior seems to go away. We also count 1—2 —3 if she does not respond to a request such as picking up her coat that she took off and dropped on the floor.

❧❦☙

It's important for Abby's sister to always be able to express her feelings. She shouldn't just have to mirror our feelings. Her feelings are going to be different, and we shouldn't feed her our feelings so that those are the only acceptable ones.

❧❦☙

There's a lot of sibling rivalry between our two sons that would be there anyway, I think. But when the early intervention teacher came to our house every week, our older son slowly caught on that there was something unusual about his brother. He got a little resentful over the amount of attention his brother got.

❧❦☙

Our oldest daughter is a real companion to Julie. But the middle one feels just caught next to this little kid who's a pain in the neck sometimes. But a four-year-old sibling would be a pain in the neck even if she didn't have Down syndrome.

❧❀❧

Josh's older brother hasn't seemed to have had problems with teasing from other kids. His friends come here all the time. They take Josh as one of the givens of the house.

❧❀❧

I was a little worried about how Hope would react when we brought our new baby home from the hospital, and she realized she wasn't the only child any more. For the most part, though, Hope is as gentle and sweet with the baby as any toddler could be. She gives the baby lots of kisses, shakes rattles for her, tries to feed her a bottle, "shh's" people when the baby is sleeping.

❧❀❧

The thing that has taken us most by surprise is how tricky it is to integrate Julie into the neighborhood. We have very nice neighbors and they think the world of Julie, but they have their own four-year-old children who are normal, competent, capable children who play together real well. There's nothing malicious, but there are all kinds of activities that go on without Julie.

❧❀❧

Our two kids are very close in age and they are pretty much best friends right now. Sure, they occasionally have trouble sharing with each other, like all little children do, but they also love playing Ring Around the Rosie, having tea parties for their stuffed animals, and watching DVDs together.

❧❀❧

I think if you had a weak marriage, Down syndrome would come as an obstacle between you. There were times when it was hard for my husband to adjust to the change in our family dynamics. Until she was about two, I was the one who was really involved in meeting all her needs. It took time away from him.

❧❀❧

There are positive and negative effects on our marriage and family, and on balance it comes out positive. It's more of a workload. It's the struggle with the educational and therapeutic activities—a whole new dimension of work that has to be split up. On the other hand, we both feel that our family is so much richer. I sometimes think life would be boring if we had all "normal" kids.

❧

One of the things about marriage is that when you have kids, you assume that those kids are going to be a part of your life for eighteen to twenty years and then you're going to go back to being a couple. But when your kid has Down syndrome, it dawns on you that this kid could be around forever. Then you go through a stage of realizing that that isn't the case—that a kid with Down syndrome can grow up and have a life too. Then it's a different emotion—like, we don't want her to leave. I know that separation is coming, but it's going to be tough.

❧

Having a baby with Down syndrome didn't diminish our desire to have more children. But the thing was, I had a hysterectomy as a result of her birth. We decided immediately to adopt more children. We definitely hate the idea of our daughter not having any other siblings. So we have planned an adoption. Everyone keeps saying, "How do you know it won't have something wrong with it?" and so we say, "Well, we could have produced one ourselves that had something wrong with it."

❧

I have a real hard time planning too far ahead. I don't mean that I muddle through each day, but I can only plan one day in advance. I don't think it's necessarily related to our baby having Down syndrome, because I have friends who have little kids without Down syndrome, and they complain of the same thing. I think someday I'll evolve out of that and I'll be able to plan ahead like I used to.

❧

With Ben in our family, there's never a dull moment. One morning when he was small, he came into the kitchen without his glasses. He is always so good about wearing them because he realizes he sees so much better with them on. I asked him where they were and he told me "in the washing machine!" What? They were not in the washing machine and they were not in the dryer, nor were they in any of the trash cans, not the big one in the kitchen, not in the toilet, and, thankfully, not in the garbage disposal, not in any of the places he told me to look. They were nowhere to be found and Ben was having a merry old time watching me search. By chance, I spotted them on the floor of his closet. When I handed them to him, he was clearly disappointed that his fun game was over.

THE DEVELOPMENT OF BABIES WITH DOWN SYNDROME

Sue Buckley, OBE, BA, CPsychol, AFBPsS

All babies develop—they grow, change, progress, and learn from the first days of life. Babies with Down syndrome develop much like other children

but at a slower rate and with some differences. In recent years, researchers have learned a great deal about how babies with Down syndrome develop, some of the reasons for their slower pace of development, and some of the factors that influence their progress. This knowledge is helping parents, therapists, and educators provide more effective environments and learning opportunities for babies and toddlers with Down syndrome, so that they can each reach their full potential and lead happy and fulfilled lives in our communities.

Most babies born with Down syndrome today will make more progress and achieve more than those born in past generations as a result of our better understanding of their needs, early intervention services designed to meet those needs and to support families, increasing access to good education, and full inclusion in their communities with other children.

This chapter sets out to share with you what we know about the development of babies and young children with Down syndrome, how fast they progress, what influences their rate of progress, and what steps you can take to ensure you are giving your child the most effective help and support. The information in this chapter is evidence-based—that is, based on the latest scientific research with references to further reading given at the end of the chapter.

■■ How Do We Describe Development?

In order to understand and describe children's development we usually divide it into five main areas—developing: 1) social/emotional, 2) communication, 3) motor, 4) cognitive, and 5) self-help skills.

Communication covers the development of all the ways a child can "get a message across" by using nonverbal communication such as pointing, gestures, and facial expressions and learning to talk using speech and language skills.

Social/emotional development includes learning how to understand and get on with other people, make friends, behave in socially acceptable ways, and understand and manage feelings. It will be influenced by a child's temperament and personality.

Motor development covers the ways in which a child develops movement skills—usually broken into gross and fine motor skills. Gross motor covers learning whole body control for skills such as sitting, standing, walking, and running. Fine motor covers hand and finger skills for picking things up, feeding, writing, and all self-help skills.

Cognitive development includes the ways in which a child develops the mental abilities of processing information, thinking, remembering, and reasoning. In early years, play activities play an important role in developing cognition as children explore their world through play, find out what things do, and solve simple problems posed by toys and puzzles. Cognitive development will be influenced by a child's curiosity and motivation to explore and persist at tasks.

Self-help describes how children develop practical independence for feeding, sleeping, washing, toileting, and dressing in the early years and later for travelling by themselves, using money, shopping, cooking, and managing personal care.

Development in each of these areas has been described in detail by those studying children's development. In each area, development progresses in an orderly sequence and later steps are built on earlier ones. For example, children point and use gestures to communicate before they use words—then they use a range of single words before they join words and use sentences. Children sit before they stand and stand before they walk. Children with Down syndrome usually progress through the same steps in each area of development. Therefore, the detailed knowledge that we have about these steps allows us to design activities to help a child reach the next step.

However, it is also important to note that progress in each developmental area may affect progress in the others, and we need to consider this when thinking about a child's learning opportunities. For example, a child's motor skills will influence social and language experience. A child who is able to move can go to the door to see who has arrived and can follow her parents around and be talked to while they are engaged in daily chores. A child who cannot move may miss out on these experiences. Similarly, delays in a child's motor skills may affect cognition and self-help skills, as fine finger coordination is needed to fit shapes in holes, build with blocks, complete puzzles, and to hold a spoon or do up buttons. Delays in learning to talk will influence a child's social development and learning opportunities.

:: What Influences Children's Development?

Many factors influence the development of any child, including her genetic make-up, family life, health, educational opportunities, and the social life of her community. While genes play a part, human development is a process (or set of complex processes) and it requires social experience from the earliest days.

Babies smile at a person as part of a social interaction, they move to get to interesting toys, they learn to talk if they are talked to, and they learn to understand themselves and others through social interaction. Babies also need to feel loved and secure in order to have the confidence to learn, explore the world, and develop their full potential. A typical, healthy baby placed in a barren orphanage will not develop in the way she could have—all aspects of her development will be stunted or distorted. Families, schools, and communities all have very significant impact on how children grow, learn, and develop, and this is equally true for babies with Down syndrome.

If we wish to help children with Down syndrome reach their full potential, we do need to understand the impact of their biology—how the presence of an extra chromosome may influence the ways in which they perceive the world, learn, and progress in each area of development. However, we must also be constantly aware that this is only a part of the picture and that their development is as much influenced by the world they live in and the opportunities it gives them as it is for other children. Please keep this in mind as you read the next section.

◼ How Do Babies with Down Syndrome Develop?

If we take a general overview, the answer to this question is that they progress in much the same way as children without disabilities in most areas of development, but at a slower pace. However, if we take a closer look, it turns out that their development proceeds faster in some areas than others, so that over time we see a pattern of strengths and weaknesses across the main areas of development. For example, for most babies with Down syndrome, social development is a strength and they are not much delayed in smiling and interacting socially, but their motor progress and progress at learning to talk is more delayed.

If we then begin to look in detail at their progress within each area of development, we also find strengths and weaknesses. For example, in communication, they are good at using gestures to communicate but find speaking more difficult—so they understand more than they can say. In cognition, they are better at processing and remembering visual information—what they see—than verbal information—what they hear. This means that both within communication and cognition we begin to see *differences* in the way that babies and children with Down syndrome are progressing and learning—not just delays.

This information is very useful in helping us to develop the most effective ways to teach and support our children's progress, as you will see in the next section. We can use their strengths to help them to learn more quickly and effectively and we can also work directly to improve their weaker areas.

∷ Social/Emotional Development

Relating to Others

The first steps in social and emotional development are seen very early as your baby looks at you and then begins to smile. Babies with Down syndrome are usually very social—they like to look at faces, to smile, and to begin to learn about other people. Babies learn to understand facial expressions, tones of voice, and body postures, as these are ways in which we convey how we are feeling.

Babies with Down syndrome often spend more time looking at faces and engaging with people than other babies do, and as they move into toddler years they continue to be interested in and engage with both adults and other children. This is good for their social learning and their ability to relate to others, but they can spend more time seeking attention from people than playing and exploring toys and the physical world. This may be linked to delays in the motor skills which are needed to play and explore, but if parents are alert to this, they can use their child's social approaches as times to play with them and show them how things work.

Managing Behavior

Another aspect of social and emotional development that begins early is learning to control one's own emotions and behavior—known as self-regulation. Children have to learn to fit into family routines and learn to wait—to understand that they cannot always do what they want. Babies begin to learn this as parents move them into settled feeding and sleeping routines which fit in with the rest of the family. Establishing routines like this in the first year is an important step towards setting boundaries and helping your child manage her own behavior.

Children with Down syndrome can be very good at understanding how others behave and sometimes they can use this good social understanding to behave in ways that are not helpful. In short, they know how to get the reactions that they want from adults, so can become quite difficult to manage or quite good at being in control and behaving in challenging ways. For example, they might refuse to go to bed, run off when you are in the street, or refuse to sit still in preschool.

Many children with Down syndrome will be easy to manage, but about a third of preschool children are more difficult—partly because they are not yet able to communicate effectively. Therefore, it is important to set boundaries, as studies show that children with Down syndrome who have more difficult behaviors at age three make slower progress through their school years, presumably because they are not able to sit still, listen, and benefit from the learning opportunities.

In addition, if we want our children to benefit from being included in day care, nursery, and preschool settings with children without disabilities, then they should be expected to behave in an age-appropriate way as far as possible. It is important to explain this to grandparents and aunties so that they do not "baby" or "spoil" your child. Finally, it is really worth helping your child to manage her behavior, as it will make family life more fun. A child with difficult behavior disrupts family life and increases stress for all members of the family.

Temperament and personality will play a part here, as some children are more placid and easygoing right from birth, and others are more active, demanding, or anxious. There is some evidence to support the view that children with Down syndrome tend to have positive personalities and to be happy, kind, and social, but there is still a wide range of individual differences among our children.

Learning with Other Children

All children learn from other children and studies show that children with Down syndrome usually make friends in middle childhood like other children. Earlier, they benefit from playing with other children in nursery school and preschool settings where they are able to model their social behavior on that of other children. This is true even though their language delays will have an effect on how they can relate. At this age, children who do not have disabilities are very accepting of differences and can be very effective friends, teachers, and supporters.

∷ Motor Development

The ability to move and to control our bodies influences everything we do. The ability to control movements smoothly and effectively re-

quires much experience and practice. The brain develops and refines learned motor plans to control walking, picking up a cup, writing, catching a ball, or stepping over an obstacle through repeated experience of the actions.

Babies have little motor control at birth but soon begin to hold up their heads, roll over, sit, creep or crawl, and walk. They also learn to reach out to grasp a rattle and steadily increase their skill at using hands, arms, and fingers for reaching, grasping, and for the fine control needed to manipulate Lego blocks or write.

Babies and young children with Down syndrome go though the same steps in motor development, but it takes longer for them to develop strength and motor control. Both need practice to develop. All motor skills are performed in a rather clumsy or less controlled way first and only improve with practice. Think of any child's first steps and how long it takes them to improve their walking to the smooth standard of an adult. Children with Down syndrome do have more flexible joints and may seem "floppy" (hypotonic), but the effects of this on learning to move are not clear. They also may take longer to develop their balance for standing and walking.

Children learn to move by moving and their brains learn to control their bodies, feet, and hands through practice. Studies show that giving babies with Down syndrome practice at kicking while on their backs using a toy that rewards kicking by playing music can result in earlier walking. In addition, giving them supported walking practice on a baby treadmill also results in earlier walking.

Individual Differences in Motor Development

Some experienced therapists feel that children with Down syndrome do not all show the same patterns of motor delay. Some are quite strong and just a little delayed; others have stronger upper bodies than lower bodies, which will affect age of walking; others have stronger lower bodies than upper bodies; and a small group are weaker and more delayed in all aspects of motor progress. We need more research into these observations to understand their significance.

We also see different rates in progress across different developmental areas. Some children with Down syndrome are early walkers and late talkers, and others are early talkers and late walkers—just as we see in other children. While other children walk at about 13 months of age on average, children with Down syndrome walk at about 22-24 months. There is wide variation around these averages for both groups.

All babies with Down syndrome should receive advice from a pediatric physical therapist (physiotherapist) with specialist knowledge of Down syndrome who can demonstrate ways in which you can help your baby's gross motor development. Later they will benefit from the advice of an occupational therapist to develop fine motor skills such as using a fork and spoon and drawing and writing.

Sports and Active Play

While early motor development may be delayed, many children with Down syndrome go on to excel at sports including swimming, gymnastics, skiing, running, and many others. Some individuals can compete with nondisabled athletes, but most achieve levels that are good for the leisure activities they provide, for their fitness, and for their social lives.

In my experience, children with Down syndrome who have good sporting skills have been given that opportunity by their families and it is worth looking for sports clubs or recreation programs that they can join from early in life. For example, in preschool years, they will benefit from swimming clubs, music and movement, and baby gymnastics groups. In addition, playing on playground equipment and learning ball skills in the park with you will all be beneficial for developing your child's motor skills.

▪▪ Communication, Speech, and Language

Communication begins when your baby looks at you and smiles, then learns to take turns in babble conversations with you. We can consider that being a competent talker requires four components: communication, vocabulary, grammar, and speech.

Communication

Communication refers to all the ways we get our message across. This could be in nonverbal ways such as facial expressions and gestures and verbal ways such as using words and sentences to deliver our message in a way that the listener can understand. Communication includes learning to take turns, to listen when someone else is talking, to make eye-contact when you are talking, and to monitor whether you are being understood. Communication skills are called *pragmatics* by researchers and therapists.

Babies begin to develop communication skills in the first months of life and then continue to refine and use them throughout life. Babies and children with Down syndrome are generally good communicators—they understand nonverbal communication from early on, make eye-contact, and turn-take in babble games. They are good at using gestures, and, even though talking develops more slowly, they are usually still good at getting their message across. Overall, their communication skills are usually considered a strength.

Vocabulary

In order to talk, we have to learn a vocabulary—to understand words and their meaning. We start this process as a baby and learn through listening and looking as our parents say "there is the cat," "here is your drink," "let's have a bath." Babies and toddlers learn the meanings of words as they hear them used in daily situations where they can "see what they mean." They learn to understand words before they can say them. This means that children understand more (their comprehension or receptive vocabularies) than they can say (their productive or expressive vocabularies).

As babies and toddlers begin to realize that everything has a "name," they often become active learners and point to things so that you will name them. As babies and toddlers begin to talk, they use single words such as "cat," "Mama," "car," "drink," "gone," and "more." Then they begin to join words together and say "Daddy gone," "more drink," "Daddy gone work." Vocabulary learning is called *semantics* by researchers and therapists.

Children with Down syndrome are later than other children to learn to talk. While typical children say their first words between 10 to 18 months and string 2 and 3 words together by around 24 months, children with Down syndrome usually start to talk from about 24 to 36 months. However, children with Down syndrome understand more than they can say due to speech-motor difficulties (discussed later) and they steadily learn more vocabulary so that vocabulary is often considered a strength by teenage years.

Grammar

Once children have a total vocabulary of 200 to 220 words and can string 2 and 3 words together, they need to learn the grammar of the language. This includes learning how to indicate possession (it is Mama's shoe), learning to indicate plurals (there are two dogs), to indicate when something happens using tense markers (jump, jumping, jumped), and how word order rules such as question forms change meaning (e.g., "Daddy has gone." "Has Daddy gone?"). These grammatical rules are called *morphology* and *syntax* by researchers and therapists.

Children with Down syndrome find grammar more difficult to learn and when young often talk in rather "telegraphic" sentences such as "me go school," or "go school Monday." They can make themselves understood but do not easily master complete sentences, probably for a variety of reasons not fully understood including limited verbal memory skills and speech-motor difficulties (both explained further later). Grammar learning is therefore an area of weakness for children with Down syndrome.

Speech

In order to talk and be understood, children have to be able to produce clear speech. This is a process for all children, most of whom are difficult to understand when they start to talk. Clear speech involves the ability to make all the speech sounds in the language and put those sounds together in words (*phonology*). It also involves being able to control your voice, put the right intonation and stresses on words and sentences, and control the speed at which you talk. These are speech-motor skills. Most children with Down syndrome have significant difficulty in developing clear and intelligible speech. There are a variety of reasons for these difficulties that are not fully understood. They include hearing loss, anatomical differences in the mouth and face, and motor planning and control difficulties. Speech is therefore an area of weakness for children with Down syndrome.

Over time, the spoken language abilities of most children with Down syndrome fall behind the understanding that they show in nonverbal ability tests. This may be because babies and young children usually learn their first language simply by listening to it. Many children with Down syndrome do not learn easily through listening due to hearing issues—about two-thirds of babies and preschoolers have mild to moderate hearing losses. They also have poor listening memory skills, which are essential for learning to talk.

The implications for these listening difficulties are that we need to use all the ways that we can to make the language visual—using signs (sign language), pictures, and print to teach children with Down syndrome to talk. We have some evidence that when we do this, they develop much better spoken language at a level that would be expected from their nonverbal mental abilities.

Signing

Studies suggest that our children learn new spoken words faster when they see a sign or picture illustrating the meaning of the word *at the same time* as they hear the spoken word. The visual input seems

to help them remember the spoken input better. Using signs and words together from the first year of life will help your baby to understand words more quickly. If signs are always used in this way, always with the words, your child will also be able to use the signs to communicate before she is able to say the words. This reduces frustration and research suggests that signing children have larger overall vocabularies in preschool years. Ordinarily, children drop the signs as soon as they can say the words—but even then, they can use the sign if their speech is not yet clear enough to be understood. This encourages them to keep communicating.

While using sign language as a bridge to talking we must also work on speech. We need to help the children develop clear speech from the first years of life through games and activities to ensure that they can hear and discriminate all speech sounds and that will improve speech clarity and fluency.

All children with Down syndrome should receive speech and language therapy from the first year of life covering all four aspects needed to understand and get messages across: communication, vocabulary, grammar, and speech. The therapist should have specialist knowledge of working with children with Down syndrome.

Using Reading to Support Communication Development

My research team and others have done extensive research that shows that many children with Down syndrome are able to learn to read in the preschool years, from as early as three years or even younger, and their ability to remember printed words can be a very powerful aid to learning to talk. Reading activities can be designed to teach vocabulary and grammar, and reading materials help a child to practice words and sentences.

The printed word makes the spoken language visual—and this means that children with Down syndrome can use their visual learning strengths to develop their spoken language. When they see and practice short sentences such as "Daddy is eating," "Billie is eating," "Mama is eating," "Jenny is eating"—illustrated with pictures of themselves and their family—it helps them to begin to join two and three words together in their speech. Later, when they see that sentences contain little words such as "the" or "a" or that a verb ends in "ed" they are more likely to learn them and use that in their speech—which helps them to overcome their grammar learning difficulty.

Studies show that reading is often a strength for children with Down syndrome through the school years. They may learn to read, write, and spell more slowly than other children, but their reading skills are often better than would be expected for their cognitive abilities and spoken language skills. About 10 percent of children with Down syndrome can read at a level expected for their chronological age if they get the right instruction from preschool years. However, any level of reading progress is a benefit, and supported reading activities can improve speech and language even for children who are not becoming independent readers. Our research has shown that reading can improve both spoken language skills and working memory skills. For further information on how to help speech, language, and literacy development, see the resources listed for Chapter 6 in the Resource Guide at the end of the book.

▪▪ Cognition and Play

Early Learning and Play

Early cognitive development is called *sensory-motor development* because children explore their world with their senses. Babies touch and pick up toys and objects and put them in their mouths—they are learning how things look, feel, taste, and what you can do with them. They are learning how information from all their senses gives them knowledge of an object. Children with Down syndrome learn in the same way, but their ability to explore may be delayed by slower motor development. For some children, it may also be delayed by sensory issues such as not liking to get their hands wet or messy. Usually children with Down syndrome slowly grow out of these sensory sensitivities.

At the next stage, children learn about cause and effect—that they can cause a toy to move by pulling the string, or make a noise by shaking—and they then move on to solving simple problems such as fitting the right shape through the right hole. They also learn about object permanence—that things continue to exist when you cover them—and they will search for hidden objects.

Babies with Down syndrome do all these things but at slightly later ages and they do have more difficulties with tasks involving problem solving as the tasks become more challenging. They will benefit from play opportunities with a "play partner" who can show them what to do but not take over. This is called *scaffolding* and we do it with all children, but may need to do more supported play for longer with children with Down syndrome. They may not see all the possibilities that a toy offers without help and may then engage in just repetitive play—banging, throwing, or lining up toys because they need help to see the next step.

Studies show that children with Down syndrome may also not persist as long as other children when trying to solve a problem and may even use their good social skills to distract you when you are trying to teach them. This means that they may lose out on learning opportunities and so slow up their progress in learning to reason and to feel pleasure from succeeding at a task. Some advice on strategies to make learning fun and effective is given later in the chapter.

Memory

Researchers have looked at the development of memory skills, and there are several ways of exploring memory. Long-term memory can include implicit memory and explicit memory. Implicit memory is the memory for skills like riding a bike which we do automatically once we have learned them, and explicit memory is memory for storing events and experiences. Children with Down syndrome have more difficulty with explicit memory—perhaps because it involves conscious recall using language.

Most research has looked at working memory—this is the immediate memory system that supports all our conscious mental activity when listening, looking, remembering, thinking, and reasoning. Information is processed in working memory before it can reach long-term memory. The working memory system includes verbal (auditory) short-term memory, and visual short-term memory components.

Children with Down syndrome usually show significantly better visual short-term memory skills compared to verbal ones. This means that they will learn more easily from visually presented information than verbally presented information. For example, illustrating the key points from a story with pictures will help your child understand and remember what is happening. She may find it very difficult to follow the story if expected to just listen. Similarly, she will learn the dance movements from watching and copying the teacher, but find simply following spoken instructions very difficult. For many children with Down syndrome, a visual timetable—with pictures to illustrate the events of the day—can help them remember what is going to happen at home or at preschool.

This finding about difficulties with verbal short-term memory is very significant, as so much information in a child's day comes from people talking to her—providing verbal information that a child with Down syndrome is going to find difficult to process and remember. In addition, verbal short-term memory is important for learning to talk—for learning single words and for learning sentences.

In addition to supporting learning with visual materials including gestures and signs, pictures, print, and computer programs, there is evidence that memory training games can improve both visual and verbal short term memory for children with Down syndrome.

Thinking and Reasoning

There is very little information on the thinking and reasoning abilities of children with Down syndrome. However, we use our language skills to think and reason. Therefore it is reasonable to assume that delayed language will create difficulties for these cognitive activities and that improved language will lead to improved cognitive skills.

Mental Age or IQ

Cognitive development or mental abilities are often measured using standardized ability tests. Most children with Down syndrome score in the mild to moderate range of cognitive impairment, but some do have more or less impairment. In my view, such test scores are not of much practical value in predicting what a child may do in her daily life, as her everyday function in academic, social, and practical situations is often better than might be expected from "mental age" or "intelligence test" scores.

I would like to add a couple of points on myths here. You may read that IQ of children with Down syndrome declines in the early years, but this is not an actual decline in cognitive abilities; it is an artifact of how IQ is calculated. IQ scores are age-related and a child's actual scores on the test are compared to same-age children to work out an IQ. Children with Down syndrome learn at a slower rate than children with average IQs who are making an "average" amount of progress per year, so, despite progressing during a year, they will often not have made enough progress to have the same IQ a year later—it will have dropped.

Another myth is that children with Down syndrome reach a plateau in cognitive development at about 7 to 8 years. This suggestion comes from very dated studies when children did not receive the education that they get now. Recent studies show continued progress for most children with Down syndrome through teenage years and into adult life on language, cognitive, academic, and social skills, especially when they are educated in inclusive classrooms rather than special education classrooms.

■■ Self-help

Most self-help skills do rely on progress with fine motor skills. Therefore the age at which a child can hold a cup or use a spoon will be a little later for a child with Down syndrome. However, progress is also influenced by practice, so it is important to let your child feed herself and not be too quick to help or continue to feed her because it saves the mess! The same reasoning applies to learning to wash themselves, dress themselves, and manage independently in the bathroom. They will be slower, but with practice they will learn.

Toilet training may be achieved a little later but most children with Down syndrome can be dry and clean during the day at 4 years of age or earlier. Toilet training—as the name implies—requires training and a routine designed to teach and reward your child. Children do not need to be able to ask to use the toilet—they can learn to signal their need for the toilet during the training process.

In preschool or nursery school, children with Down syndrome should be expected to hang up their coats, put away shoes, and take their lunchboxes to the right place, just like the other children. They should also take their turn to give out pencils, collect books, tidy up, and take messages, just like all the other children. It is so good for a child's self-esteem to be able to be independent and take care of herself. Over time, independence in self-help skills can be a strength for children with Down syndrome, provided they are encouraged to be self-sufficient.

‼ Overview—Development at 5 Years

While there is considerable individual variation in progress, at age 5 most children with Down syndrome have good social understanding, can relate to others, make friends, and learn to behave in socially appropriate ways. They can fit into a typical preschool and kindergarten and follow the rules. Most children will be toilet trained, and are able to feed themselves, use a fork and spoon, and drink independently from an open cup. They will be able to undress, and put some clothes on but still need some help with dressing and fastenings. They will be walking, climbing stairs, and beginning to run and kick/catch large balls. They will be beginning to draw and write.

Most children will be talking as their main means of communication—some using short sentences, some 2- or 3-word sentences, and some still using single words or signs. Some children will be reading words and sentences. Most children will know common colors and shapes and be beginning to count. They will be enjoying the same children's TV programs as other children and will enjoy listening to stories and sharing books.

∷ What Influences Progress

Genetic Variance

Children with Down syndrome are not all the same. Like any other group of children, they vary widely in personality and temperament, abilities, and aptitudes. They have an extra chromosome, but this is an extra copy of their own family genes. Therefore, they may well show family traits and be more like their own families than like each other. For example, if a family trait is mathematical or spelling ability, then we may see this in the child with Down syndrome. Similarly, if there is autism in the family, we may see it in the child with Down syndrome.

Children with mosaic Down syndrome, who have less of the extra chromosomal material in their cells, tend to have the same profile of strengths and weaknesses as other children with Down syndrome—sometimes to a lesser degree. They may or may not develop more quickly in some or all areas.

Family Environments

Like all other children, the progress of children with Down syndrome is influenced by their families—by the love, attention, expectations, guidance, and opportunities that parents, brothers and sisters, aunts, uncles, and grandparents provide.

Families can help in all areas of their child's development, but it is important to keep this in perspective. The aim is not to try to help your child "catch up" with children who don't have Down syndrome or even other children with Down syndrome—it is to help them achieve their own potential. There are some areas of development, including communication, behavior, or self-help skills, where it is usually easier for family influences to make a difference. There may be some other skills—math, for example—where, try as you might, your expectations and the opportunities you provide may not enable your child to achieve as much as you would like.

Parents often say that they feel guilty because they are not doing enough. We certainly do not want you to feel like that. The aim is to give your child quality time and quality parenting—just like any other child—not more or less.

Health

Any child's progress will be affected by serious illness and periods of hospitalization. Some babies with Down syndrome have serious medical problems at birth, and this could affect progress. Babies with cardiac defects may make slow progress until their hearts are repaired, but then they usually catch up quickly. Some babies develop complications after surgery which can affect long-term progress, as can the onset of epilepsy in infancy. Some babies do seem to be more disabled and progress more slowly than others for reasons we do not understand at present. Some children have additional physical disabilities such as a hemiplegia (damaged motor control of one side of the body). Any additional disability may affect progress and should be treated as it would be in any other child.

One issue which can be overlooked is sleep. Many babies and young children with Down syndrome do not sleep well. They may be restless sleepers, may have sleep apnea, or be early wakers. Any reason for poor sleep should be investigated, as lack of sleep will have negative effects on learning and on day-time behavior. It will also cause stress for the rest of the family. Once any health-related sleep problems have been addressed, you should get behavioral help if your child will not settle at night, wakes in the night, or wakes early, since this is usually learned behavior which can be changed.

There is no scientific evidence that taking supplements of vitamins and minerals has any effect on the development or health of children with Down syndrome. Controlled trials have shown no benefits and it is not even clear that the ingredients sold as "targeted nutritional interventions" are actually safe. They can have side effects and even make children reluctant to eat if the supplements are hidden in foods and affect the taste.

Hearing and Vision

Children with Down syndrome are at greater risk of hearing and vision impairments. These will both have an impact on developmental progress and it is very important that they are diagnosed and treated. Mild to moderate hearing loss, which may fluctuate if it is due to conductive loss, will have an effect on learning to talk. The support of hearing aids, signing, and a teacher of the deaf should all be available in addition to surgery to insert ear tubes or T-tubes, if appropriate (see Chapter 3).

Similarly, any visual impairments should be treated promptly and appropriately. Research into visual development is ongoing, and the use of bifocal glasses is helping many children to develop their acuity and focusing skills.

Autism

It is possible for a child with Down syndrome to also have autistic difficulties, though this is not always easy to diagnose. Figures from various studies suggest that some 7 to 10 percent of children with Down syndrome may also have an autism spectrum disorder.

Children with autism or autistim spectrum disorder show impairments in social understanding, empathy, and relating to others; in communication; and in imagination and play. They may also show sensory sensitivities—for example, they may not like being touched or loud noises—and they may develop repetitive behaviors. All these behaviors, on their own, do not indicate autism. Other children can also show any of them. The symptoms listed *all* need to be present for a diagnosis of autism spectrum disorder to be correct and allowance must be made for the expected developmental delays in language and cognitive development that are part of having Down syndrome. Many children with Down syndrome have phases when they show sensitivity to touch and noise or engage in repetitive play, but they certainly do not have social impairments or autism.

Children with greater levels of cognitive impairment are more likely to show autistic-like behaviors and more severe delays in communication and play. Whether it helps to label them as having autism is unclear. In some communities, the label may result in the child receiving more appropriate therapies and instruction. In other communities, it may lead to lowered expectations for them rather than more effective teaching and support. More delayed children need help to learn to communicate and to move on from repetitive play, and if these are seen as a symptoms of autism rather than cognitive delay, they may not get the right kind of help.

If you are worried that your child may have some additional difficulties because she is progressing more slowly than most other children with Down syndrome, then seek the advice of your early intervention team or pediatrician.

■ Early Intervention

Early intervention services and support help both families and children. Families benefit from information and from feeling in control—so do go and find the information, support groups, and services in your community.

Research shows that most families cope extremely well with bringing up a child with Down syndrome and generally experience less stress than families with children with other disabilities. One reason for this may be the social strengths and positive personalities of most  children with Down syndrome. Studies of family adjustment and coping show that it helps to make full use of services and family networks to help you. They also show that families whose members communicate well and support one another do well. In my many years of experience, I would stress that the most important thing for a child with Down syndrome is to be a much loved member of a happy family—like any other child. Children with Down syndrome learn all day, every day, from being loved, talked to, played with, and involved in family life just like any other child. The reason for stressing this is to encourage you to keep early intervention and extra therapies and teaching in perspective.

I have already written a great deal about special needs and ways we can help our children if we understand their development. My knowledge and practical experience indicate that extra teaching, games, and activities will help them to develop, but few early interventions have actually been scientifically evaluated. Where they have, the evidence shows that parents are the best therapists and the best "therapies" or interventions are those that are delivered by parents at home. The therapies or teaching activities should ideally be developed to be part of everyday routines or play, or take no more than 20 to 30 minutes of additional teaching time in a day.

If your child with Down syndrome is to be part of a happy family, then it is important that family life continues normally and is not turned upside down by time given to going to or doing therapy. It is clearly a bit of a balancing act, as your child with Down syndrome does have additional needs, but it is so important not to undervalue the learning your child has during all her waking hours as part of ordinary family activities—shopping, playing, walking in the park, visiting Grandma, collecting other children from school, eating, bathing—all provide social learning and opportunities to keep talking to your child about what she is doing and experiencing.

■■ Early Education and Therapies

It is clear that your baby and toddler with Down syndrome will benefit from early education programs, physical therapy (physiotherapy), occupational therapy, and speech and language therapy—provided these professionals are experienced in working with children with Down syndrome and work with you to share their knowledge and to show you how to help your child at home. Equally important is the opportunity for your child to play with other nondisabled children in an inclusive nursery school, preschool, or kindergarten where she will hear other children talking and see them playing and behaving in age-appropriate ways.

■■ Learning Activities at Home

When engaging your child in learning activities at home, it is important to make the activities fun and reward her efforts. I would encourage you to read books with your child from early in life, as this is a good way to get her to sit still and attend. Children with Down syndrome usually love books and get the same benefit from them for language learning and later enjoyment of books as other children. Learning to sort shapes and build with blocks, match pictures, and complete puzzles are all tasks that can encourage attention and learning through imitation. You can take turns with your child—you fit one shape through the hole, she fits the next—to make it fun rather than pressure her to perform. Teaching your child games will improve her ability to sit still and attend, as well as to learn, if you can make them fun and support her in these ways.

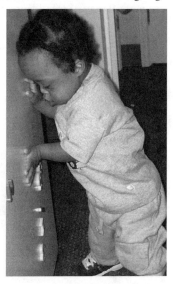

I would also encourage *errorless learning*—that is, you prompt your child to complete a task successfully. For example, you guide her hand to match pictures correctly the first few times and then begin to reduce your help by letting her place the picture on her own once it is in the right position. Errorless learning prompts success, leads to faster learning, and helps to make the learning games fun.

It is also important to know when to help and when to wait a bit, as children need to be able to solve problems themselves and to persist in finding a solution. However, the solution must be at just the right level of difficulty and toys can be simplified to prompt success. For example, just give your child one shape for the shape sorter and cover all the holes but the correct one, then give one shape and cover all but two holes, then two shapes and two holes—so that you gradually increase the difficulty but prompt success. Similarly, adapt a puzzle by only taking out one shape, making it easy to complete, then two shapes, and so on. Likewise, with a memory game which involves finding matching pairs among a set of cards, only use two sets to start with and then three, adding more as your child can manage them.

Many children with Down syndrome enjoy computer activities and there are many good learning programs that can be used from 3 and 4 years of age. The computer uses our children's strengths. It presents everything visually and they choose an answer with the mouse. They do not have to talk to show they understand. The computer can also go at their pace and it does not get irritated if they get it wrong! Computer games are a good way of providing practice on a range of learning activities.

∷ Special Needs and Community Inclusion

This brings us back to an issue that I raised earlier—that if we are to give our children the best possible opportunities to develop their

full potential, we need to meet their special additional needs but in a fully inclusive world. This is the challenge that I have just outlined for families—the importance of providing your child with an ordinary family life while also meeting her special needs. It is equally important that your child can go to the same places, activities, and clubs in the community that her brothers and sisters and friends go to. Children with Down syndrome will learn how to be successful in the community by being there, and this is so important for their adult lives.

∷ Special Needs and Education

The same principle applies when your child reaches school age. Research studies show that children with Down syndrome have better speech, language, and literacy skills, learn more, are more socially confident, and have fewer difficult behaviors if they are fully included in regular classrooms with appropriate planning and support. We still have some way to go to develop fully inclusive school systems, but we need to work for this, as it also changes the attitudes of all other children, and those other children will be our children's work mates and neighbors when they reach adult life.

:: In Conclusion

I have shared a great deal of information in this chapter which I hope will help you to understand and support your child's development. However, the most important piece of advice I can give is to simply love and enjoy your child—you will experience great joy and pride in her progress. My daughter with Down syndrome, Roberta, is 38 years old at the time of writing and she has brought great love and joy to all her family throughout her life. She has a partner, lives in the community in supported housing, works part-time, and enjoys life to the fullest.

:: Parent Statements

I can't emphasize enough how important it is for parents to know about typical development. For example, you need to know how a child gets into a sitting position to help your child. Otherwise when you plop him down to sit, and he has his legs widespread, you're doing more harm than good. Also, you need to know what comes next. You may see your child starting to do something and not realize it's a move toward the next step, particularly if it's your first child.

❧

With our first baby, we just expected the development to happen, but with Chris every milestone is a great success. When he crawls or feeds himself with a spoon we're very happy, and we tell everyone about his progress. Other people might think we're going overboard, but we're very proud of every small victory.

❧

There really is a wide range of capabilities among kids. You can't predict how your baby will develop. You can only provide the best kind of stimulation that you can as a parent, and deal with what is there genetically. During the first couple years of Emily's life, I think I had an advantage because I didn't have anyone close to me who had a baby her age, so I wasn't constantly comparing her with anyone.

❧

When I was pregnant, I had this picture in my mind that my baby would be a super achiever—doing everything three months early. So it was kind of hard to wait a little while longer for our daughter to do things.

❧

Our local early intervention program is quite willing to provide physical therapy to help with gross motor development. But the program is really reluctant to provide speech therapy to infants and toddlers, and it doesn't even have enough speech therapists to go around. This seems really cockeyed. Every adult with Down syndrome I've ever met can walk, climb steps, etc. quite adequately. But all of them have at least some trouble with articulation or other aspects of speech. That's the area of development I'm most concerned about.

❧

Every time I see a kid with Down syndrome who is around the same age as my daughter, I watch him to see whether he can do things my daughter can't. If my daughter can do more things, I secretly feel happy. I know that sounds mean spirited, but I think it's more that I am looking for signs that my daughter may be a "high functioning" kid with Down syndrome. I've heard lots of parents of kids with Down syndrome say they never compare—they just rejoice in every bit of progress their child makes—but unfortunately, I don't have that attitude yet.

❧

I don't feel anxious about Isabella's development right now, but sometimes I wonder what it's going to be like when it's time for first grade, or when she's a teenager. I try not to spend a lot of time worrying about the future because I really don't know how she'll do. She's doing pretty well now: I hope she'll keep it up.

❧

A new parent might wonder, "Will he smile? Will he hug me? Will he play? Will he recognize me?" From our experience, that's not something to worry about. You may feel a little frustrated when he doesn't do what Johnny-Next-Door is doing, but you'll find over time that he just reaches those stages a little later, but he'll reach them just the same.

❧

My feeling is that our son's horizons are unlimited. Quite realistically, I don't expect him to be a nuclear physicist, but I do hold out hopes that he will be quite independent and have a fulfilling life. I think any parent can be happy with that.

❧❧❧

I think you have to be careful not to blame every problem with your child's development on Down syndrome. For example, our eighteen-month-old daughter was having trouble learning to feed herself with a spoon. The OT said it was because she had "poor separation" of the top lip from her tongue. But I think the real reason was that up until then, we almost never let her try to feed herself because we didn't want to deal with the mess. We hadn't given her the practice she needed.

❧❧❧

There aren't guarantees for any child. Even if somebody is born with a normal set of chromosomes or perfect health, you don't know what's going to happen to that person. They could get sick, or they could grow up perfectly healthy but have some inability to cope with life. There are a lot of people in the world who have normal capabilities but don't know how to use them or who use them for bad purposes.

❧❧❧

I used to go to preschool with Abby one day a week and come home and feel that I had to push because I wasn't enough seeing progress in this or that area. I often thought Abigail would never count to ten, and now she can go well beyond that. It can get frustrating when teachers and therapists are reminding you over and over of the things you need to do, and you don't see change from one week to the next. But you're not going to see changes every week, especially when you're monitoring your child's development almost too closely.

❧❧❧

Sometimes it seems as if Liam doesn't progress at all for several months and then all of a sudden he'll take off like a rocket, and the progress is extremely noticeable and a real thrill. In our other children, the plateaus are a lot shorter. When he does progress, it's more noticeable.

❧❧❧

One day I was sweeping the kitchen floor when Ben, my little guy, toddled in looking for me. When he saw what I was doing he went to the kitchen closet and grabbed the dustpan and brought it to me. I was thrilled to my very toes to realize again how observant and really smart Ben can be!

❦

Besides having Down syndrome, my daughter was born six weeks prematurely as a twin. I'm never completely sure whether delays are due to the Down syndrome, the prematurity, or being a twin.

❦

Sometimes people find that once they have a kid with special needs, they learn a lot about child development. It makes bringing up your other children extremely interesting. I can watch Josh's younger brother for hours. It's so fascinating because of what I've learned from Josh about the learning process—how children learn gross motor skills, fine motor skills, speech. It has deepened our enjoyment of the baby because we know so much more about the process.

❦

To get Isabella to learn well, you have to hype her up. Music is one of the ways we do it. We use music with a purpose—following directions, sequencing activities, learning concepts. Get her excited and she learns better.

❦

Our son tries really hard to do some things, like climbing up the stairs. There are other things he couldn't care less about. He reached a point where he got really turned off about doing certain things he didn't like, such as trying to scribble with a crayon.

❦

We've had a hard time just leaving Ravi to enjoy his quiet time by himself. I feel I should be holding him, stimulating him, dangling a rattle in front of him. It's as if we have a higher standard of care because he has Down syndrome.

❦

Our child's younger sister has been one of the biggest motivators for her. She sees her sister riding a trike, she wants to ride a trike. She sees her sister using a computer mouse, she wants to use a mouse. She sees her sister flipping her coat over her head to put it on, she wants to do it too. She's very competitive with her sister—in a good way.

❧❀❧

Parents shouldn't have any mental barriers about what their child can do because you really can't predict that. We were constantly finding that Chris could do things that we had no idea he could do. If we hadn't been working with therapists and other people who knew what to look for, we just wouldn't have known. The most striking example was when we first met with the speech therapist. We had no conception that he could understand words. She got him a ball and a telephone and some of his toys, and she asked him, "Where's the ball?" and he pointed to the ball. Then she asked, "Where's the telephone?" and he pointed to the telephone. We were just so amazed and felt very bad that we didn't know he could do that.

❧❀❧

*I love reading to my daughter—first, because it's a nice, quiet, one-on-one bonding activity. And second, because it's such a great way to work with her on communication skills and concept development. Even though we often read the same books over and over, there's always something new you can point out—a color, the number of kittens on the page, one object that's **under** another one, etc.*

❧❀❧

Sam has a really long attention span when it comes to looking at books. He likes to point out things we ask about, but will also pore over books on his own. He started holding them the right way up at an early age—I think the early intervention teacher was somewhat surprised. Once she was testing him, and she kept handing him a book that was upside down to see if he'd turn it right side up, and he did every time.

❧❀❧

You have to figure out what's the most important thing to strive for at each developmental stage, just like you do in every child's life. Then you have to give that input. Once you've figured out what is most important, you need to let the rest roll off your back, which isn't always an easy thing to do.

▪▪ References

Abbeduto, L., Warren, S. F., & Conners, F. A. (2007). Language development in Down syndrome from the prelinguistic period to the acquisition of literacy. *Mental Retardation and Developmental Disabilities Research Reviews 13,* 247-61.

Baddeley, A. & Jarrold, C. (2007). Working memory and Down syndrome. *Journal of Intellectual Disability Research 51,* 925-31.

Bray, M. (2008) Speech production in people with Down syndrome. *Down Syndrome Research and Practice 12* (3).

Buckley, S. & Bird, G. (2001). *Memory Development for Individuals with Down Syndrome.* Portsmouth, UK: Down Syndrome Education International.

Buckley, S. (2001). *Reading and Writing for Individuals with Down syndrome—An Overview.* Portsmouth, UK: Down Syndrome Education International.

Buckley, S., Bird, G., & Sacks, B. (2001). *Social Development for Individuals with Down Syndrome—An Overview.* Portsmouth, UK: Down Syndrome Education International.

Buckley, S., & Johnson-Glenberg, M. C. (2008). Increasing literacy learning for individuals with Down syndrome and fragile X syndrome. In J. E. Roberts, R. S. Chapman, & S. F. Warren (Vol. Eds.), *Communication and Language Intervention Series: Speech and Language Development and Intervention in Down Syndrome and Fragile X Syndrome* (pp. 233-54). Baltimore: Paul H. Brookes.

Buckley S. J. The significance of early reading for children with Down syndrome. (2002). *Down* Syndrome News and Update *2* (1),1 (and case studies in this issue). (www.down-syndrome.org/practice/152)

Cebula, K. R. & Wishart, J. G. (2008). Social cognition in children with Down syndrome. *International Review of Research in Mental Retardation 35,* 43-86.

Fidler, D.J. (2005). The emerging Down syndrome behavioral phenotype in early childhood: Implications for practice. *Infants and Young Children 18,* 86-103.

Fidler, D. J. (2006). The emergence of a syndrome-specific personality profile in young children with Down syndrome. *Down Syndrome Research and Practice 10* (2), 53-60. (www.down-syndrome.org/reprints/305)

Roberts, J. E., Price, J., & Malking, C. (2007). Language and communication development in Down syndrome. *Mental Retardation and Developmental Disabilities Research 13,* 26-35.

Snowling, M.J., Nash, H. M., & Henderson, L. M. (in press). The development of literacy skills in children with Down syndrome: Implications for intervention. *Down Syndrome Research and Practice 12* (3). (www.down-syndrome.org)

Ulrich, D. A., Ulrich, B. D., Angulo-Kinzler, R. M., & Yun, J. (2001). Treadmill training of infants with Down syndrome: Evidence-based developmental outcomes. *Pediatrics 108* (5), 84.

7

EARLY

INTERVENTION

Mary Wilt, BSN, RN, CCM

When my daughter Emily was two weeks old, I received a phone call from the person destined to be my earliest ally in encouraging her development: my Early Intervention Service Coordinator. From the day Emily was born, her pediatrician and other members of her medical team had been mentioning this thing called "early intervention," and giving me the phone number to call my local program. Finally, with a little trepidation (since I had no clear idea what "early intervention" was), I made the phone call that brought support and expertise into our family's life. Together with her Early Intervention Team, I took the first steps to ensure Emily's success by laying the groundwork for future learning and development.

While early intervention services have changed substantially in the sixteen years since Emily was an infant, the benefit of working with a team of highly motivated professionals who understand infant and child development and are experts on community resources has remained the same. The aim of early intervention is to support maximum development of infants and toddlers within their families and communities, and it can be a valuable aid for your family, too.

❚❚ What Is Early Intervention?

"Early intervention" (EI) is both a philosophy and a service. It means just what it says: intervening early in a child's life to encourage growth and development. Many different professionals are involved in providing EI services, including specialists in motor skills, language and communication, learning acquisition, and social-emotional development. But EI is family-focused and family-directed. Since each

child is uniquely situated in his own family and community networks, EI is tailored to the specific needs of that child and his family. The child's specific areas of strengths and weaknesses are taken into account, as well as the specific context of his daily living: who he spends time with, what his family likes to do in leisure time, and opportunities he has to interact with others in his community, such as church or play-groups.

In the United States, infants and toddlers from birth to three qualify for EI if they have (or are at significant risk of having) developmental delays or disabilities. While each baby with DS is a unique individual, the presence of extra genetic material almost always causes recognizable developmental delays. Currently in the U.S. and in most countries with EI programs, babies with Down syndrome qualify for EI services based on diagnosis alone. Even if your baby does not demonstrate any delays when tested, he or she is still eligible for EI services. This can ensure that the team of early intervention professionals will monitor your baby's development and, if necessary, intervene to help him keep making the most developmental growth possible.

Although EI is individually tailored, it is also based on research into effective treatments for specific problems. For example, a majority of children with Down syndrome have low muscle tone, which may cause differences in the way they stand or walk. Because this is a known problem, EI services should plan to address this specific issue. In other words, how can low muscle tone best be addressed in this individual child in his individual circumstances? Does he need a specific therapy program or can we incorporate activities to help with low muscle tone during play-group or when he is with the infant teacher?

Another example of a common problem that calls for individualized intervention might be speech delays. Many children with Down syndrome will have delayed speech. But EI professionals should ask questions such as: How will we help this specific child communicate? What strengths does he already have, and what skills does he still need? Does he need an alternate means of communication (such as sign language or a communication board)? Does he need a specific therapy or program? Or is his speech delay best explained as part of a general developmental delay, and best supported in ways that encourage total growth and development?

■■ Who Provides Early Intervention?

Early intervention is not a single entity or stand-alone program. In the United States, each state has established its own programs for providing the service known as early intervention. These programs are usually under the direction of a state education agency, a state public health agency, or a state agency providing services to individuals with

disabilities. Because EI is provided by different agencies in different states, the way services are delivered to families will also vary.

In Canada, early intervention is a provincially delivered program. Although each province receives funds for programs from the federal government, they are each responsible for providing regional programs. Currently, there are large differences in kinds of programs and ages served. In other parts of the world, there is also great variability in kinds of programs offered and even whether services are provided at all.

Regardless of where you live, a good EI program will have profession-

als on staff who have expertise in infant and toddler growth and development, including (but not limited to) the professionals listed below

A good EI program will also recognize that you or your child's primary caregiver are going to be providing most of your child's early intervention. The program will therefore ensure that you or your child's primary caregiver are educated about your child's developmental strengths and weaknesses, and trained in strategies to help maximize his development.

Educators

Early childhood educators are known by different titles in different states. These teachers have degrees in education or child development, and are experts not only in normal growth and development, but also in teaching techniques. Often these teachers have had extra course work in special education. They can evaluate a child's current development and devise strategies for teaching new skills, or for supporting and expanding emerging skills.

Educators can help parents devise learning environments and activities in the home or daily living setting to support and encourage child development. They can also teach these techniques to parents and family caregivers. For example, some children with Down syndrome will have problems learning to imitate adult movements, a necessary step to learning how their actions influence their environment. A teacher would help parents understand why this is an essential learning skill. She would show them how to incorporate imitation activities into regular home routines in a fun way, demonstrating how they can use toys or regular household items to play with their baby and reward his attempts to imitate.

Occupational Therapists

Occupational therapists (OTs) help children or adults to develop, recover, or maintain daily living skills. For babies and toddlers, these essential living skills include eating, drinking, and playing. OTs are experts in adaptive techniques: that is, they help adapt the environment or tools so that your child can function well in his daily living environment. They will observe your child at home and play, and devise ways to improve your child's ability to participate in daily activities.

Sometimes this involves direct work with your child's fine motor skills, for eating or performing age-appropriate activities in play. For example, many children with Down syndrome have difficulty with fine motor control (controlling small muscle movements) in the hand. They may understand, for instance, how to put a puzzle together, but lack the fine muscle control needed to fit the pieces in the right places. Play is an essential skill for a child: it is *essential* that he be able to play and have fun doing so! Not only can an OT suggest specific activities to improve finger control; she may also recommend adaptations to the puzzle (or other toys) to make it easier to put together until your child's fine motor skills improve. She can show your family how to encourage your child to use these muscle groups in other activities and how to incorporate specific fine motor activities into everyday routines.

Physical Therapists

Physical therapists (PT) help children or adults with movement disorders or delays to maintain and improve movement skills and to prevent further movement difficulties. In addition, they can assist in adapting the environment to help the person accomplish daily living tasks involving movement.

The PT may work directly with your child to improve gross motor skills so he can participate in family activities and age-appropriate play. For example, most children with Down syndrome have specific problems related to low muscle tone. This low tone may cause differences in how they stand and how they walk, in addition to delaying walking in general. The PT can work directly with your child, using specific exercise and motion routines to encourage muscle strength and to counteract the effects of low muscle tone. However, since the PT will only be working with your child for a limited amount of time each week, he or she will also show your family the techniques for use at home. The PT can also recommend seating, standing, or walking equipment specially designed to help infants and toddlers with low tone, if this equipment is necessary for your child.

Speech-Language Pathologists

Speech-Language Pathologists (SLP) are professionals who spe-cialize in the study and treatment of human communication, including speech and language. SLPs provide "speech therapy," but also help with communication and swallowing skills. An SLP can help your child directly

improve his ability to speak, or may help him learn other ways to commu-nicate if his speech is delayed and he needs another way to tell you his wants and needs. SLPs can also assist children who struggle with oral feeding or swal-lowing, because of their knowledge of oral-motor development.

Because Down syndrome is a complex disorder that involves both physical and cognitive delays, it is tempting to dismiss speech delays as "just part of the syndrome." Some-times parents will hear that their child with Down syndrome does not "need" speech therapy—perhaps because "his

speech is delayed at the same rate as his general cognitive ability" or "his speech is in line with his global development." You should not accept this kind of argument as a reason to deny your child speech-language therapy. It appears that there are some specific differences in the way babies with Down syndrome develop pre-speaking abilities, and also in the way they develop memory and oral-motor abilities. So, it is not true that the speech problems children with Down syndrome encounter are simply part of a slower development in general.

All babies with Down syndrome should be evaluated by an SLP who is experienced in Down syndrome-specific issues. This SLP can then provide therapy to your child directly, or can supervise early intervention services to make sure they incorporate specific speech-language goals.

Most children with Down syndrome eventually learn to speak orally. However, if your child's oral speech is still significantly delayed when he is preparing to leave EI and enter preschool, be sure to consult with the SLP about alternative means of communication. This may involve a simple picture board device, or instruction in basic sign language, or a combination of approaches. This kind of planning cannot be left until the last moment.

Because speech delays and differences are so pervasive in Down syndrome, all children should at least have an SLP as a consultant on their EI team, and many will need direct speech-language services. This may be a difficult point for many parents to make if their EI program tends to deny speech-language therapy for children who have not met certain specific prerequisites or does not include professionals who are knowledgeable about the communication delays associated with Down syndrome. Nevertheless, being informed will help you advocate for including speech-language professionals on your child's team.

Audiologists

Audiologists are experts in hearing and can diagnose and treat hearing loss or deafness by providing hearing therapy and properly fitted and appropriate hearing aids. All babies who receive EI services will have screening tests for hearing, which means they will be evaluated to see if they might have some degree of hearing loss. If a screening indicates your baby may have a problem, an audiologist can evaluate further. He or she can assist your family and the other professionals working with you to understand your baby's unique hearing needs. For babies who have a hearing loss, an audiologist is part of the EI team on an "as needed" basis, for testing and recommendations for hearing aids or other devices to assist with hearing.

Infant Mental Health Specialists

An Infant Mental Health Specialist (IMHS) concentrates on helping families and children develop and improve their relationships. He or she may come from a variety of professional backgrounds, including social work, psychology, or nursing. An IMHS is specifically trained to support infants, toddlers, and their parents or other caregivers. This specialist works with families and infants, directly and indirectly, to help them establish a healthy emotional bond. These specialists may also be part of the evaluation team because of their expertise in understanding parent-child relationships. They may also serve as consultants to the primary provider of services for individual children.

Most families of children with Down syndrome will not need the services of an IMHS. Simply having a child with developmental needs doesn't indicate a need for mental or emotional support. However, if your family experiences problems, an Infant Mental Health Specialist can offer counseling and support. Although raising an infant and toddler with Down syndrome is much like raising any infant and toddler, some families encounter problems while everyone is learning to understand and provide for the child's special needs. Sometimes sadness or grief becomes prolonged and a parent may realize that depression has set in, interfering with parent-child bonding. The IMHS will use specific evaluations designed to look for parent-child relationship problems and work with you to sort them out. He or she may be an ongoing member of your IFSP team, or may just work with you for a specific amount of time. Family support and counseling to enable families to care for their children with special needs is an important part of early intervention.

Social Workers

Social workers are professionals who assist individuals and families in meeting the challenges of everyday problems they encounter in their daily lives. A social worker's aim is to help people find the resources and supports available in their community to solve environmental and social problems. For example, they can help a family solve problems related to housing, employment, or medical care. Social workers are specifically trained in crisis management and emotional support, as well as resource management. Social workers may function as the service coordinator for an early intervention team, or as an Infant Mental Health Specialist, or they may be used by families only for a short time to help them resolve a specific social need.

Again, simply because you have a child with Down syndrome, does not mean you will need every service available! However, if your family needs the services of a social worker, you should be able to get this assistance through the EI program.

Registered Nurses

Registered Nurses (RNs) are professionals trained in promoting health, preventing illness, and diagnosing and treating human responses to health problems. Many registered nurses are experts in maternal-child and child health. In addition, nurses are trained to understand environmental and social issues that may affect a child's health or the developing mother-child relationship.

If your state or local EI programs are administered by a health department, your family may have a Registered Nurse as your service coordinator. Many programs administered by other agencies employ RNs to provide service coordination for children who have multiple health issues. However, while some children (including those with Down syndrome) have health problems, the federal special education law does not provide for direct nursing care services except in very limited circumstances. In other words, Registered Nurses on EI teams do not provide nursing services per se, but rather provide care coordination or teach families about specific health issues.

Service Coordinators

In the United States, "service coordination" is a required service for families receiving early intervention. Each child and family eligible for EI must be provided with one service coordinator who coordinates all of a family's EI services, regardless of what agency provides them, and who acts as the "single point of contact" between parents and those agencies. This service coordination is provided at no charge to families.

Because there are so many different models or programs for providing EI, it is not possible to say exactly how your child's program will provide a service coordinator. Some agencies provide what is known as "dedicated" service coordination, which simply means that the service coordinator does nothing else for families. Or your program may require the EI team to decide among themselves which of the people who provide services to your family will act as the service coordinator. For instance, if your child receives services from an educator once a week and sees other team members less often, your team may decide that the educator is the best person to be the service coordinator. Regardless of the program or agency that provides your family's EI services, there will always be a service coordinator appointed at no charge to you.

It is your service coordinator's job to assist you not only with the services that are being provided to your child, but also with *accessing* those services. It is his or her job to help you. If anything is preventing you from getting the full benefit of your child's program, discuss this with your service coordinator. Sometimes, for instance, families are not satisfied with one of their EI service providers, or having trouble finding a good time to meet with a service provider. Or, maybe you have not discussed some financial hardships with your service coordinator and she does not know how they are affecting your family and your child. Parents should not feel shy about talking to the service coordinator about any problem that comes up. She is there to help you problem solve and to find help for issues that affect your family's ability to receive early intervention services.

:: What Is an Early Intervention "Team"?

The early intervention team is simply the people who gather together to:

- evaluate your child's development,
- make recommendations based on that evaluation,
- make plans for providing services to address any areas of concern,
- provide the services agreed to, and
- conduct reevaluations and progress assessments when needed.

The sections below discuss how your baby's team will work with you to help pinpoint the areas where your family and your baby need support and then address those needs through individualized planning for specific interventions and therapies.

:: The Evaluation

Before an infant or toddler can begin receiving EI services, his development needs to be evaluated. An evaluation is necessary to get a picture of your baby's specific abilities and needs. Babies with Down syndrome are unique. Because your EI team will use this evaluation to plan for your baby's specific interventions, it's important for them to understand his unique strengths and weaknesses. This will help ensure that services are based on your child's current development and not on some cookie-cutter or textbook idea of what "a child with Down syndrome" might need.

Evaluations are also used for eligibility purposes if a baby doesn't have an automatically qualifying condition. For example, children with

Down syndrome automatically qualify for services based on having a condition that is considered to have a high probability of resulting in developmental delays, and so the evaluation is done to determine individual needs rather than to determine eligibility. For children who do not have a known condi-tion, the evaluation process also serves to determine if they have a developmental delay significant enough to qualify for services.

Many states have streamlined the referral pro-cess for children with Down syndrome, and a representa-tive of your local EI program may contact you very soon after your child's birth to discuss the evaluation process. If you are not contacted, you may request an evaluation at any time. Most hospital nurseries and pediatrician's offices will have contact information for your local EI program. Or you may visit the NICHCY (National Dissemination Center for Children with Disabilities) state-resource web page, or call them toll free at 800-695-0285. (See the Resource Guide.)

The team will use a variety of tools or tests to do your baby's evaluation. They may use standardized tests of infant development, checklists, observation, and informed clinical judgment (which means the evaluator uses information he or she has gained on the job to evaluate your baby, when a particular test does not address a specific concern). It is important to get observations from different kinds of tests and from different professional disciplines, to get a good evaluation across all areas of development.

Evaluations are often done in a familar setting, such as your home. Sometimes the evaluation is done in a center specifically designed for infant and toddler use. Regardless of setting, most evaluations are "play-based" assessments, done to observe your child's development in all areas while he is engaged in play. The evaluation team may use different tests specifically designed to measure development in one or more areas, but they will use a child-friendly approach through play. The team will look for specific developmental strengths and weaknesses while your child is playing and interacting.

Often parents say, "Well, it just seemed like they were *playing* with my child! I didn't really notice they were *doing* anything!" The team may sit on the floor with your baby and hand him familiar toys to watch how he reaches for and handles the objects. They will observe what he does with specific toys to assess his problem solving and thinking. They will listen to his responses when they point to pictures in a book. They will see how he seeks comfort if he gets upset during play. All of these pieces of what looks like ordinary play are parts of a good developmental assessment.

You are an important part of the evaluation team, just as you are an important part of the whole EI process. You will be present during the evaluation, and your input will be sought. This can be very stressful for parents, who may feel as if the evaluation is a sort of "judgement" or a test that can be "failed." But developmental assessments are not at all a "pass-fail" event! This is a snapshot portrait of one short amount of time in one of your child's days, designed to help team members understand, in a general way, your child's individual needs and strengths. If you know that your child can ordinarily do something that he is not doing for the evaluators, feel free to speak up about it. But don't try to complete a task for your child or interupt the interaction between the child and other team members unnecessarily. Your team will ask you many questions during the assessment, such as what sounds or words your child uses and what kind of movements he makes. This information is as important to the evaluation as the play observation, and will be included.

Getting the Results of Your Child's Evaluation

As soon as the evaluation is over, the team will go over the results with you. All areas of development will be scored separately: physical, cognitive, adaptive, communication, and social-emotional. Because this is a developmental assessment, the results will usually be given to you in developmental ages. "Developmental age" is a term used to describe the age at which children ordinarily are able to do certain physical, social-emotional, language, and learning skills. Developmental ages have been determined over many decades by testing hundreds of thousands of children to come up with typical developmental ages.

If your child is being evaluated shortly after birth, in all probability the developmental age scores may not differ significantly from his actual calendar age. However, there may be a wider gap between developmental and calendar age as your child grows. For example, if your child is being evaluated at 12 months old, you might hear that he has expressive speech at the 8-month developmental level.

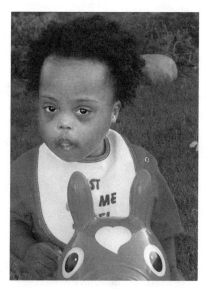

Allowing your wonderful new baby to be evaluated is often traumatic for parents. It is not intended to be this way! But it can be very hard to hear your little one described in terms of development, even when you may expect some differences to appear. It may seem that you are only going to hear all the things that are "wrong" with your baby, but this is not the purpose of an evaluation. Although the early childhood professionals are evaluating your baby for possible developmental delays, they will remember that he is a real and whole person. They will also share with you all the positive things they find during their evaluation process. In fact, they are required to discuss your child's strengths as well as any perceived deficits. If this important piece of the evaluation report has been skipped, make sure you ask! The whole team should be thinking of your child's strengths, because they will build on his strengths as they plan to work on areas that are less strong.

Especially if your baby is very young, he may not show any developmental delays when he is evaluated. This doesn't necessarily mean he won't qualify for services (see below). However, this also does not mean that he won't eventually show some delays in development. The majority of children with Down syndrome have developmental delays. Because of this, your child will automatically qualify for early intervention, even if his first evaluation doesn't show any significant delays. Don't decline EI services just because this very early evaluation shows scores "within normal limits." Very early evaluations don't adequately predict future abilities.

In addition, early intervention evaluations shouldn't be thought of as a predictor for future IQ scores. Although an infant or toddler with a cognitive delay caused by Down syndrome will generally still have a delay in later childhood, there is no direct correlation between certain developmental age scores and specific IQ scores. That is, even if your baby tests as being quite delayed in one or more areas when he is very young, it does not mean that he won't be able to make good progress with these skills later. Likewise, a normal developmental age score in one area will not adequately predict future normal scores in that area. A developmental evaluation in EI is used to plan for *one* baby: *your* baby. The scores serve only to look for areas of relative strength and weakness. They are not useful as standardized tests or absolute predictors of future development.

■■ Eligibility

In the United States, early intervention is provided under the federal law known as the Individuals with Disabilities Education Act (IDEA). (See Chapter 8 for more information on IDEA.) Under IDEA, certain requirements must be met in order for a child to be "eligible" to receive services. One of the purposes of the evaluation is to determine

whether the child is eligible. In order to receive early intervention services under IDEA, the child must either have: 1) a developmental delay in one or more areas evaluated, or 2) "a diagnosed physical or mental condition which has a high probability of resulting in developmental delay."

Most children with trisomy 21 (regardless of type) will be found eligible for EI because of the known diagnosed condition.

■■ The Individualized Family Service Plan (IFSP)

After the evaluation is done, it is time to gather the team together and decide how to proceed. The plan that emerges from the team process is called an Individualized Family Service Plan (IFSP). This is a family plan: it addresses not only your child's developmental goals but also services needed to support your family in meeting the developmental needs of your child. An IFSP is both the planning as it occurs and the plan that emerges and is written down. In other words, it is a process of planning and not simply the drawn-up plan for services. The evaluation results are only one part of this planning. In addition, your goals, wishes, and dreams for your child are an essential part of the IFSP.

The discussion during this planning process should take place in an orderly manner, with the following steps:

1. Review your child's current development

With the other team members, you will go over the results of your child's developmental assessments. This is the time to add any important information you have about your child or make comments. You may wish to add information from your pediatrician, for example, or get questions answered about specific results in certain areas of the assessment.

2. Identify your family's strengths, priorities, and concerns

An IFSP is designed purposely to be a family plan, and your priorities and concerns are an integral part of it. For example, your major concern might be that your son isn't talking, and you want to make this a priority. One of  your family's strengths may be that you are fortunate to have many extended family members in your immediate area and often visit each other. The team should be able to come up with some plans for improving your child's communication skills using the many opportunities presented by having extended family to visit with.

3. Identify outcomes (goals) based on developmental and family assessment, and how your team will monitor or measure them

An IFSP should focus on family outcomes—which are the benefits that families hope to receive from EI services—and not solely outcomes for the child. After all, children grow and develop in the context of a family, not as little individual units in isolation from others. Nevertheless, many of the outcomes (or "goals") on your child's IFSP will relate to specific measurable progress that the team wants to see in specific developmental areas. These outcomes are determined with you as a team member, and your team will devise not only the outcomes themselves, but also the ways of measuring the outcomes to see if progress has been made.

Outcomes are determined by thinking about what your child is currently doing, what you would like him to be able to do, what your family's priorities are, and what your family needs to help your child achieve a given outcome. Let's say you would like your child to be able to communicate. What? When? Why? And how will you measure progress?

Thinking more about this large outcome, you may decide you would like your child to be able to tell you when he is hungry, thirsty, or tired. You would also like him to be able to tell Grandma these things when he visits her. It's important to your family because your son gets frustrated and cries when people cannot understand him. Your team looks over the results of the evaluations and together comes up with goals, using both developmental test results as a general guide and your priorities and concerns. Together, you decide that your son will learn to use sign language to express five words: drink, eat, more, hug, sleepy. He will be able to do this all the time, at home and at Grandma's house. Your team writes this outcome or goal down as part of his IFSP.

To see if the outcome (the goal of learning five signs) is being met, the team will observe to see whether your child uses these signs all the time, at home and at Grandma's house. Your team may further break down the large outcome into smaller objectives, such as having your child learn one new sign at a time, each over one month. It's up to your team to decide how often, when, where, and who will measure your child's progress toward the outcomes you decide on. Your IFSP can be reviewed and revised at any time, as goals are mastered or changes are desired, but by law, it needs to be reassessed every six months.

4. Decide on the services necessary to reach these outcomes

Now that your team has decided on outcomes, it's time to decide which services might be necessary in order to achieve them. Using the example above of learning new signs for words, it might be necessary for a speech-language pathologist to work directly with your child and family to learn these new words and ways to incorporate them in family life. However, the infant educator on your team may already be very skilled at both teaching these common signs and demonstrating ways to use them in everyday childhood experiences. If so, it may be more appropriate for the educator to work with your family on this particular outcome.

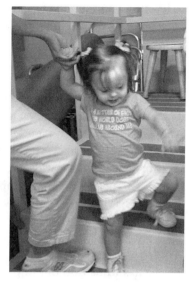

It is easy and tempting to break down all outcomes by certain categories or realms, and decide that only certain specialists can appropriately work on those outcomes. But all EI team members are experienced in guiding early childhood growth and development, and the appropriate service needed should be individualized to your child's particular and specific circumstances.

There will be times when only a specific profession can provide a specific service. If, for example, your child's evaluation reveals that he has specific gait or standing problems (not just a general delay in walking), these problems would require specific therapy by a physical therapist. Likewise, specific language problems caused by hearing loss (not just a general delay in oral speech) would require the services of a specially trained speech-language pathologist and/or audiologist. Focus on your child's outcomes and then let the outcomes and your child's specific needs guide decisions about the services your child needs.

5. Decide on the natural environments in which your child will work on goals and receive services

All children have the right to belong to and fully participate in their communities, and one of the most important goals of EI is to help children with disabilities be included in all aspects of family and community life. Research shows that infants and toddlers are much more likely to develop skills during the everyday routines of ordinary life, in their typical settings such as their homes, day care settings, or playgrounds. In addition, in the United States, programs are required to provide early intervention services in these typical settings (so-called natural environments) to the maximum extent appropriate to the individual child. (See the section on "Natural Environments" below for more information.)

6. Identify your service coordinator specifically

You have the right to know specifically who is providing service coordination to you, because the service coordinator has certain responsibilities to the IFSP team. He or she is the person who ensures that your family's IFSP is carried out, that all the services are being provided, that any coordination with other agencies or insurance is provided, and that your child's specific transition needs are addressed when he is getting ready to leave early intervention and move on to preschool.

As mentioned above, in many states, you will be assigned a service coordinator who will provide no other service to you than service coordination. This person may have training in any area of child development or human service, such as social work, nursing, education, or counseling. In some states, you will choose your service coordinator from among the team members who will be providing services to your family.

7. Discuss transition out of early intervention

In the United States, children with disabilities usually "age out" of early intervention when they reach the age of 3. See the section on "Transition" below.

▪▪ Approaches to Providing Services

There are several ways that professionals on an EI team might work together to provide evaluations and services to children and their families. Currently, the most common approach to team services in the United States is transdisciplinary. However, many programs still provide services using other approaches, and it is possible you may encounter other methods or "team philosophies." The three most common approaches (transdisciplinary, multidisciplinary, and interdisciplinary) are discussed briefly below, to help you understand the terminology you may hear as part of the EI process:

The Multidisciplinary Approach

Traditionally, many EI programs used a multidisciplinary approach to provide services. That is, professionals from different educational backgrounds provided individual assessments of specific developmental areas, and provided discipline-specific treatment for the child. For example, if a child had many developmental concerns and showed delays in both motor and language skills, a physical therapist would provide "physical therapy" to address the physical concerns, and a speech-language pathologist would provide "speech therapy" to address the language problems. The professionals from each separate discipline would develop goals and objectives for the child's IFSP.

The multidisciplinary approach has fallen out of favor since we now realize that this approach can lead to fragmented care, missed communication between team members, and lost opportunities to encourage emerging skills in other developmental areas. When each service provider develops specific goals and objectives for one area of development, they may not relate to other areas of concern or what other providers are doing.

The Interdisciplinary Approach

A variation of the multidisciplinary approach is called the inter-disciplinary approach. In this approach, a team of providers from many different professions comes together to conduct a group assessment of the child and to develop an IFSP. In this way, all team members know what other team members are working on and when the plan will be reassessed. However, each area of developmental concern is still addressed by individual providers, so that a child who has many areas of concern may still see several different professionals in different places and at different times. Each professional is still primarily concerned with addressing one area of growth and development.

While interdisciplinary programs still exist in many places, the majority of early intervention programs have moved toward a revision of this concept called "transdisciplinary" teams.

The Transciplinary Approach

A transdisciplinary approach to services doesn't diminish the number or type of professionals involved in early intervention teams. Rather, it changes the emphasis to team cooperation as opposed to having different professionals focus on specific realms of practice. This approach is supported by research into how infants and young children learn. It also reduces fragmented care and encourages families and professionals to look at the whole child and not just narrow areas of development.

In fact, one of the major philosophies behind EI is that of transdisciplinary team support. Your baby's development is an integrated process, with one area developing at the same time as all other areas. Early intervention professionals who practice in a transdisciplinary manner have an understanding of developmentally appropriate practices. Your child's language skills, for example, develop along with his motor and cognitive abilities, in an orderly fashion and at predictable times.

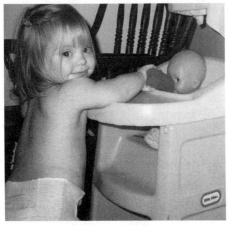

Your *individual* child's development may differ more in one area than another, but that particular area of development is never happening all by itself.

"Transdisciplinary" means that one early childhood professional will take the lead to provide support for your child in all areas of development, regardless of that professional's clinical or educational background. EI systems that use this approach may refer to this person as the "primary service provider." All qualified early childhood professionals, regardless of degree or specialty, understand child development. The primary service provider will be the main person providing EI services to your child. For example, if your child has both cognitive and speech-language delays, your team (including you) will decide on outcomes (goals) related to those areas of concern. You will decide what the goals will be, how you will measure them, where your child can best learn them, and who will provide the services in that environment. Your team may decide that the best person to be the primary service provider is your early childhood special educator.

That doesn't mean the educator is now suddenly a speech-language pathologist! It means that, while working on specific learning goals in your child's natural environment, the educator will also work on the outcomes listed on the IFSP for language acquisition. She can do this because she has expertise in early childhood learning *and* because a speech-language pathologist on the team helped devise the language outcomes and thinks they can be addressed by the educator.

Obviously, not every developmental need can be addressed using this transdisciplinary approach. As explained above, if your child has certain specific problems, such as a hearing loss or oral-motor problems, he may need a speech-language pathologist for specific therapy. If so, the SLP who works on speech and language with your child could *also* provide services to help with your child's cognitive and motor delays, if the team decides this is appropriate. For example, when the SLP comes to your home to work on language skills at your kitchen table, she can also incorporate techniques she has discussed with the physical therapist to encourage your child to walk to the table.

This approach is sometimes as difficult for professionals to understand as for parents. It can also be difficult for professionals trained in a specific discipline to allow another early childhood professional to perform therapy that has traditionally been their role to perform. However, when teams work together in a transdisciplinary manner, each professional plans with all the other team members, and together with the family, the team decides who will be the primary provider of EI services. If other specific treatments or therapies are needed, they can always be added.

In transdisciplinary teams, the individual therapists and other professionals are mostly involved during the evaluation and planning phase of the IFSP. The members of the IFSP team decide what areas of development are of the greatest concern, discuss the family's priorities, and then decide who will provide what services. The professional with expertise in the area(s) of primary concern or priority is generally selected as the primary provider, as discussed above.

Parents often hear this approach described as "cost saving." Or they may worry that "the speech therapist should not be providing physical therapy." In truth, the approach was never intended to save money, but instead, to recognize the actual way children grow and develop in families and communities, in an integrated way. Nor is the speech therapist acting as a provider of physical therapy, but as a provider of early intervention services. The primary provider—whoever that is—always requires a team to work with, made up of professionals from all areas of expertise who can be called upon as necessary for advice.

A transdisciplinary approach may not be helpful if your child's development in a particular area is atypical and he needs certain techniques only practiced by a particular specialist or discipline. For example, your child may have a general delay in walking that is not out of line with his other general areas of development. If so, your team may decide (with input from a physical therapist) that some good techniques to encourage walking is all your child needs at present and that these can be incorporated into the EI services provided by your primary service provider. Or, your team may decide that a physical therapist should meet with you and your child for a consultation and to develop a home exercise program that will then be monitored by your primary service provider.

However, children with Down syndrome often have specific gait or stance problems. Physical therapy may be needed to address specific goals related to these individual areas of need. If your child's individual needs require specific professional therapies, these can (and should) be incorporated in the IFSP.

Another example might be a child with severe eating problems who will not allow food to be put into his mouth. This is not a general delay in development, but a specific problem requiring specific expertise. This child may need an expert in oral-motor feeding therapy to help him learn to tolerate food in his mouth.

Transdisciplinary approaches are currently becoming common in early childhood settings, as well as in EI. As your child approaches school age and you begin to think about including him in regular classroom experiences as much as possible, this kind of transdiscplinary approach will become important. For instance, if your child goes to a regular preschool, you may see a transdisciplinary approach in action when the SLP comes into the room during class and works with a group of children around the table. Has she suddenly stopped being a speech-language pathologist because she is now "teaching" a group of students their letters? She will leave the teacher with specific instructions on how to support your child during classroom work. If the teacher puts these plans into practice and uses them to encourage your child's speech, has she suddenly become an SLP? Or, a physical therapist may show the teacher how to use a walking device or place your child in a seat that gives her needed support. When the teacher does these things, is she now a PT? Of course, the answer to all those questions is "no." These are examples, though, of transdisciplinary practices in action.

∷ Natural Environments

Early intervention is optimally provided in a "natural environment"—that is, in a place where babies or small children ordinarily live or play. In fact, IDEA *requires* that EI services be provided in natural environments "including the home, and community settings in which children without disabilities participate," unless the team decides that the child cannot achieve his goals in such an environment.

Because the definition of "natural environments" includes "community settings in which children without disabilities participate," if your child attends a typical daycare or preschool, your EI team can decide to provide services in that setting as well. However, because you are the most important component of the learning plan for your child, your team may be reluctant to provide services if

you are not available. If your child attends such a program full time, or if he is at a babysitter's house daily, services can be provided in these settings. However, a careful EI team will discuss ways to include you in the teaching (and learning) that will be going on.

If your team jointly decides that your child's goals cannot be met in natural environments for a good reason, your child may receive services in a specialized setting. This might be a classroom setting in which only children with disabilities or developmental delays receive services, for instance. Or, in some circumstances, a therapist's clinic or office may be the setting. For instance, if your child is deaf and requires a specific communication instruction technique that can only be found in a classroom for deaf children, your team may decide he needs to be in this setting to make progress toward his specific language outcomes.

Remember, you have the right to receive EI services in natural environments unless your team makes an individualized decision that your child can't achieve his goals there. Because many EI programs have been around for many years, some have maintained specialized, center-based programs that serve only children with developmental delays or disabilities. However, your child should not have to receive EI in a specialized center just because it exists, or because it is more convenient for staff, or less expensive for the program. Your child should not be removed from a natural environment without a serious discussion during an IFSP meeting.

■■ Common Questions/Concerns about Early Intervention

My Team Disagrees with My Pediatrician— Now What?

Remember that the term "early intervention" describes a particular service for children. It is not a medical or health-related service, per se. Nor is an EI agency like a "home health" agency, where professionals receive orders from physicians to provide a certain amount of therapy of a certain type for a certain length of time. This can often cause misunderstandings between the pediatrician, the parents, and the EI professionals, particularly because a pediatrician has valuable information for your early intervention team. And it is made worse in states where EI systems bill insurers for services provided (see below). It can be very confusing.

What often happens is this: you take your child to the doctor and the doctor writes a prescription or order for a particular service: for example, "Physical Therapy (PT) twice a week for 60 minutes." The physician has a good reason to think your child needs help with walking, for instance, and in his experience, PT can provide this help.

Yet when you meet with your IFSP team about this, the team decides that this is not what your child needs to meet the outcomes listed on the IFSP. This *does not mean* that your team is making medical decisions, nor trying to save money, nor disagreeing with your doctor. It means that, for the outcomes you have listed on your IFSP, the team does not agree that specific service is needed and therefore it will not be provided under EI.

You have some options, if this occurs. You can decide your team is right, and you don't need more services because the IFSP already addresses walking and you feel confident about the services being provided. Or, you can request a reassessment and a new IFSP, and try to get more specific goals related to walking that show the need for specific PT services. Or, you can try to supplement your EI services using other sources, such as using health insurance benefits or your own money to pay for private therapy. (Depending on your insurance coverage, your pediatrician's prescription may be useful in obtaining payment for certain kinds of therapies.) Or, you can decide you have an issue that you cannot agree with your team about, and that you need specific help to come to an agreement. See the section on Due Process Rights, below.

Should We Try to Supplement Our IFSP?

It is important to acknowledge that an IFSP will probably not contain all the services that might benefit your child. For one thing, your IFSP will concentrate on only specific developmental outcomes—and a limited number of goals means limited amounts of services. There are many other services you will hear about from other parents, read about in books and online, and find out about at seminars and presentations. Many of the professionals who make up your team will not have specific information about every new therapy or treatment you have found, and they may also disagree with you about the need for that specific item.

This is a good time to call the member services number on your insurance card, get copies of your plan's benefits explanation, and advocate for those services you cannot get through EI.

Many parents who can afford to do so decide to pay for physical, speech, or other therapies out of their own pockets. This may be an option for you. Many therapists are willing to see your child for a consultation and make recommendations for you to follow through with at home, and then monitor your child's progress infrequently. This may help you to keep costs down.

Whether or not you are able to swing private therapy, find a way to get your baby and family involved with other infants and children. The hope of early intervention is that your child will learn to function in the context of family and society, so find places in which you can explore your community and other children.

All learning experiences that benefit children in general will also benefit your child with Down syndrome. For example, many young children with Down syndrome benefit from movement or music classes for infants and toddlers. Many recreation centers have activities for babies or toddlers, including swimming or play groups. Your local library may have story-time and other fun family programs. You are your child's primary teacher. Many of the discussions you will have with the professionals involved with your child will give you insight into ways to support your child's learning in other areas.

Do We Have to Be Constantly Doing Therapy with Our Child?

When you have a new baby with Down syndrome, sometimes it can seem like there is always something you "have to" be doing. Instead of seeming like a help, early intervention can seem like just some more "stuff" you have to do; some more appointments to be kept and therapists to see. EI, though, is *supposed* to be helpful to your family. With its emphasis on natural environments, EI is supposed to bring services to you, to be part of your everyday routine, and to show you how to incorporate developmentally appropriate activities into everyday occurrences. Your

service provider(s) should be helping you figure out how you can use natural parts of your ordinary life to encourage your child's growth and development.

Let's say your child is learning "object permanence." That is, he is beginning to learn that objects are still there even when they are hidden. You can work on this over and over during a "therapy session" . . . or you can introduce it in play any time of the day when you play peek-a-boo with a scarf. Not only is it more fun to simply play with your baby when he shows an interest in playing, it is a more effective way to teach. A child sitting and working on "object permanence" is working on a task you set for him. A child playing peek-a-boo is having a great time with a loving parent and coincidently learning object permanence at the same time!

If EI is beginning to feel like just "one more chore" or "one more appointment," and causing you stress instead of feeling like a support, speak up! You can call your service coordinator and discuss your concerns, or decrease the amount of services. Or you can take a break from early intervention for a while.

There is no "magic" number of therapy hours, and no "magic" type of specific therapy yet found that will prevent all the developmental effects of that extra twenty-first chromosome. If EI is a burden rather than a help, then you can decide how much or how little you want to take advantage of it. Early intervention is just a part of the whole experience of supporting the growth and development of children with special needs. A loving family, proper medical care, and a stable home with toys and books are all just as important in ensuring your child's optimum chance at a great future in school and adult life.

Why Are Other Children with Down Syndrome Getting Better Services?

The answer has to do with the federal law that provides for early intervention, the Individuals with Disabilities Education Act (IDEA). First, as described above, the IDEA stipulates that EI programs be individualized. Your child will receive only those services that your IFSP team agrees are necessary for him to meet his unique outcomes or goals. So, even though you may think that your child would benefit from the same service or frequency of service that another child is receiving (for example, one hour of speech therapy a week), he may not receive it if:

1. his IFSP does not include outcomes/goals that support the need for that service,
2. the members of your IFSP team think that he can achieve those goals without that service, or
3. your EI program uses the transdisciplinary approach and the primary provider is expected to help your child achieve all his goals.

Second, IDEA gives the states a great deal of latitude in deciding what services to offer and whether and how much to charge families for them. To understand why your state (or community) may not provide the same level of services as another state does, it helps to understand a little about the history of the law, as discussed in the next section.

:: A Short History of Early Intervention

Early intervention is not a new concept. People have been interested in teaching young children for many years in the expectation that

encouraging learning in infants and toddlers would have a positive effect on later development. In 1968, the U.S. Congress authorized nationwide demonstration projects intended to develop program models for the education of children with disabilities from birth to third grade. These projects were established across the country by private and public nonprofit agencies, but did not provide services to all children. Gradually, some states began to offer early intervention services to their citizens, but many areas of the country had no programs. Even the first national legislation guaranteeing public education for students with disabilities (the Education for All Handicapped Children Act in 1975) only mandated services to children of school age.

Eventually, thanks to advocacy work by both parents and professionals, public laws began to ensure services to younger children. In 1986, states were required to provide services to preschoolers in need of special education. At the same time, Congress established a grant program to encourage states to set up programs for infants and toddlers. This part of the law is currently known as "Part C" of the Individuals with Disabilities Education Improvement Act (IDEA) of 2004.

It is important for parents to remember two things about the current law: it is not permanently authorized and it does not mandate that services be free of cost. IDEA 2004 is a special education law and guarantees that school-age children with disabilities receive a free, appropriate, public education (FAPE). The part of IDEA 2004 that guarantees services to school-aged children is permanently authorized—it will not expire. It is often referred to as a civil rights law, because it guarantees that children with special education needs receive their civil right to an education just like any other student.

However, the part of IDEA 2004 that includes services to infants and toddlers (Part C) is currently authorized only through 2010. It is not a civil rights law. Instead, it is a federal grant program that provides states with some funding to establish EI programs. States that apply for the grant money must comply with the federal requirements established under Part C, but are otherwise free to run their programs by their own standards. This includes the right to bill families for services, in certain circumstances. Children receiving services under Part C are not guaranteed a free, appropriate education.

What does this mean to you as a parent? It means that the services your child receives in your state may differ significantly from services in another state. It means you may have to pay for some of those services, or that your insurer can be billed for some services. However, the law is very clear: services cannot be withheld because a family lacks the ability to pay for them. All states receive Part C grant money, and all states are interested in providing services to qualifying infants and toddlers. Your local EI team will work with you to ensure you receive the services you need.

■■ Transition: What Will We Do After Early Intervention?

Most children leave early intervention at the age of three. (IDEA 2004 gives states the option of continuing EI until age five, but this is not currently an option in any state.)

In the United States, most children with Down syndrome who have aged out of early intervention are eligible for special education services through the public school system in their state. Special education simply means specially designed instruction, at no cost to parents, to meet the unique needs of a child with a disability. (In Canada, although specifics may vary from province to province, most children with Down syndrome will also be eligible for special education services in the school system.) Special education includes both specialized teaching and "related services" (for example, speech or physical therapy) that are needed for the student to achieve the goals of his specially designed instruction. This specially designed instruction plan is referred to as an Individualized Education Program (IEP).

Eligibility

In early intervention, a child who has a condition with a high probability of developmental delay (such as Down syndrome) will automatically qualify for services. But the same is not true when a child moves on to school services. To be eligible for special education services in public school (in the U.S.), a child has to be found to meet one of the categories of eligibility under the federal IDEA law. For a child of three, this usually means he must meet the state's definition of "developmentally delayed." (He could meet other categorical definitions, but the majority of children with Down syndrome will fall into the "developmentally delayed" definition.)

The definition of "developmentally delayed" varies from state to state, but is usually based on a percent of delay across one or more areas of development as measured by a valid evaluation. For example, some states require a 50 percent delay. Other states have no specific percentage but instead try to define a qualifying delay, such as "development that qualified personnel determine to be outside the range of 'normal' or 'typical' for a same-age peer." Children are found to be eligible for special education if they require specialized instruction and related services because they have an eligible degree of developmental delay.

There are other categories, as mentioned above, that allow a child to be found eligible for special education. Currently, the other categories specified in IDEA are: mental retardation (intellectual disabilities); a hearing impairment (including deafness); a speech or language impairment; a visual impairment (including blindness); a serious emotional disability (referred to as "emotional disturbance"); an orthopedic impairment (physical disability); autism; traumatic brain injury; an "other health impairment" (one that affects strength, vitality, and alertness, is due to a chronic or acute health problem, and adversely affects educational performance); a specific learning disability; deaf-blindness; or multiple disabilities.

The category under which your child is found eligible for special education services is simply that: a qualifying category. It is just a means of determining eligibility. The category itself should not be used as a planning tool. For example, you should not be told that your child must go to a particular school because that is where your district serves preschoolers with a given category of disability, or that he cannot work on reading goals yet because he was determined to be developmentally delayed. The category should not be the plan, the curriculum, or the setting. Those are individualized decisions based on your individual child, and not the category under which he or she qualifies for services!

No parent who has had a beloved toddler evaluated to determine whether he is eligible for special education will tell you this is an easy or painless moment. Even though the intent of the evaluation is solely to determine the need for special education and assist in planning for that education, it feels judgmental. Parents should firmly remember that the evaluation is to determine eligibility for a program. It is not an evaluation of worth or human dignity, or future potential. It is very helpful to find other parents  who have already experienced this moment, if only to reassure yourself that you are not the only parent experiencing the pain and sorrow that might be involved.

The Goal of Special Education

The goal of special education is—quite simply—education. It is no longer simply a matter of encouraging or supporting your child's development, although this is an important educational goal for toddlers and young children. Special education is designed to provide optimal learning for children with disabilities, enabling them to a quality education to the greatest extent possible. Early Intervention was focused on getting your child ready for learning. Special education is focused on providing that learning.

What this often means is that services you have been used to receiving in EI will stop. The focus will switch to specialized instruction, with the goals of helping your child attain a public school education in the regular curriculum to the greatest possible extent. The focus, in other words, will move to how to get an appropriate public school education for your child, and this is, after all, a wonderful goal.

While your child was in EI, he may have received therapy services such as physical therapy. This therapy was provided to meet goals listed on the IFSP. Or perhaps your child received occupational therapy, because he was working on goals related to the need to manipulate small objects so that he could participate in play at day care, or so that he could eat with a spoon and fork.

In public school, however, therapies are only considered "related services." They are provided to enable your child to benefit from the special instruction he is getting. Therefore, the need for OT (for instance) would be determined by looking at the education goals for your child: what does he need to be learning in the classroom? If there is an education goal that requires the assistance of OT to make sure your child can progress toward that goal, then OT may become part of the plan and be included as a related service. For instance, if one of the preschool learn-ing goals is that children will learn to separate small toys into categories, and your child lacks the fine motor ability to do this, an OT may work on this particular goal with your child.

In preschool and school, your child's education plan is called an Individualized Education Program (IEP). It will be based on the evaluations done to determine if he is eligible, the level of performance he demonstrated in those evaluations (information from you and other sources can also be included), and a team plan to address those areas where your child is determined to need special education. The process of developing an IEP is a team process, and you are again part of this IEP team as you were part of your IFSP team.

But the emphasis will now be: how can my child get a public school education? What kind of specialized instruction is needed? Where will it occur (what kind of classroom or setting)? Who will provide the instruction? How often? And what kind of related services (such as PT or speech-language therapy) does he need to benefit from the specialized instruction?

Although you may lose some therapies you received through EI, the good news is that school services are free by law. Any related service provided on an IEP is part of the "free appropriate public education (FAPE)" to which every special education student in the U.S. is entitled. Public school services are free to all qualified students, and this includes all students in special education, whether or not they are receiving additional services through an IEP.

Special Education Settings

Once your child has received early intervention services in natural environments you will find it easy to understand the need to provide special education services in similar settings.

The Individuals with Disabilities Education Act (IDEA) is intended to provide a public school education for students with disabilities that is as similar as possible to any other public school student's education—as long as it provides that student with an appropriate education. Obviously, the closer a student can get to a classroom setting where the neighborhood children are all learning together, the closer his experience will be to the ordinary public school curriculum and learning environment.

By law, students receiving special education services must be educated in the "least restrictive environment (LRE)." This term in intended to convey that services for children *with* disabilities are to be provided in the same kinds of settings and in the same kinds of schools that provide services to children *without* disabilities, except in clearly defined circumstances. For example, once your child begins kindergarten, he should attend a typical elementary school, typically the same one that the other children in the neighborhood attend, preferably in the same classroom as all the other kindergarteners.

Of course, this doesn't mean that your individual child, for reasons related to his own unique needs, might not be better able to receive an education in some other kind of setting. That is a decision that the entire IEP team—which includes the parents—should make. But where a child will attend school should never be an automatic assumption. Nor should all children with a particular categorical label be placed in segregated settings by policy.

At the preschool level, there may be fewer options for your child to be educated with typically developing children than there will be once he enters kindergarten. This may be the case if your county or state does not provide a free public education to most preschoolers without disabilities. For instance, your school district may have a program for preschoolers from lower income families, and this may be the only program where preschoolers with disabilities can receive an education in an inclusive setting at public expense.

When families are dissatisfied with public preschool programs, they sometimes choose to send their child to a private preschool at their own expense. In this instance, it may still be possible for your child to receive some public school special education and/or related services in his private school. For instance, the speech-language pathologist may come to your child's private school and provide therapy there. There are specific rights and processes in both federal, state, and local levels that may help you get this kind of accommodation. You can contact your local department of special education to find out what your specific rights are.

Making a Smooth Transition to Special Education

Planning for your child's transition into special education is a required part of early intervention, and your service coordinator should be assisting you all along to think about this transition. Here are some tips, however, that might make things go a little smoother:

1. Begin thinking about the transition *out* of EI as soon as you get *into* EI. This may seem premature, but it's not. Thinking ahead will help you find good resources and save you some of the last-minute worry.
2. Find other parents who have transitioned out of EI and talk to them, to get ideas of what they liked and disliked about the process. Your EI service coordinator should be able to help you find local support groups, or you can contact the NDSS or NDSC for possible local groups.
3. Begin talking to staff at your public school special education department. Let them know you have a child who will be making the transition to preschool in a few years. Ask them how you can best gather information from them: Do they run a parent resource center? Do they have tours of facilities? Do they offer their own preschool transition classes for parents?
4. Follow up on leads from other parents and the school system itself. If possible, tour some specific settings. Try

to get a feel for the teaching styles, staff-to-student ratios, classroom environments, and other features that you think would help your child be a successful learner in preschool and beyond.

5. Begin to familiarize yourself with preschool and kindergarten curricula. Most school systems (either on the local or state level) have published their grade level curriculum, and you should be able to find it, perhaps by contacting your local elementary school or by looking on the school system's website. Think about what is expected for early childhood curricula, and what children are expected to learn in order to go on to be competent readers and learners. This will help you begin to visualize your own child's inclusion in the regular curriculum, and what he might need to benefit from a preschool or kindergarten education.

‖ Conclusion

By now you may be overwhelmed or confused by all this new information, and all these new terms and descriptions, laws, and programs. You may think you need to learn it all at once. But you don't! Early intervention programs are there specifically to help new parents, and the vast majority of families find EI both helpful and comforting. You have a lovely new baby and are the most important person in your baby's life. EI is there to support you and your whole family as you encourage your child's growth and development. The infant and toddler years go by so fast! Relax, get to know your baby, and enjoy these early days. You will learn as you go along, and emerge a stronger, more confident parent and advocate for your child.

‖ Parent Statements

Early intervention was really helpful to me because I learned a lot about how to play with my baby. For those couple years, I was constantly striving to stimulate her. I was always making time to play with her and doing early intervention activities, whereas before I probably would have done my housework instead.

❧

It was handy having the physical therapist come to our house and see how Sophie got around the obstacles there. For instance, we had a sunken living room with a step down and the PT advised us about how to help our daughter negotiate that step before she was comfortable with stairs.

❦

In the beginning, it seemed like the early intervention people were always coming when Anthony was too sleepy or irritable to cooperate. So, I would just chat with them about how he was doing and get some tips on how to work with him on different skills. After he started needing less sleep, I felt like we accomplished a lot more.

❦

The parent is always ultimately the case manager.

❦

The whole idea of learning about development and teaching my baby was intimidating in the beginning. I had this picture that I was going to have to work with Hannah ten or twelve hours a day. I remember at first trying to do that, but I couldn't keep up with it. Finally I got to the point where I could relax a bit and just enjoy her. And she's probably better off now.

❦

It's a good thing to set aside specific work times if you can. But the best approach to teaching is an incidental approach anyway. Whatever comes up in the routine of the day can be made into a learning experience.

❦

When we were in the midst of early intervention, I found it helpful to think through my day and choose a couple of times when I knew I would have time to focus on teaching specific things. For example, there was a nice, twenty-minute stretch when I was driving to day care that I could provide lots of good language stimulation by singing and talking to Abby. And then at bedtime, my husband and I were always less stressed than we were in the morning, so it was easier to work on self-help things like taking off socks.

❦

I find myself now in the position of being very protective of new parents I talk to. I let them know they still need to be who they are and that it's just fine to go for four days without doing a thing, if that's what they feel like doing. If that's the way they need to react to their child, that's the way it is. You just can't let your life revolve completely around your child.

❦

Some of the people on our early intervention team tend to make really vague suggestions, such as "Encourage her to keep trying when something is difficult for her." I've found we get the most useful advice if we ask for specific solutions to specific problems. For example, for the longest time Hope wouldn't hold her own bottle. We asked all the therapists what to do, and one gave us a suggestion that worked—using a bottle straw to help her understand that this was something she could do.

❦

The people in the early intervention program pushed us to use Total Communication—signs plus speech—from the start. I wasn't crazy about the idea, because I thought it might delay the development of speech. The first time Hope used the sign for "more," though, I was hooked. It made me look at her in a new light—as a little person who knew her own needs and could make them known very capably.

❦

Learning signs hasn't interfered with our daughter's speech development at all. Often she learns to say the word very shortly after she's learned to use the sign. She learned to sign "bear," and then started saying "beh"; to sign "apple," and then say "a-pull."

❦

Often I've wished I had someone I could go to for advice on my "normal" child. Early intervention seemed like such a great deal—having someone to turn to when I couldn't figure out how to approach a problem—and my special-needs child wasn't the only one to present me with problems!

❦

The teachers in our program were good. I would go to them really frustrated and feeling unable to set aside an hour to do the things they wanted me to do. But the case manager said, "Look, there are ways that you can incorporate these things into your daily routine—when you're changing her, dressing her, when you're bathing her, and feeding her." When I tried to do that, usually it went a whole lot better.

❧❀❧

I've pretty much given up trying to do therapy-type work with Ethan at home because he's totally turned off to it right now. But if we just play, then he can learn a lot of things. We have to fake him out. We got these wonderful toys—puzzles, pegboards, and blocks—and all he does is ignore them. I guess he figured out that they were educational.

❧❀❧

Some of Hope's therapists have preconceived ideas about what little kids with Down syndrome are like. Even though each child theoretically has his own IFSP, it seems like some of the therapists do the exact same activities with every child with Down syndrome. For example, my daughter crawled very well on her hands and knees at ten months, and there was this other kid in the program who couldn't budge an inch on his own. And yet, the PT kept doing the same exercises with both of them on the therapy ball.

❧❀❧

*To keep the goals on my child's IFSP current, therapists periodically haul out different checklists of skills and behaviors and ask me if he can do certain things. Sometimes when he can't do something, it's because he hasn't had much chance to practice a particular skill. For example, he can't identify x number of clothing items by pointing because I haven't spent enough time saying things to him like, "OK, let's put your **shirt** on now. Can you hand me your **shirt?** Isn't this a nice **shirt?**" So, sometimes these tests are more a test of your parenting skills than your child's skills.*

❧❀❧

It frustrates me that Hope will hardly ever demonstrate what she can really do when someone is assessing her skills. The teacher will try to get her to do something, and she'll just sit there like a lump. So, I'll say, "But she does this all the time when we're alone." Then the therapist will say, "Well, that may be, but let's work on it some more so she can do it more consistently." I guess it's more important that she be able to do something that she can show, but I hate to waste time working on skills she's already accomplished.

◈

Fortunately, we have lots of family around to help give our son his therapy and that's made it a lot easier on us. But even so, we do feel under pressure a little. You know, you think that if you have any free time and the kid is sitting there, you should do some exercises with him. There was a time when we pressured him too much and he started refusing to do anything and was throwing all his toys around.

◈

When we first learned that Ravi needed different types of therapy, we overdid it. Sometimes we would do exercises with him until he cried. Then we realized that it was just too much and that we were pushing him too hard. Now we try to make it fun for him, and that's been much more effective. We get little gems of time when we feel we are effective, and over time it adds up.

◈

With the educators, you have to trust your feelings and perceptions because you know your child best. We had one therapist who was very good, but whose voice was very shrill, and our son would get upset. It was interfering with his lesson even though the things she was doing were good. So we changed therapists, and found one who got along better with our son.

◈

I feel very strongly that if you have a child with special needs, you need to explore every option, even if it's an option that doesn't appeal to you at first. I checked out every program, and I talked to many therapists. My husband and I sat together and made lists of the advantages and disadvantages of each thing.

◈

I think that with our child a physical therapist was vital in the first year. After the first year, a speech therapist was vital, and once she turned three, an occupational therapist was vital.

❧

A good special education teacher can provide parents with a lot of important information that will carry through for the rest of your child's life—especially in terms of teaching you to be your child's advocate.

❧

We feel as if our work has paid off. The early intervention program has been terrific. It was important because we learned too. They really taught me how to help Jayden, and I think that was invaluable, just because I didn't know that much about how to play with babies. I just knew the bare minimum. I can't believe how much I've learned.

❧

The teachers at my son's preschool were very interested in working with him and learning about his special needs. They were especially excited over his accomplishments, maybe because he worked harder than the other kids to achieve things. They also felt more protective, perhaps, toward him than the other children.

❧

When Sophie was in preschool, the county special education office sent a teacher once a week to observe her in class and advise the teachers about how to work with her. The teacher would leave a note for us with her observations and suggestions. That was somewhat helpful, but nowhere near as useful as the home visits we'd had in early intervention.

❧

There was a period during the preschool years where our daughter only qualified for speech-language therapy because she wasn't testing as delayed enough to need any other services. Frankly, I enjoyed the breather from having to do other types of therapy with her.

❧

When our child was preschool aged, the school offered to send a school bus to take her to and from speech therapy at the local elementary school. (The school housed a Head Start program so it was considered the least restrictive environment.) We weren't nearly ready to let her go off in a big school bus by herself, so I drove her myself.

❧❀❧

Our school district doesn't readily volunteer information about all the programs they have available for kids with disabilities. You have to talk to other parents about what kind of programs they are aware of, search the school website, and keep pestering your team members to find out all the available options. I'll bet it's pretty much the same in many communities. If you don't like the first, or second, or third program they offer you, keep asking what else is available!

❧❀❧

If I hadn't had to work full time, I don't know if we would even have sent our child to preschool. Sometimes I think I could have done a better job teaching him at home. But he did pick up a lot of social and language skills that he needed in kindergarten just by interacting with the other kids.

❧❀❧

When it was time for Sophie to transition from early intervention to school-aged services, our service coordinator was really great. She knew we wanted Sophie to be in full inclusion and she backed us up in all the meetings we had leading up to her transition out of early intervention. We never really considered any other kind of placement.

8

LEGAL RIGHTS AND HURDLES

Jo Ann Simons, MSW

■■ Introduction

When you found out you were going to be a parent, you probably had some mixed feelings. I know I did. I was excited about the journey of parenthood and becoming a family. I could not wait to tell the world, or whoever was willing to listen. I wanted a baby to hold and to love. I dreamed of great athletic accomplishments and academic achievements. Like you, I had big dreams, too.

I was also a little nervous about having enough money to take care of a baby and having enough money to pay for a college education. I worried about having enough time to work and enough time to sleep. If you have other children, you probably wondered how you could find the love for another child. Sometimes, I worried myself sick with thoughts of what would happen if we were not there. Who would take care of our baby and raise him like we would want?

You worry about all these things when you are having a baby. But, if your baby is born with Down syndrome, like mine and yours, you worry about a whole lot more. At first you may worry all the time. That is why this book was written in the first place; to provide you with accurate information about raising a baby with Down syndrome, to ease your worries, and to welcome you into the family of Down syndrome.

This chapter is going to explain to you the legal and related protections that are in place in the United States for your baby. In a legal sense, this is the best time in our country's history to become a parent of a baby with Down syndrome. We have laws that guarantee your child an education. We have laws that prevent discrimination against people with Down syndrome. There is a law that gives parents the right to take time off to care for their child and not be afraid of losing their jobs.

There are government programs that can provide assistance to low income families. These programs can help with supplementing income and by providing medical insurance. There are also housing and food programs that can be useful. There may be some tax benefits that may be helpful to you as well.

The importance of some of the issues covered in this chapter will not become apparent to you during the first few years of your baby's life. They are discussed here to give you some basic and important information. You do need to make sure that you begin to plan for your child's future, however. You **must** have a will. You will **need** to think about the unlikely possibility that you might not be here to raise your child, and decide who will take care of your child with Down syndrome and any other children you have or may have in the future. You need to make sure that you do some estate planning, even if you do not think you have any assets.

While every effort has been made to ensure that the information contained in this chapter is accurate, this chapter is not intended to provide legal, accounting, or estate planning advice. Instead, we hope that you will have enough background information to ask the right questions and know when to get professional advice when you need it. As in any situation with your child with Down syndrome, other parents will often have the best advice for you.

▪▪ Education for Children with Disabilities

No law has done more to help individuals with Down syndrome and other disabilities than the law that guarantees your child's right to an education. These rights were established through the tireless efforts of families who came before you. Prior to this time, public schools routinely excluded children with disabilities. Instead, families were encouraged, by their physicians and other professionals and often by their families, to send their children away to state-run institutions. The rationale was that their children would receive training at these facilities. Families were encouraged not to visit their children and sometimes they were encouraged to forget they even existed. Babies with Down syndrome who were sent away received little or no education in these

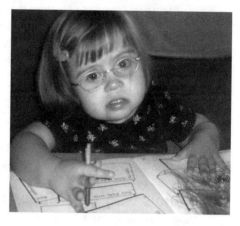

crowded and often wretched places until the 1970s. Then, it took legal action and media attention to get government officials to take notice.

While many families chose to place their children in residential institutions, other families rejected the notion that their children needed to be sent away from their families and communities. Instead, they worked with their children at home and quietly began banding together with other families. By the early 1950s, families had begun to put notices in newspapers, looking for other families who were raising their children at home. These informal groups often began their own nursery schools in church basements. As these groups became more organized, they become part of the newly established National Association for Retarded Children, which is now The Arc of the United States.

Because of these efforts, some schools voluntarily educated some children with mental retardation and established classes for children who were "educable" or "trainable." No groups of children were more discriminated against than children with Down syndrome, who were easily identified, and almost always labeled "trainable." Since reading and other academic skills were only taught in the "educable" classrooms, a generation of children with Down syndrome never had the opportunity to learn to read. Instead, they spent their limited school time learning very few useful skills.

> *Many years ago, I was in a support group and mothers were talking about their children learning to read. Another mom, much older than I, seemed in shock. Her son was in his 20s and didn't read. In fact, he had never been given the opportunity to learn to read. A few months later, this same mom reported to all of us that she had hired a tutor and her son was learning to read. I shudder to think how many people with Down syndrome never learned to read because they were sent to the "trainable" classroom.*

It was not until 1975, when Public Law 94-142, The Education for All Handicapped Children, was enacted, that children with disabilities were guaranteed a "free and appropriate" education. The law has been amended several times and is now called the Individuals with Disabilities Education Act and commonly referred to as IDEA.

Individuals with Disabilities Education Act (IDEA)

The purpose of IDEA is to guarantee a free public education for children with disabilities. It is coordinated by your Local Educational Authority (LEA). The "LEA" is just the bureaucratic term for your local school district or school system. Part B of the law covers students from

the age of 3 to 21 and Part C covers children from birth to 2 years of age and is discussed in Chapter 7.

Since families want what is best for their child, they often want to make sure they are living in the "best" school district, one that will provide the best services for their child with Down syndrome. Some families do their own research and look at per pupil expenditures for regular and special education students. Others speak to advocacy organizations for recommendations. The truth is that some school systems *are* better than others. But it is not realistic for every family to move into those communities. Income and job locations are powerful barriers for many families. If large numbers of students needing special education services moved into only a few communities, it would not take long for those districts to be so burdened that they would cease to be best. To create as equal a playing field as possible, IDEA contains many safeguards for families.

There are four major elements, or protections, of Part B of IDEA. While the statute, as written, is complex, you can understand the law's relationship to your child with Down syndrome and your role in your child's education by understanding the following four major areas:

1. Free Appropriate Education (FAPE),
2. Least Restrictive Environment (LRE),
3. Individualized Education Program (IEP), and
4. Due Process Protection

Free Appropriate Education (FAPE)

In this situation, "free" does really mean free. While you may have had to pay for some early intervention services, you are not required to pay for your child's education once she enters the public school system. Under certain circumstances, your child might even attend a private school at no cost to you—but only if the LEA approves of, and arranges for, her to go there. However, if you decide to send your child to a private school based on your religious preferences, for example, you will have to pay for tuition. Your child will still be eligible for free related services such as speech-language therapy, though.

Although you do not have to pay for your child to attend a public school, if your child receives Medicaid, the LEA is required to use your child's Medicaid benefit and bill Medicaid for any eligible services, such as speech, occupational, or physical therapies. This is because Medicaid is considered the payer of first resort. Medicaid will be discussed more fully later in this chapter.

Some school districts may ask you to provide your private health insurance information so they can pursue that source for reimbursement. Some school districts have sought this alternative as one way to address the rising costs associated with special education. You are under no obligation to provide your health insurance information. In fact, you should consider any request like this very seriously, as health insurance companies often have lifetime limits in certain categories of care. Many of our children with Down syndrome have complex medical issues and you might want to consider your child's lifetime need for care before allowing your school district to tap into your private health insurance. On the other hand, you might be very interested in helping your school district cope with special education costs.

"Appropriate" is a hard concept to define. According to the dictionary, appropriate means "suitable for a person, condition..."—and there is the challenge. What is appropriate for one student with Down syndrome may not be appropriate for another. "Appropriate" for one may be a private school and for another, it may be the same classroom in the same school where other neighborhood children go.

It could be suggested that the regulations are intentionally vague so that each student can be treated according to her needs. It is important to remember that the education your child receives will permit her to achieve the educational goals set for her in her IEP (Individualized Education Program). You should know, however, that "appropriate" does not necessarily mean "best." Just because there may be ways to make your child's education better, does not mean the school system will have to do them.

Least Restrictive Environment (LRE)

The law states that "... to the maximum extent appropriate, children with disabilities, including children in public or private institutions or care facilities, are educated with children who are nondisabled; and special classes, separate schooling or other removal of children with disabilities from regular educational environment occurs only if the nature or severity of the disability is such that education in regular classes with the use of supplementary aids and services cannot be achieved satisfactorily."

This is the section of the law that guarantees that history will not repeat itself and our children will not be segregated into special classrooms or schools, unless you agree to the placement. This entitles your child with Down syndrome to be educated with the other students her age from your neighborhood—to be served in an "inclusive" setting.

Today, some students with Down syndrome in the United States are fully included in elementary, middle, and high schools with students who do not have disabilities. Some students with Down syndrome have even graduated from college. Students with Down syndrome are learning more as their opportunities for access to the regular curriculum have increased.

Inclusion is different from mainstreaming. Mainstreaming was an educational concept, often used in the 1980s and 90s, in which students with Down syndrome or other disabilities spent a portion of their day in the "mainstream"—a regular classroom. Mainstream opportunities were most often lunch period, a gym class, or a music class. Our children then spent the majority of their day in a special education class, often referred to as a self-contained classroom, away from their peers who did not have disabilities.

Inclusion is an entirely different value and it is based on the concept that each child has the right to be educated in the setting where she can have the maximum contact with typically developing peers while still achieving her educational goals. Another way to say it is that the "least restrictive environment" is the setting that is the closest to the one where your child's typical peers are educated. The LRE is different for different students, however.

It is important to understand that least restrictive environment is not synonymous with inclusion. What is the least restrictive environment for one child is not necessarily the least restrictive environment for another child. If your child is unable to learn what is expected of her in any given classroom setting, then that setting is not the least restrictive environment for her. There may be a number of reasons why you might consider a less inclusive classroom for all or part of the day at some time in your child's education. Among the reasons for you to consider may be that your child with Down syndrome uses sign language to communicate and you believe she needs to be in a classroom where all teachers use total communication. Other reasons may be that your child learns best in an environment that is free from distractions or in a setting where staff are better able to work on a particular challenging behavior, like suddenly leaving a room. Still another reason may be that your school may not be able to offer all the elements of your child's Individualized Education Program (which is discussed later) in your district.

Every parent hopes that their child, with or without Down syndrome, will be a "super star." When your child has Down syndrome, it might mean you hope that your child will be able to participate in regular classrooms and typical school activities all of the time. Many students with Down syndrome will. However, some children may need to spend part or even all of their day in another educational setting. Some students with Down syndrome may be in inclusive programs for some of their educational years, and in other years be in a more specialized environment. Things change and you need to be open to change as well. You know your child best.

Inclusion will always remain the goal for our children in other areas of their lives besides school—sports, religious activities, employment, etc. Sometimes we do not always get there. But we never give up trying.

Our neighborhood school welcomed our daughter into an inclusive kindergarten class. The teacher had been a special education teacher, so she was very knowledgeable about different learning styles, and there was a classroom aide who helped any child who needed it. Our daughter sometimes needed instructions repeated and extra time to finish up her work, but she made good progress in reading and math, and became friends with a quiet little boy who was even shyer than she was. At the end of the year, there was no question that she should go on to an inclusive first grade class.

Individualized Education Program (IEP)

Before your child can receive special education services, she must be "referred" for special education. Your early intervention program may initiate this process or you can make the referral yourself. The referral must be in writing and should state that your child is in need of special education services. After the referral is made, the school district must determine whether or not your child is eligible, which they will accomplish through an evaluation. You might think that the school system already has sufficient documentation to determine your child's eligibility, but the school will almost always conduct its own evaluation any way.

I wanted our school system to know Matt long before he turned three so that they would know about his needs. I did this by sending the special education department all his evaluations from early intervention and from other professionals working with him, beginning when he was 18 months old. I figured this way, he wouldn't just be a typical "this child is turning 3" referral from early intervention.

▪▪ Universal Design for Learning and Inclusion

Universal Design for Learning (UDL) is a concept that is borrowed from architecture and product design. Universally designed places or products are designed to be accessible to all users, regardless of age or disability. Likewise, Universal Design for Learning considers the needs of individuals who have diverse learning profiles at the outset when a curriculum is being designed, so the curriculum is more accessible to all learners. This is a different approach from what usually occurs. Usually, the curriculum is modified for a student with disabilities *after* it is developed. UDL is meant to support all learners, rather than relying on the old method of adapting the curriculum for each special education student.

Here are two examples of how Universal Design for Learning is integrated into the curriculum. All students need to learn how to create meaning from or understand what they read. In a book based on UDL principles, embedded prompts help early readers think about the meaning of the story. The embedded prompts can be turned off as your child progresses. Or if your child is a nonreader, she may use software that reads the same text aloud to her that the other students are reading to themselves. As your child begins to learn to read, the read-aloud feature can be turned off. Other features such as speed, highlighting, and repeating words are also available.

If you are lucky, your school system may already be applying UDL to the curriculum. If not, you might want to attend workshops on UDL yourself and advocate for some of the techniques you learn to be used in your child's classroom. For more information on UDL, visit www.cast.org. If you are really excited about this concept, you can download existing books or create your own using this technology at http://bookbuilder.cast.org. This emerging concept has great applicability to students with Down syndrome.

Evaluation and Eligibility. With your consent, your child will be evaluated "in all areas related to the suspected disability, including, if appropriate, health, vision, hearing, social and emotional status, general intelligence, academic performance, communicative status, and motor abilities" (34 CFR Sec. 300.532). The evaluation will be conducted by professionals representing your child's areas of need. For a

child with Down syndrome, the evaluation team usually includes a special educator, speech-language pathologist, occupational therapist, physical therapist, and a psychologist. Depending on your child, there could be evaluations by other professionals. For example, if your child has diabetes, a nurse may evaluate your child to make sure she receives appropriate services. If you disagree with any part of the evaluation, you can request an independent evaluation, at the school district's expense. (See Chapter 7 for more information about evaluations.)

Your child will be declared eligible for special education if she is determined to have one of the qualifying disabilities listed in IDEA *and* if that disability has an impact on her ability to learn. (See Chapter 7.) If she is eligible, the next step will be to develop an individualized education program (IEP) for her. The IEP is a legally binding document that describes how the school will work with your child and what special services your child will receive to enable her to meet the goals that you and school personnel individually choose for your child.

My child's eligibility category was "speech and language disorder" in kindergarten. This didn't turn out to be a very helpful label for her because the school took that to mean that her only delays were in speech and language. As a result, the classroom aide didn't routinely help her pay attention or stay on task like she did with the other students who had IEPs. In first grade, we got our daughter's category changed to "other health impaired" with the help of a letter from our doctor explaining the impact that Down syndrome has on strength and alertness. After that, the school changed our child's case manager from a speech-language pathologist to a special education teacher, and she was better able to suggest goals and accommodations for all areas of our daughter's learning.

Special Education and Related Services. The IEP will set out: 1) the *special education*, and 2) *related services* your child will receive. Special education means specialized instruction designed to help a student with disabilities learn. Related services are those that are required to help a child to benefit from special education. Related services include, but are not limited to: audiology, counseling services, health services, occupational therapy, parent counseling and training, physical therapy, psychological services, recreation and therapeutic recreation, school health services, service coordination services, social work services in schools, speech-language pathology, transportation and related costs, and assistive technology and services. Obviously, not every student will receive all of these related services. The services that your child receives will depend on her needs, as identified during the evaluation.

I knew that my child was entitled to transportation services. But, he was only three years old and my only child and I headed out to work at the same time as he needed to be at school. I liked taking him to school myself and having the opportunity to see his teachers every day. After my second child was born, we took advantage of the school-provided transportation. This worked very well until Sam went to middle school and he told me that middle school kids got picked up by their parents. In high school, he just got a ride with kids in the neighborhood. It seemed counterproductive to me to have him included in all areas of academics and then have him transported to school in a "special education" bus.

When our child was in early intervention, she received speech-language therapy, physical therapy, and occupational therapy. But she stopped receiving physical therapy once she entered preschool special education because her gross motor skills didn't hold her back from doing anything the other kids did. In elementary school, they started cutting back on her OT, going from direct services (where the therapist worked individually with her on her handwriting) to consultative services (where the therapist only

*advised the teachers about any fine motor difficulties our daugh-
ter was having). After a couple years, they dropped OT completely
and she just had speech-language therapy.*

Goals. The IEP will also include descriptions of the goals that your
child is expected to meet—usually over the course of one school year.
Goals must be written for all areas where your child is determined to have
needs. Goals will be written for academic areas such as reading, writing,
math, and science, but may also be written for developmental skills and
functional skills that your child needs to acquire in order to succeed. For
example, your child might have goals related to developing handwriting
or keyboarding skills, waiting her turn, staying on task, or organizing
materials. She may also have goals relating to physical education.

Annual goals must be measurable so that you and your child's
teacher can easily tell whether she has achieved them. In the past, IDEA
required short-term objectives for all students, which were intermediate
steps toward meeting the long-term goals. Although objectives are no
longer required for most students, you can still request them. Otherwise,
there must be benchmarks to be able to measure progress. Often families
believe that short-term goals are the best way to measure success toward
the often larger annual goals. An example of a long-tem goal may be
for your child to learn to tell time on an analog clock. Short-term goals
might include: learning to tell time on the hour, then the half-hour, then
by 15 minute increments, and then by 5 minute increments.

*Looking back at all the goals that Sara had as a child, there is no
doubt that the academic skills were most important. But now that
she is older, I am also glad that there were goals that addressed
her fine and gross motor skills. She was able to practice the motor
skills she learned in art classes, bowling, and horseback riding.
She learned some great skills that she will be able to enjoy her
entire lifetime.*

*We sometimes have to struggle with our school to get them to truly
individualize goals for our child. They tend to want to use "boiler
plate" goals that they have used for other children in the past. In
fact, our school system has a whole database of goals for teachers
and it's much easier for them to use those goals than to work with
us to develop truly individualized goals. To get teachers thinking*

about ways to better tailor goals to our daughter's needs, it helps to remind them of specific instances when she struggled with class work or homework. For example, I save things she has written, and then show them to the teachers at IEP meetings to back up the need for a particular goal in reading or writing.

IEP Meetings. Your child's IEP will be written by a team of people at one or more IEP meetings. IDEA describes the IEP team as "a group of people who are responsible for developing, reviewing, and revising the IEP." This group consists of a regular education teacher, a special education teacher, a representative of the school district, other individuals invited by the school or the family, and someone who can interpret the results of the evaluation. Students are included when they are older. You must remember that you are an equal member of the team and the team may not make recommendations and modifications to the IEP without your knowledge and participation.

The IEP meetings can be intimidating—all those professionals talking about your child. I always brought someone with me to those meetings for support. It helps to bring a spouse or a friend— someone who cares about your child and could help you if there were any disagreements.

Extended School Year Services. Families are often interested in extended school year services (ESY) for their child. This refers to services that are provided during the summer vacation for students who meet eligibility criteria. Whether or not your child needs ESY will be determined by her IEP team. Your team will discuss whether your child will regress (lose ground) a great deal over the summer without continued instruction, whether she is on the brink of learning an important new skill, whether she has a great deal of trouble making the transition back to school after a break, and other issues. Regression is not the only standard used to determine eligibility for extended school year services. After all, all students regress during the summer, and that is why classes in September are often a review of the previous year's material.

Some families prefer that their child go on family vacations or attend camp in the summer, even if she qualifies for ESY. Other families determine that their child really benefits from extended school year services.

*I never wanted ESY services for Emily. The school district offered
classes with some silly recreation services. The summer was the
best time for Emily to be with typical kids and do typical things.
We sent her to regular day camp beginning when she was three
years old and she just continued with regular summer camps.*

*In our school district, they only offer ESY at a couple central loca-
tions rather than at many neighborhood schools. I think they try
to make it as inconvenient as possible to discourage parents from
asking for it.*

Due Process Protection

IDEA gives parents the opportunity to question the decisions that
the school district makes about their children. You may question any
decision related to your child's identification, evaluation, placement, or
free and appropriate education. You may hear this called "due process
protection" or "procedural safeguards."

There are 4 ways you can question decisions. They are:

1. Resolution;
2. Mediation;
3. Due process; and
4. Civil complaint.

The first step in formally questioning a decision you disagree with
is to file a due process complaint with the local education agency with a
copy to the state education agency. Filing a due process complaint does
not mean that you will necessarily proceed to a due process hearing.
Holding a due process hearing is a fairly drastic step that can drain a
family's energy and finances. For this reason, there are other steps that
should be taken *before* you proceed to a due process hearing. Once the
LEA receives due process notification from a family, the LEA must offer
to hold a "resolution meeting." At this meeting, the parent discusses the
facts that form the basis of the due process complaint. This provides an
opportunity for the LEA to settle differences informally.

The participants in the resolution meeting may include representa-
tives from the special education administration and IEP team members.
The family will want to consider asking an advocate to attend with
them. The school district may not have an attorney present unless the
parents are accompanied by an attorney. If an agreement is reached

in the resolution meeting, it is binding and enforceable. If you do not agree with the results of the resolution meeting, the request for a due process hearing may continue.

As an alternative to having a resolution meeting, you and the school district can agree to go directly to the next step—mediation—or directly to a due process hearing.

IDEA requires each state to offer mediation. Mediation is conducted much like a legal proceeding, but is a much less formal proceeding. A neutral mediator tries to broker an agreement between the family and the school district. It is important to know that mediation is voluntary. The results agreed upon in mediation are also binding and enforceable in any court.

If neither a resolution meeting nor mediation is satisfactory to your family or the school district, either of you may request a due process hearing. A due process hearing is conducted by a neutral hearing officer who listens to what the parents, school staff, their witnesses, and their lawyers have to say about the alleged violation of IDEA and then decides who is right. Generally, your complaint must be filed within two years of the date of the action that you are disagreeing with and you must give notice to the other party. The notice needs to include identifying information about your child, the nature of your concern, and a proposed solution, if you are aware of one. For example, you might believe that the classroom where the school district has placed your child is not the least restrictive environment for her and you may propose a different classroom. The school district then responds with an explanation, including options considered and reasons they were rejected, evaluations and assessments used, and relevant factors that led to the school system's decision. After all proper notifications are made, a hearing officer is assigned and a hearing date scheduled. The hearing officer must be independent of both the child and the school system and possess sufficient qualifications.

If you do go to due process and are not happy with the hearing officer's decision, you may file a civil complaint in court. In fact, your case could go all the way to the Supreme Court, although this is a rare, costly, and emotional journey. You should also know that IDEA allows for the court to order families to pay the attorney fees for the school district if the parents' case is determined to be frivolous or unnecessary litigation. If you prevail, however, the court may order the school district to reimburse you part or all of your attorney fees.

Whether you decide to try to settle your differences by resolution, mediation, a hearing, or by bringing a civil complaint, you will need excellent representation. In addition to attorneys who specialize in special education law, there are also specially trained and certified special education advocates. Most families start by using an advocate for resolution, mediation, and some hearings. They then depend on the advice of their advocate as to when and whether to hire an attorney. This saves money. If money is not an issue, you can hire a lawyer for your resolution meeting and mediation. School districts have attorneys on retainer to represent them in actions with families. School systems are also aware that many families are not able to pay for legal representation. Some school districts will decline mediation in order to force a family to go to the more time consuming and costly due process hearing. They do this because they know that most families do not have the resources to pay attorney fees.

Each state has a federally mandated Protection and Advocacy System (P&A) to protect the rights of individuals with disabilities. There may be attorneys there who may be able to assist you in a dispute with your school. To locate your state's P&A, contact the National Disability Rights Network (see the Resource Guide).

Perhaps the best advice I can give you is to become educated about your child's rights to a free and appropriate education. For instance, attend any workshops that are offered in your community about IDEA or visit the U.S. government's website on IDEA (http://idea.ed.gov). Your child's education is simply too important a subject to leave in the hands of your school district.

No Child Left Behind Act (NCLB)

This federal law, a law distinct from IDEA, has areas of interest and concern to families with a child with Down syndrome. This law was originally passed in hopes of making sure that all students can read and do math at grade level by 2014. Testing occurs annually in grades 3 to 8 and once in high school. There are ramifications for schools whose students fail to make "adequate yearly progress" (AYP). Since students in a variety of subcategories, including those in special education, are all supposed to make AYP, schools with many special education students are feeling pressures to have special education students exempted from testing.

The goal of NCLB is critical for special education students, who are often left behind. Before NCLB was enacted, many schools did not count the scores of students with disabilities when they reported their progress. Under NCLB, the achievement of students in special education is under much more scrutiny. This has resulted in greater efforts being made to teach the general curriculum to students with disabilities, and greater accountability for successes and failures.

School districts are allowed to give alternative testing to a small percentage of special education students. However, when this is done, children are often not given access to the regular curriculum or held to the highest educational standards possible. While the government and Down syndrome advocates in Washington monitor and develop acceptable solutions, families need to make sure that their child is not automatically offered alternative testing. Since all of our children will have different abilities, you want to make sure that the testing bar is set at the right height for your child. Alternative testing is appropriate for some children with Down syndrome, but others will be challenged to achieve more if they are expected to take the same tests as typically developing peers.

Ms. Dune (the special education teacher) said I couldn't do the work. I wanted to try. I am at a new school and I take earth science and U.S. History. I want Ms. Dune to come see me at my new school and see that I can do the work. I think other kids with Down syndrome should have the chance to do regular work.

■■ Estate Planning

As the parent of a child with Down syndrome, you will soon learn about the world of estate planning. There are basically two parts that families of children with disabilities should be concerned with—a will and a special needs trust. Both are instruments that require the skills of a knowledgeable attorney to prepare. You will also begin to hear about financial planners; I will discuss them separately at the end of this section.

Wills

Every adult should have a will, or Last Will and Testament, but many adults in this country do not have one. It is a difficult concept for many of us to have to plan for the distribution of our estate and the care of all our minor children. That is exactly why you must have a will. You have a child with Down syndrome and you must make these decisions that are in the best interest of your baby.

Some people think they can make their own will using forms available to download for free on the Internet. However, there are special considerations when you have a baby with Down syndrome that only an attorney familiar with the issues knows. This is not the time to call upon a family friend who happens to be a lawyer. I have seen many instances when smart and well-intentioned lawyers, who were not aware of the special laws and situations that come into play when you have a child with a disability, unintentionally hurt the future of a child with Down syndrome.

Having a Will to Name a Guardian

You have probably already thought about what would happen in the unlikely event that you, your spouse/partner, or the other parent, were not able to care for your child. If you do not have a will that names a guardian, the court will appoint one. Anybody can petition the court to be named your child's guardian, and more than one person can petition the court. This sets up the possibility of a family battle as well as the possibility that someone could be named guardian that you would not have chosen.

In deciding who will be your child's guardian, you need to consider what is important to you. You will have to look at each potential guardian and think about the qualities of that person and the home where he or she would raise your child. Many families naturally look at other family members as potential guardians. Parents often consider their children's aunts and uncles or their grandparents (if they are fairly young), but you may want to consider other relatives or close friends.

In choosing a guardian, you might want to consider some of these factors:

- Do we share values and morals?
- Does the home have the kind of environment where my child will thrive?
- Are their children of similar age?
- Will my child's religion be practiced?
- Will there be enough resources to care for my child with Down syndrome?
- Does this person live in our community?

It is also important to name a successor guardian in the event that the guardian you originally named is not able to serve as guardian. This eliminates the need to revise your will if the need for a successor guardian arises.

I have one sibling. We are not particularly close and he does not live in our community. My husband has siblings, too. But after much thought we decided that one of my first cousins, who shares our children's religion and has children the same age, would be the best choice for a guardian, even though she lived halfway across the country.

We made our will before we had any kids, but it stipulates that in the event we did have kids, my sister would be the guardian. After our child with Down syndrome was born, I never actually went back to her and asked her if she would still be willing to be the guardian. I know this is a huge oversight and I need to revisit this issue with her soon, but I keep putting it off.

▪▪ A Letter of Intent

Now that you understand the importance of making a will for naming a guardian, you can move on to another big worry for families—how do I convey my wishes and information about the needs of my child? Many families before you have also worried about this very thing. Several different organizations and individuals have developed templates to make it easy for you to put down everything from important medical information to favorite bedtime routines for your child. While this type of document is generally referred to as a "Letter of Intent," different authors call it different things. My agency and I developed such a form and we call ours "Footprints for the Future." You can download it for free at www.theemarc.org, under "Resources."

Having a Will to Distribute Your Assets

The other important reason for having a will is to distribute your assets. Again, if you do not have a will, the court will distribute your assets according to the laws that govern your state. That is the last thing you want to happen if you have a child with Down syndrome, because it could have far reaching and long-lasting negative effects on your child.

This brings us to one of the most difficult concepts for new families to accept. In order for your child to be eligible for all of the various government benefits and many programs she will likely need as an adult, your child must not have too much money in her name. In fact, generally speaking, as of 2008, your child must not have resources of more than $2000 to qualify for Medicaid or for Supplemental Security Income (SSI). Resources include real estate, bank accounts, cash, stocks, and bonds. Some income is also counted. While there are some exceptions, if you leave your child money or other property outright in your will, that bequest will likely render her ineligible for needed benefits until those resources are spent. Even if you have a young child, paying attention to these details is important.

A good lawyer, familiar with the rules for government benefits, will make sure that your will contains the kind of language that will ensure your child's eligibility for all the benefits she may be entitled to receive. There are basically two ways to do this within a will. You can:

1. Decide not to leave any assets to your child with Down syndrome—this is called disinheriting your child and it requires you to state that you are not leaving any assets to your child. Many families find this option unappealing.
2. You can have your attorney create a trust within your will specifically worded to maintain government benefits and to provide for additional needs for your child. See "Special Needs Trusts," below.

Unfortunately, our children must remain poor to be eligible for most of the programs that will be of benefit to them as adults. This is because the programs were established to assist individuals with financial needs.

A few families do not have to worry about these issues because they have adequate personal financial resources and they do not intend to rely on government benefits. Even in the rare situation where a family has vast wealth, however, it is wiser to make other financial arrangements for the child.

It may be hard to imagine your child as an adult when you are still busy with diapers and hoping for a full night's sleep. But, the day will come and some of the services your child will need will only be available if she qualifies financially for them.

Special Needs Trusts

You might think, as I did, that only people with lots of money have trusts for their children, thinking of the stereotypical "trust-fund baby." I learned quickly that I needed to have a trust for my son with Down syndrome to provide and protect him. Initially, as a new parent, I was able to accomplish this through our will, but it became obvious to me that I would have to have a "special needs trust" to fully protect him. You do not need any money to establish a special needs trust, but once you set one up, it is there for the future and you might someday have funds to put in it.

A special needs trust, when properly designed by an attorney knowledgeable in this area, enables you to leave money to be used to benefit your child. Your child will never be able to access the assets of the trust or make decisions about the distribution of the trust. Instead, a trustee will make these decisions on behalf of your child. This enables your child to still maintain eligibility for government benefits, if the trust is drawn up correctly, because your child will never have control of the assets. The government, therefore, does not view the funds in the trust as assets belonging to your child.

When you set up a special needs trust, you name a trustee. In most cases, the trustee will be you and your spouse, and you will also name a successor trustee. Many families think about naming a young

grandparent and later, the child's brother or sister as trustee. The trust will also specify how the remainder of the trust will be distributed upon the death of your child, who is called the beneficiary.

The important thing to remember about naming a trustee is that this individual will be the gatekeeper of the trust. You need to be very careful that the person you name as the successor trustee will not be tempted by any possible personal gains from the trust. For example, I have seen a situation where the parents named the brother of their daughter with Down syndrome as the trustee, with the remainder of the trust to be given to the brother's children upon the death of his sister. The parents were probably confident that their son would provide for all the unmet needs of their daughter. Unfortunately, it has not played out that way. The brother distributes very little of the trust to the sister. I think this is because he is thinking that if he keeps the trust assets, his own children will benefit. I am not saying that this will happen in every family, but you have to be aware of what kind of financial pressures the trustee may be under in the future. Even with this information, I have named our daughter as the successor trustee for our son's trust.

When you establish a special needs trust, it is important to notify any of your relatives who might wish to make monetary gifts to your child with Down syndrome. They need to know that they should direct their gifts to your child's special needs trust, rather than to your child, unless they are sending her small sums, such as for a birthday present. I have met with my parents' attorney to make sure that any gifts they make to Jonathan go directly into his special needs trust.

Life Insurance

Life insurance is another one of those items that all parents need to consider once they have a baby. Having a baby with Down syndrome makes it even more important to think about your life insurance needs and your ability to afford it. There are several different life insurance products, and while they are generally not considered the best investment plan, life insurance may have a place in a total strategy for your baby's future.

There are two basic types of life insurance:

1. Term life insurance, in which you choose the amount of insurance you want (e.g., $100,000, $200,000, $500,000) and then purchase a policy in that amount for a specified "term" of 10, 20, or more years at a set annual rate for that period of time. If you die during the term of the insurance, your survivors receive the face value of your policy, but if the term has expired before you die, your policy becomes worthless.

2. Whole life or universal life, which has an investment component in addition to life insurance. This form of insurance is expensive and you have to pay fees and commissions. As a purely investment strategy, there may be better products to save for retirement, but this type of insurance makes sense for some families.

Many young parents purchase inexpensive term insurance to be paid upon their death to help either the surviving spouse or the guardian to pay for their child's expenses. Since the premiums on these policies can get expensive as the insured person gets older, some families prefer whole life policies, which actually build cash value the longer they are held. Whatever path you take, you want to make sure that nobody, including yourself or well-meaning relatives, purchases any life insurance for your baby with Down syndrome. This will only complicate future benefits for your child because life insurance policies, except for small burial accounts, are considered assets. In addition, it is very unlikely that your child with Down syndrome will need any of the benefits that life insurance provides.

After our children were born, my husband and I shopped around
for life insurance policies with higher pay-outs. This is pretty easy

to do online and we were able to purchase quite a bit more cover-
age for not that much more money. Since we listed our children's
guardian as the beneficiary, this gives us some peace of mind that
our children would be well cared for in the event of our deaths.

■■ Financial Planners

Many financial services companies and independent individuals
offer financial planning services specifically geared to families who have

children with special needs such
as Down syndrome. These professionals can generally be divided
into two groups: those who receive
commissions for selling you products and those who charge a fee for
their services. After all, these are
trained individuals and need to be
paid for their services somehow.

Not everyone needs a per-
sonal financial planner. Some people do their own taxes and some
people are comfortable doing their
own financial planning. This is
another area that you will want
to become educated about—for
example, by attending workshops conducted by financial planners.

In picking a financial planner, you should check their credentials,
and, more importantly, get references from other families or your local
Down syndrome parent group or Arc. You also have to have a personal
comfort level with any advisor.

I think I went to five workshops on financial planning before I
was actually ready to make an appointment with one. I brought
my parents with me since they were going to be a large part of
insuring Jon's future. In the end, I bought a "second to die" life
insurance policy on my parents' lives. It is a type of life insurance
that insures two people, in this case, my mother and father. It pays
when the second person dies and is a less expensive alternative.
I could afford this policy since my parents were able to "gift" me

money to help with the annual dividend. As it turns out, it has been the worst investment I ever made. Jon's future has been ensured and my parents have lived a very long life. I could have done better if I had invested in the stock market, but having my parents around is worth it.

A Special Word for Grandparents and Others

Your baby with Down syndrome can receive all the love and attention from grandparents and other relatives and friends that they can give. When it comes to money and other assets, however, your child with Down syndrome cannot be treated the same as your other children. Some grandparents are in a position to buy savings bonds, establish a bank account or trust, or transfer stock to your child with Down syndrome. They might even want to establish an educational fund. They must not.

Anybody who wants to provide for your baby with Down syndrome must pay attention to your child's need for future benefits just as you do. Grandparents are especially at risk for unknowingly making financial planning mistakes when it comes to their grandchild with Down syndrome. You will have to get involved and make sure that these wonderful and well-meaning relatives have wills that do not jeopardize your child's future.

▪▪ Taxes

As the parent of a child with Down syndrome, you may be entitled to some important deductions and credits on your tax return. To get you on the right path, every new parent must have a date book to record medical and related appointments for their baby and all the members of the family. Use it to record every medical, therapy, and early intervention visit—both those you pay for and those you do not pay for. Be sure

to record appointments you go to without your baby, as well as appointments for other family members. Write down the location of the visit, the mileage, tolls, and parking fees. This will become the cornerstone for determining whether you will be able to meet the threshold for taking advantage of the "Medical and Dental Deduction."

You may only deduct the amount of eligible deductions that is more than 7.5% of your adjusted gross income, so you will want to make sure you don't miss any expense. Some examples of items you can deduct are the following:

- Health insurance premiums and co-pays
- Transportation to get medical and related care (using standard mileage rates)
- Prescription drugs
- Eyeglasses and hearing aids
- Nursing care
- Therapy
- Cost of meals and lodging related to receiving hospital care
- Tutoring under some circumstances
- Special education (such as tuition at a private school for children with disabilities) with a doctor's recommendation
- Medical conferences related to your child with Down syndrome

If you are a parent of low or moderate income, you may be eligible for the Earned Income Tax Credit. The age limitations are waived for our children. If you pay for childcare so that you can work or look for work, like all parents, you may be eligible for the Child or Dependent Care Credit, depending on your income. There are special credits for those of you who adopted your baby with Down syndrome.

For a full discussion of tax topics, visit www.irs.gov and type any keyword you need information on into the search area. You can also phone 800-829-1040 for live assistance. You may also want to consult with a tax advisor.

We always did our own taxes. We didn't find them too compli-
cated and it was like a challenge to see how many deductions we
could find. We liked having the extra money instead of giving it
to a tax preparer.

You can reduce your tax burden if you take advantage of an employer's 125 Plan or Flexible Spending Plan. These employer- and govern-
ment-required plans allow employees to pay for medical and childcare
expenses with pre-tax dollars under a payroll deduction plan. You should
see your human resources department for more information.

None of us like to pay taxes. However, taxes take on a whole new
meaning when you have a baby with Down syndrome. That is because
many wonderful programs for our children, such as early intervention
and the right to a free and appropriate education, are paid for with tax
dollars. There is also important research being carried on to help us understand more about the ways our children learn and behave, as well as
research to understand how the extra chromosome affects our children
and to develop ways of possibly reducing some of its effects. The medical breakthroughs that have occurred, thanks to our tax dollars, have
improved the lives of our children and given them the opportunity to
live healthy and productive lives. In addition, when your child becomes
an adult, she will be entitled to the many financial benefits, job training,
housing, and other benefits that are financed with tax dollars.

❚❚ Anti-Discrimination Laws

There are several important landmark pieces of legislation that
protect individuals with disabilities from discrimination. While these
laws are not specifically designed for people with Down syndrome, your
child will be covered by them as a person with a disability. Here is an
overview of the most important laws:

Section 504 of The Rehabilitation Act of 1973

Section 504 prohibits discrimination against individuals with
disabilities by any program receiving federal funding, and this includes
schools or activities sponsored by schools. If a child with disabilities
does not qualify for assistance under IDEA, this law ensures that she
will have equal access to school activities. Although the law does not
cover services such as therapies or assistive technology that cost the

school money, it does require that schools make adaptations or modifications to the environment, instruction, or materials that enable the student to have an equal opportunity to learn.

Sometimes children with Down syndrome are so "high functioning" that they do not meet the eligibility criteria of IDEA. If that is the case for your child, Section 504 would ensure that your child's educational needs are met. For example, if your child only needs classroom accommodations, such as more time for assignments or seating at the front of the class, Section 504 would guarantee those accommodations.

Since most children with Down syndrome do qualify for special education under IDEA, Section 504 adds little to their rights and entitlements at school. It does, however, guarantee your child an equal opportunity to participate in extracurricular activities unless this would require unreasonable modifications or a "fundamental alteration of the program." While each school district might interpret this a little differently, let me provide some examples. If your child with Down syndrome wants to participate in the school chorus and needs assistance getting up and down the risers, that is a reasonable accommodation. Or, your daughter may enjoy playing on an intramural team where there are no try outs to make the team. The other kids don't necessarily like your child slowing them down, but the school has to let her play anyway. However, if your son with Down syndrome wants to manage the varsity basketball team, but he requires supervision when traveling to away games, cannot keep a shot chart, and is not alert enough to get out of the way of play—that is, even with accommodations he could not perform most of the duties of a manager— it would not be a violation of Section 504 to deny him the manager position.

I never used Section 504 for my child with Down syndrome, but my other child has ADD and no other disabilities. I used 504 so that

she could be seated at the front of the class and not be distracted by
other students and so she could receive extra time on tests.

Americans with Disabilities Act

Not too long ago, people with disabilities were routinely discriminated against in many areas of life—employment, housing, transportation, and public places, to name a few. The Americans with Disabilities
Act of 1990, or ADA, is our country's first comprehensive law for people
with disabilities and is considered a landmark civil rights law. People
with Down syndrome are protected under the ADA.

The ADA has four accessibility requirements. They are:

- Title I—Employment,
- Title II—Public Service,
- Title III—Public Accommodations,
- Title IV—Telecommunications.

Title I—Employment

This section makes it illegal for employers with 15 or more employees to discriminate against individuals with disabilities who are
otherwise qualified. In addition, an employer is required to make reasonable accommodations to qualified employees or applicants.

This section of the ADA also provides you, as a parent, protection from an employer who might not hire or promote you because he
or she thinks you might miss too much work caring for your child (the
association clause).

Since you have a baby with Down syndrome, this section of the
law may not be of particular interest now. The important thing to know
is that when your child enters the workforce, you can expect her to be
treated without discrimination.

My son got his first job—working after school at the local super-
market—when he was fourteen. He was treated like any other
applicant. He was allowed to take the training video home for re-
inforcement and to have a job coach assist him until he was ready
to do the job by himself.

Title II—Public Service

This section is fairly simple. Under ADA, all buildings that are open
to the public must be accessible. In addition, state and local governments

may not discriminate against individuals with disabilities. This means that people with disabilities must have equal opportunities to benefit from all programs, services, and activities that are available to the general public. This includes recreational activities and classes, social services, courts, voting, transportation, public education, and meetings.

Although this section may not appear to be all that relevant to families with babies with Down syndrome, we have gained much from this section of the law. Since our children are often delayed in walking and toilet training, curb cuts and ramps make life much easier for those pushing strollers and carriages. In addition, the privacy and room available in accessible restrooms make it much easier to take young children to the bathroom.

Title III—Public Accommodations

This section has the most applicability to families of babies and children with Down syndrome. Title III mandates that restaurants, hotels, theaters, shopping centers and malls, stores, libraries, parks, private schools, day care centers, and other places of public accom-

modation (any building or activity open to the public) cannot discriminate on the basis of disability.

For example, children with Down syndrome cannot be excluded from a daycare center or family daycare on the basis of their disability. Daycare centers, like the other examples above of places of public accommodation, are required to provide "auxiliary aids and services" to people with disabilities unless to do so would "fundamentally alter" the services provided or create an "undue burden." For example, a daycare center would be required to continue changing your child's diapers past the age when other children at the center are toilet trained if diaper changing is a service provided to some children at the center and the center is already equipped with diaper-changing facilities. The daycare center would not, however, be required to change your child's diapers if no other children receive the service and the center would need to hire an additional staff person to change your child.

When my son with Down syndrome was born, I was afraid I would not be able to return to work. My fears were unfounded. The day-care center welcomed him when he was twelve weeks old, coordinated visits by the Early Intervention therapists, and the staff and children even learned sign language.

The ADA ensures that families of children with Down syndrome will have access to camps, community swimming pools, bowling alleys, movie theaters, and other recreational settings and guarantees your child the right to participate in these programs. It does not mean that your child does not have to follow reasonable rules related to participating in the programs. For example, if there is a rule that children in diapers cannot use a swimming pool, your child has to comply with the rule. In this case, everyone in diapers is being treated the same, and the rule protects everyone's health. Likewise, if an amusement park requires that children be above a given height to ride a roller coaster, you and your child must abide by that rule if she is too short, even if other children her age are tall enough to ride.

If a child needs an aide to help him or her participate in a summer camp or class, our county recreation department will supply a free volunteer to help—as long as you ask a couple weeks in advance. A lot of the volunteers are high school kids who need to do some kind of community service to graduate, so it's a nice way for teenagers in the community to get to know something about kids with Down syndrome.

Title IV—Telecommunications

This section requires telephone companies to provide 24-hour-a day relay services for people who have speech impairments or hearing loss. A relay service enables someone who is deaf or hard of hearing to communicate by telephone via an operator who translates speech into text or another format the deaf person can see. Since some people with Down syndrome have hearing losses, this section of the law may be of use to your child in the future.

Family and Medical Leave Act of 1993

Families who have a baby with Down syndrome are often busy with more than the usual number of medical appointments, as well as with keeping up with early intervention services. Understandably, they can have a more difficult time balancing work and home life with the needs of their baby. Prior to the passage of the Family and Medical Leave Act, families often had to make agonizing decisions about caring for their baby and maintaining their job. This law addresses the needs of working parents by allowing employees to take unpaid leave from their jobs to care for sick family members or in the event of their own illness. Among other protections, the law allows employees twelve work-weeks of unpaid leave every twelve weeks to care for a new baby, to handle adoption or foster care issues, or to care for a sick child, spouse, or parent.

Under the law, employees can take leave without fear of being terminated or being moved to a lower job upon their return. However, only employers with 50 or more employees must comply with the law, and an employee must have worked for the company for at least 12 months and 1250 hours during those 12 months to qualify for leave.

The Health Insurance Portability and Accountability Act (HIPPA)

Most of us are familiar with the Health Insurance Portability and Accountability Act (HIPPA) because we have to sign forms in medical offices stating that we understand how our personal medical information will be used and the lengths that will be taken to protect our

confidentiality. What you may not realize is that this law protects and improves American workers' health insurance coverage. The most important elements for families with a child with Down syndrome is that it severely limits the use of preexisting conditions in enrollment in health insurance plans.

There are two things for you to know. First, group health plans cannot exclude a preexisting medical condition from coverage for more than 12 months (18 months for later enrollees). Second, if you are switching to a new insurer, your new plan must cover the preexisting condition, as long as the person with the preexisting medical condition had previous continuous health coverage for at least 12 months (or 18 months for late enrollees). This is true provided you do not let your old insurance lapse for more than 62 days before your new insurance takes effect. Even if your insurance lapses for 63 days or more, a group health plan can't exclude a preexisting condition for more than 12 months (or 18, if you are a late enrollee). This reduces or eliminates the exclusion period for coverage of medical conditions such as heart problems or sleep apnea that babies or children with Down syndrome may have.

▪▪ Health Insurance

Besides your love, there is probably nothing more important for your baby than having adequate health insurance. Health insurance should be available to everyone, but, while great strides are being made, there are still many individuals in the United States without health insurance. The importance of health insurance cannot be overstated since our children need access to quality medical care and the related services that accompany health insurance. Families should not be forced to make career decisions based on the availability of health insurance, and families should not have to pay exorbitant fees to obtain health insurance.

Most families will find that their baby does not change their health insurance status, but some health plans discriminate against individuals with preexisting conditions such as Down syndrome. This is based on the assumption that your child might develop health conditions that are costly.

There are programs in all the states to assist families obtain health insurance for children. This is primarily done through the Medicaid program. (See below.) Eligibility for Medicaid is based on the income of the family and each state has different eligibility criteria. The other way to get Medicaid eligibility is through the State Children's Health Insurance Program (SCHIP). This program provides health insurance to children whose family does not meet the low income levels required for Medicaid eligibility but who cannot afford traditional health insurance. Each state has different eligibility criteria and benefits and determines whether co-payments are required. The federal government has centralized eligibility and application procedures at Insure Kids Now! (www.insurekidsnow.gov or 877-KIDS-NOW/543-7669).

Every child who is eligible for Medicaid is also eligible for a valuable program for children with disabilities called EPSDT. This stands for Early Periodic Screening, Diagnosis, and Treatment. This program provides for regular checkups and complete physical and mental health care from birth and up to a child's eighteenth, nineteenth, twentieth, or twenty-first birthday (depending on your state).

▪▪ Federal Government Benefits

While benefits available through the federal government do change, the basic underpinnings of the programs that will be discussed here—Medicaid, Medicare, Supplemental Security Income, and Social Security Disability Income—do not regularly change. For instance,

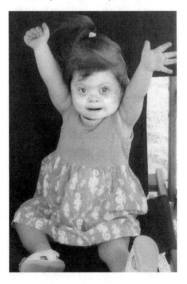

although income guidelines and some of what is covered may change, the basic eligibility for people with Down syndrome has changed very little over the years.

The rules for these programs are very complex, and most people find them very confusing. With the exception of the right to a free and appropriate education, all other benefits from the federal government are meant to assist those in financial need and to act as a safety net for people. These government benefits almost always use income or what is called a "means test" to determine eligibility. As long as your child with Down syndrome is under 18, the government will almost always consider the income of the parents when determining eligibility. There are some exceptions to this rule, so it is always best to do some of your own research. This underscores the importance of making sure your child with Down syndrome remains "poor" so that as an adult, she will meet the means test or income eligibility for many programs.

Medicaid

The Medicaid program provides health benefits to eligible people. Most often these are low-income individuals. Although the general guidelines for Medicaid are established by the federal government, each state establishes its own eligibility requirements. Some of these state-specific guidelines address individuals with disabilities.

While your child is under 18, she will probably not qualify for Medicaid unless your family's income is below the income cut-off that has been established for your state. The exception is if your child has very complex and significant disabilities, beyond just Down syndrome. In that case, she may qualify under a waiver program, sometimes called the Katie Beckett waiver. In this program for children with severe disabilities, the family's income is not considered. It was named for a girl from Iowa, who was dependent on a respirator and had to live in a hospital in order for Medicaid to cover her large medical bills. Her mother fought and won a battle with the federal government to have her cared for at home, with the special equipment she needed, instead of a hospital. It made fiscal sense since it was much cheaper to care for her at home.

Once your child becomes an adult, she will most likely qualify for Medicaid coverage. Again, this is because once your child reaches adulthood, the federal government looks only at your child's income and assets, not your family's. Medicaid is the primary payer of health-care benefits for adults with Down syndrome in this country. This will become an essential benefit for your child with Down syndrome when she becomes an adult. Medicaid is also the primary health insurance program for low income people in general.

Unfortunately, this important benefit has its flaws. Physicians, dentists, and other healthcare professionals can choose whether to participate in the program, which means they can decide whether to accept Medicaid as a form of payment. Since the Medicaid reimbursement rates are notoriously very low and payment is often delayed, many healthcare professionals have decided not to accept Medicaid patients. This creates a two-tier medical system. Individuals with private health insurance are free to go to anyone who accepts their health insurance, but those on Medicaid are limited to healthcare professionals who will accept the low and often late Medicaid payment. Many parents of children with Down syndrome therefore go to great lengths to ensure that their children have both Medicaid and private insurance.

One way that families ensure access to medical care is to take advantage of all health insurance offered by their employers. Most health insurance programs allow for coverage for children who are permanently disabled even after they are no longer a full-time student.

However, you must apply for this exception according to the rules of your health insurance company. This is usually necessary when your child reaches the age of 18 or is no longer a full-time student.

An individual also qualifies for Medicaid when she qualifies for Supplemental Security Income (SSI). (See below.) Remember, too, that your child may gain access to Medicaid through the SCHIP program described above.

The access to health care through Medicaid, while not perfect, is essential for adults with Down syndrome because the majority of adult services are funded through the Medicaid program. For more information about Medicaid, contact the Centers for Medicare and Medicaid Services (see the Resource Guide).

My son was well aware that he had received a significant amount of money for his Bar Mitzvah. About a year after, he asked, "Where did my Bar Mitzvah money go?" It was a difficult question since the money had been "redistributed" so that it would not affect his eligibility for services in the future.

■■ A Note about Adult Services

It is probably hard to imagine your beautiful baby as an adult, but that day will come and you will be thinking about other things besides diapers and those first words. You will probably be thinking of making sure your child has a meaningful life: a productive way to spend her day, a good place to live, people to provide support to her, and access to quality medical care.

Although the funding for these services and supports differs among our states, every state uses the Medicaid program to pay for some—and, in many cases—all of these services for individuals with disabilities such as Down syndrome. In some cases, if an individual is not eligible for Medicaid, he or she cannot receive the services. In other cases, you might be allowed to purchase the services. These services and supports can be quite expensive and only the very wealthy would find paying out-of-pocket reasonable. This is why it is essential to make sure your child always remains eligible for Medicaid.

Supplemental Security Income (SSI)

The Supplemental Security Income Program is administered by the Social Security Administration but is not a part of Social Security. Funds from the program come from U.S. Treasury funds rather than from Social Security taxes. Supplemental Security Income (SSI) provides monthly payments to people with low income who are aged 65 or older or to people with low income who are blind or have a disability. Your child with Down syndrome may qualify based on your family income. In some cases, your child with Down syndrome may qualify for SSI as described below.

SSI Program for Children

For SSI purposes, a child is either under 18 or under 22 if attending school. To be eligible, a child must have a disability that is expected to last and that results in severe limitations. However, childhood eligibility always considers the parents' income and resources. This is called "deeming." Deeming is done because it is assumed that a parent's income and resources are available to the child. There are several conditions when deeming does not apply, but they are not particularly relevant to most families. However, when your child reaches the age of 18, only your child's income and resources will be considered in determining eligibility. This is another reason why it is essential for you to consider strategies to keep your child "poor" when doing your financial planning. Although your child may just be a baby now, make sure that you apply for SSI benefits for her as soon as she turns 18. Contact your local Social Security office or visit the website at www.socialsecurity.gov.

Social Security Disability Income (SSDI)

Social Security Disability Income (SSDI) is another federal program that provides monthly benefits to qualified individuals. This program is paid from the Social Security Tax to which all workers contribute. When our adult children have worked and paid into the Social Security system long enough, they may receive SSDI benefits in addition to their SSI benefit. In addition, your child with Down syndrome may also be eligible for survivor benefits upon the death or retirement of a parent. When a parent becomes disabled, retires, or dies, the adult child with a disability may receive a SSDI monthly payment based upon the parent's Social Security benefit.

Medicare

Although Medicare is most often recognized as a health insurance program for people 65 years of age and older, some people with disabilities under the age of 65 are eligible, as are individuals with end-stage renal (kidney) disease. When people with Down syndrome become eligible to receive SSDI, they automatically become eligible to receive Medicare as well. This creates a group of individuals referred to as having "dual eligibility," meaning they receive Medicaid and Medicare.

Medicare is our national health program for the elderly and it is a Social Security program—not a need-based program like Medicaid. Since everyone over 65 is eligible for it, all healthcare providers accept it.

Medicare, however, does not have the far-reaching benefits of other services of Medicaid. Medicare has 4 parts:

1. Part A is hospitalization insurance.
2. Part B is medical insurance.
3. Part C allows participants to enroll in private health plans.
4. Part D is prescription drug insurance.

Housing Assistance

The availability of affordable housing is one of our country's challenges. Individuals and families should not have to spend more than 30 percent of their gross income on housing, yet many Americans spend 50 percent or more of their income on this expense. If you spend more than 30 percent of your gross income on housing, then you are considered burdened by the cost of housing and can have trouble paying for other necessities such as food, clothing, and utilities.

Public housing was established to address some of the housing needs for low-income families, the elderly, and people with disabilities. These housing units can be single-family houses or apartments. The U.S. Department of Housing provides money to local housing authorities to administer the housing units. They are generically referred to as subsidized housing projects.

Housing authorities also administer federally funded housing choice vouchers. The housing authority, usually using a lottery process, awards vouchers to people who have applied for them. The lottery system is necessary because there is not enough funding to subsidize housing for everyone who needs it. The individual or family holding the voucher then locates a housing unit whose owner has agreed to rent it to someone with a housing voucher. The owner receives a direct subsidy from the housing authority, and the family/individual pays the balance of the rent. These vouchers are also commonly referred to as Section 8 vouchers.

Some families with a child with Down syndrome use this housing voucher program if they meet the income requirements. However, many more adults with Down syndrome benefit from this valuable program. It allows individuals who are living on SSI or SSDI to rent or own their own homes, while only paying 30 percent of their income for housing.

In addition to federal rental assistance programs, there may be state or local programs or other local organizations that can help you with your housing needs.

My adult daughter wanted to live in her own apartment. We just weren't ready for her to really live away from us. We had an area of our house that we were able to convert into an apartment for her. When her name came up on the Section 8 list, she was able to use her voucher to rent the apartment we created for her.

Food Stamps

The federal Food Stamp Program is designed to make sure that low-income families receive assistance to purchase food. Using an Electronic Benefit Transfer card (EBT), qualified individuals and families can buy eligible food in authorized stores. The card is filled monthly with a predetermined amount and users draw down each time they use the debit-like card. This assistance can be very helpful to both low-income families and to families who may find themselves temporarily in a difficult financial position—for instance, due to the loss of employment. This can also be a very important benefit for our adult children. Most adults with Down syndrome will qualify for the Food Stamp Program when they are no longer living in their family home.

■■ State Government Assistance

In addition to the federal benefit programs described above, there are some assistance programs that are state funded. These are often programs provided by your state developmental disability agency. In some states, this agency is called the Department of Mental Retardation, Division of Developmental Disability, or some variation of a similar name.

Eligibility for services and supports and the services provided vary widely by state. What is important is for you to find out right away whether your state has a family support program that you might be eligible for. These valuable programs might provide you with a cash subsidy, access to respite care, or any of a number of other supports for your young family. While some of these programs may be Medicaid funded and be subject to the eligibility criteria discussed above, many of the programs are funded with state dollars. If only state dollars are used, states are free to establish their own eligibility criteria.

Although all states have family support programs, they vary considerably in eligibility and benefits. To find out about your state, contact the state agency that is responsible for individuals with mental retardation, developmental disabilities, or intellectual disabilities. You may also want to contact your local chapter of The Arc or your Down syndrome support group for more information.

■■ Conclusion

I hope that you will return to this chapter in the months ahead when you need the information or when you are ready to learn about the areas discussed here. It is a lot to take in right now. The most important thing you need to do now is to love and enjoy your beautiful baby. There will be the right time to learn more about financial planning, your educational rights, and the many legal protections and concerns that will come up. And they *will* come up. Do not ignore them. Learn about them and make some plans. It is all part of the wonderful journey you have begun. From someone who has been on that journey for a long time, it just keeps getting better and I would never have wanted not to be on it.

AFTERWORD: WELCOME TO HOLLAND

Emily Perl Kingsley

I am often asked to describe the experience of raising a child with a disability—to try to help people who have not shared that unique experience to understand it, to imagine how it would feel. It's like this......

When you're going to have a baby, it's like planning a fabulous vacation trip—to Italy. You buy a bunch of guide books and make your wonderful plans. The Coliseum. The Michelangelo David. The gondolas in Venice. You may learn some handy phrases in Italian. It's all very exciting.

After months of eager anticipation, the day finally arrives. You pack your bags and off you go. Several hours later, the plane lands. The stewardess comes in and says, "Welcome to Holland."

"HOLLAND?!?" you say. "What do you mean Holland?? I signed up for Italy! I'm supposed to be in Italy. All my life I've dreamed of going to Italy."

But there's been a change in the flight plan. They've landed in Holland and there you must stay.

The important thing is that they haven't taken you to a horrible, disgusting, filthy place, full of pestilence, famine, and disease. It's just a different place.

So you must go out and buy new guide books. And you must meet a whole new group of people you would never have met.

It's just a *different* place. It's slower-paced than Italy, less flashy than Italy. But after you've been there for a while and you catch your breath, you look around .... and you begin to notice that Holland has windmills ....and Holland has tulips. Holland even has Rembrandts.

But everyone you know is busy coming and going from Italy...and they're all bragging about what a wonderful time they had there. And for the rest of your life, you will say "Yes, that's where I was supposed to go. That's what I had planned."

And the pain of that will never, ever, ever, ever go away...because the loss of that dream is a very significant loss.

But... if you spend your life mourning the fact that you didn't get to Italy, you may never be free to enjoy the very special, the very lovely things ...about Holland.

GLOSSARY

Abstractions—Concepts, symbols, and principles that cannot be experienced directly, such as time and space.

Accommodation—A change made to the way information is presented or to the way a student responds that does not change the content or degree of difficulty of what the student learns. Examples include: extra time to complete tests or class work; use of a keyboard in place of hand-writing; dictating answers rather than writing them; assistance with note taking.

Acuity—How clearly an individual sees—at a distance and close up.

ADA—See Americans with Disabilities Act.

Adaptive behavior—The ability to adjust to new environments, tasks, objects, and people, and to apply new skills to those new situations.

Adenoids—Pads of lymph tissue located behind the nose and nasal cavity.

Advocacy groups—A wide variety of organizations that work to protect the rights and opportunities of children with disabilities and their parents.

Alpha-A-Crystallin Gene—The gene that controls the amount of protein in the lens of the eye. This gene may be related to the development of cataracts.

Alpha-feto protein (AFP)—A protein present in the blood of pregnant women. Abnormally low amounts of it may indicate that the fetus has Down syndrome.

Amblyopia—Loss of vision in one eye that can be caused by a variety of eye problems, including nearsightedness, farsightedness, and crossed eyes. Typically, it occurs when one eye has stronger vision than the other and "takes over" for the weaker eye.

Americans with Disabilities Act (ADA)—A federal civil rights law that prohibits discrimination by employers, government agencies, and public accommodations against people with Down syndrome.

Amniocentesis—A method to test the cells of a fetus for possible genetic defects. A needle is inserted through the mother's belly and a small amount of amniotic fluid is withdrawn. The chromosomes within the cells are then tested.

Amniotic fluid—The liquid that surrounds an embryo in a woman's uterus.

Amyloid Beta Protein Gene—A gene that controls the production of certain proteins in the brain. May be related to Alzheimer's disease.

Antibiotics—A group of drugs that kills bacteria that cause illness.

Articulation—The ability to move and control the lips, tongue, jaws, and palate to form speech sounds correctly and clearly.

Assessment—An evaluation of the strengths, needs, and developmental progress of a child. In the public schools, assessments are used to help design education services.

Astigmatism—An irregularity in the shape of the eyeball which prevents light waves from focusing properly on the retina. Blurred vision (usually correctable with glasses) results.

Atlantoaxial instability—Instability in the joints of the upper bones of the spinal column.

Atria—The two upper chambers of the heart.

Atrial septal defect (ASD)—A defect—often a small hole—in the wall between the two upper chambers of the heart.

Atrioventricular canal defect (AV Canal)—A defect in the structure of the heart in which the walls of the two upper chambers and the two lower chambers may be deformed.

Attention span—The length of time a child stays on task or is able to pay attention to one thing (attending).

Audiogram—The graph showing results of a hearing test. An audiogram shows what frequencies (pitches) an individual can hear, and how loud (at what decibel) the sound has to be for the individual to hear it.

Audiologist—A professional trained to evaluate and measure hearing and hearing loss. He or she also fits hearing aids.

Auditory—Having to do with sounds; the ability to hear.

Auditory Brainstem Response (ABR)—A test that measures electronically the brain's reception of sound. It is used to measure hearing in babies and children who cannot respond to sound with words or gestures. Also called auditory evoked potential, auditory evoked response, and evoked response audiometry.

Babbling—The sound a baby makes when he combines a vowel and consonant and repeats them over and over again (e.g., ba-ba-ba, ga-ga-ga).

Bell curve—A curve on a graph that shows the distribution of characteristics in a population. These curves are used to show the range of human intelligence and developmental skill acquisition, as well as many other characteristics of populations.

Beneficiary—The person designated in a trust or insurance policy to receive any payments that become due.

Bilateral—Relating to or affecting both sides of a child's body; of importance in developing skills. For example, holding a piece of paper with one hand and scissors with the other is a bilateral skill.

Blood Pressure—The pressure the flow of blood exerts on the arteries.

Bone Marrow Transplant (BMT)—A treatment for leukemia in which healthy bone marrow is transplanted to replace cancerous bone marrow.

Brachycephaly—A condition in which the back of the skull is somewhat flatter than usual.

Bronchitis—Inflammation of the bronchial tubes, the two branches of the windpipe.

Brushfield spots—Light spots on the outer part of the iris of the eyes, often an outward manifestation of Down syndrome.

Cardiac—Having to do with the heart.

Cardiac catheterization—A surgical diagnostic technique in which a catheter is passed into the heart so that blood pressure and blood flow can be measured and viewed.

Cardiac surgeon—A doctor who specializes in heart surgery.

Cardiologist—A doctor specializing in diagnosing and treating heart conditions.

Case Manager—The person on a child's educational or medical multi-disciplinary team who is responsible for coordinating all members of the team. May be referred to as Service Coordinator.

Cataracts—A disease of the eye that causes the lens to become cloudy or opaque.

Catheter—A flexible tube that is used to provide or remove fluids from the body.

Cause and effect—The concept that actions create reactions.

Chemotherapy—A treatment for leukemia (and other diseases) that uses chemicals to kill cancer cells.

Chorionic villus sampling (CVS)—A method for testing the chromosomes of an embryo at nine to eleven weeks of pregnancy. A small number of fetal cells are removed from the chorion (the outside of the placenta) through a catheter inserted through the cervix into the uterus. The cells' chromosomes are then tested.

Chromosomes—Microscopic rod-shaped bodies in the nucleus of every cell of the body that contain genetic material.

Clinical geneticist—A doctor who specializes in the study and diagnosis of genetic disorders.

Cognition—The process of perceiving, thinking, reasoning, and analyzing.

Cognitive disability—*See* Intellectual disability.

Colic—A condition of some young infants in which the baby has abdominal pain.

Communication skills—Broadly, the ability to receive and express information and emotion, whether through speech, gestures, written words, etc.

Conductive Hearing Loss—Decreased hearing acuity resulting from difficulty in sound transmission in the middle ear (often due to middle ear fluid).

Congenital—A condition that exists at the time of birth.

Congenital heart defect—A defect of the heart present at birth.

Congestive heart failure—*See* Heart failure.

Consequence—The result of an action.

Coordination—Synchronized, balanced, or harmonious muscle movements.

Cradle cap—A patch of crusty dry skin on the scalp of newborns that flakes off over time. This condition is normal in babies.

Crawling—To use the arms and legs to move the body along the floor with the abdomen on the floor.

Creeping—To use the arms and legs to move the body along the floor with the abdomen off the floor.

Critical region—The part of the number-21 chromosome thought by some researchers to be responsible for the majority of differences seen in Down syndrome.

Crossed eyes—A condition in which one eye is turned inward while the other eye looks straight ahead. Also known as esotropia (when eyes turn inward) or exotropia (when eyes turn outward), this condition can cause double vision.

Cruising—Standing and moving on two feet while holding onto a support such as a table.

Cue—Input that prompts a child to perform a behavior or activity.

Culture—A medium in which microscopic organisms are grown, such as blood samples used in karyotypes.

Cyanosis—A bluish color of skin caused by a lack of oxygen in the blood. This can occur in babies with heart defects.

Cytogeneticist—A doctor who studies chromosomes.

Daughter cells—The two cells created during mitosis that are exact copies of the parent cell.

Development—The process of growth and learning during which a child acquires skills and abilities.

Developmental pediatrician—A doctor who specializes in the development of infants and children.

Developmental delay—A label that may be used under IDEA to qualify children aged 3-9 for special education services. The label may be used for children who are experiencing delays in physical, cognitive, communication, social, and/or self-help skills.

Developmental disability—A disability or impairment that begins before age 18, causes a substantial disability, and is expected to continue indefinitely.

Developmental milestone—A developmental goal that acts as a measurement of development progress over time, such as an infant rolling over between two and four months of age.

Dietitian—A professional with a degree in nutrition or dietetics who is registered and may have a state license. This professional offers advice and counseling regarding improving or modifying food intake for optimal nutrition.

Discretionary trust—A trust in which the trustee (the person responsible for governing the trust) has the authority to use or not use the trust funds for any purpose, as long as funds are expended only for the beneficiary.

Disinherit—To deprive someone (such as a person with a disability) of an inheritance. Parents of children with disabilities may do this to prevent the state from using their child's assets to pay for his care.

Disjunction—The process by which chromosomes separate during meiosis.

Dispute resolution procedures—The procedures established by the IDEA and regulations for the fair resolution of disputes regarding a child's special education.

Diuretics—Drugs that increase the flow of urine, resulting in a decrease in the amount of fluid in the body. They are often used to help children with heart defects to reduce the heart's load because accumulated fluids tend to stress the heart.

DNA—Deoxyribonucleic acid, the spiral-shaped molecule in genes that carries hereditary traits.

Down syndrome—A common genetic disorder in which a person is born with forty-seven rather than forty-six chromosomes in all or some of his cells, resulting in developmental delays, low muscle tone, characteristic physical features, and other effects.

Dramatic play—Play involving imagination, role-playing, and games of make-believe. The ability to engage in dramatic play is regarded as a measure of cognitive and social development.

Dual Diagnosis—The diagnosis of two disorders in one individual. In the Down syndrome field, the term usually refers to Down syndrome plus an autism spectrum disorder.

Due process hearing—Part of the procedures established to protect the rights of parents and children with disabilities during disputes under the IDEA. These are hearings before an impartial person to disputes related to the identification, evaluation, placement, and services by a child's educational agency.

Duodenal atresia—A narrowing or blockage of the first part of the small intestine.

Ear tubes—Also called pressure equalization or myringotomy tubes or grommets, these small tubes are inserted in the eardrum to allow the fluid to drain from the middle ear and also ventilate the middle ear.

Early development—Development during the first three years of life.

Early intervention—Providing therapies and other specialized services to infants and toddlers to minimize the effects of conditions such as Down syndrome that can delay early development.

Echocardiogram (EKG)—A painless test that uses high-frequency sound waves to create an image of the heart.

EEOC—Equal Employment Opportunity Commission. A federal agency that is responsible for resolving employment discrimination complaints under the Americans with Disabilities Act. Complaints must first be made to the EEOC before a lawsuit may be brought.

Egg—The female reproductive (sex) cell.

Electrocardiogram (ECG)—A medical instrument that measures the electrical impulses of the heart. These measurements show a cardiologist how a heart is functioning and can reveal heart disease.

Electrode—A small device placed on the body to transmit the electrical activity in a specific body part to a machine. The machine then records and interprets the activity—for example, to aid in the diagnosis of seizures, heart defects, or sleep apnea.

Embryo—A baby in the earliest stages of development in the uterus.

Endocardial cushion defect—Defects or deformations in the walls between the chambers of the heart.

ENT Physician—A medical doctor who specializes in diagnosing and treating problems in the ear, nose, and throat. Also known as an otolaryngologist.

Epicanthal folds—Small folds of skin in the inner corners of the eyes. Often present in babies with Down syndrome.

Epilepsy—A neurological condition in which a person has recurrent *seizures.*

Equilibrium—Balance.

Esotropia—*See* Crossed eyes.

Estate planning—Formal, written arrangements for handling the possessions and assets of people after they have died.

Ets-2 gene—This gene, found on the number-21 chromosome, is called an oncogene. It is involved in cancer or leukemia.

Eustachian tube—A small tube running between the middle of the ear and the back of throat that controls air pressure in the ear and drains fluids from the middle ear. This tube may become blocked by fluid as the result of ear infections or allergies, which can lead to a temporary loss of hearing.

Evaluation—The process of determining the developmental level of a child. Evaluations are used to determine whether a child needs educational services, as well as to determine what types of services he needs.

Expressive language—The ability to use gestures, speech, and written symbols to communicate.

Extension—The straightening of the muscles and limbs.

FAPE—*See* Free Appropriate Public Education.

Farsightedness—A condition of the eye that causes near objects to be seen blurred and objects in the distance to be seen clearly. Also called hypermetropia, this condition can be corrected with eyeglasses.

FBA—See Functional behavior assessment.

Fine motor—Involving movements of the small muscles of the body, such as those in the hands, feet, fingers, and toes.

Flexion—The bending of the muscles and limbs.

Folic Acid—A water-soluble vitamin in the B-complex group.

Fontanels—The soft spots of the skull; the spaces between the separate bones of the skull.

Free Appropriate Public Education (FAPE)—The basic right to receive appropriate special education services without charge to the family established under the Individuals with Disabilities Education Act.

Functional behavior assessment—A systematic way of determining the function that a behavior serves for a child (for example, to obtain a cookie or to get out of doing something). Conducting an FBA involves figuring out the antecedents of the behavior (what happens before it) and studying the consequences (what happens after the behavior—what benefit the child receives from it) in order to determine what the child is communicating through his behavior.

Gastrointestinal system—The stomach and intestines that function to digest food.

Generalization—Using a skill learned in one situation or setting in another situation or setting. Using information about an object or concept to make conclusions about a similar object or concept.

Genes—Contained within the chromosomes, genes contain a person's hereditary material and determine specific traits such as eye color and susceptibility to certain illnesses.

Genetic Code—The pattern of proteins on human DNA that determines hereditary traits.

Genetic Information Nondiscrimination Act (GINA)—A U.S. federal law intended to keep insurance companies from using genetic information to establish eligibility or premiums for insurance and to prevent genetic information from being used to discriminate against employees.

Genetics—The study of genes, chromosomes, and heredity.

Genome—The entirety of an organism's hereditary information that is encoded in its DNA. Also, the complete genetic sequence of one particular chromosome—that is, a map of every gene found on that chromosome and its location.

Genotype—A person's complete set of genes, including those that do not result in any observable characteristics. This is in contrast to the *phenotype,* which refers to the genetic characteristics of an individual that are observable. For example, a brown-eyed child may actually have genes for both brown eyes and blue eyes. His genotype (which is not directly observable) includes genes for both brown and blue eyes, but what you can observe—his phenotype—is brown eyes.

Germ cell—The cell that results when a sperm cell (male) combines with an egg cell (female).

Giemsa banding—In genetics, a technique in which the chromosomes are stained with a special solution to aid in karyotyping. The stain produces a pattern of lighter and darker bands on the chromosomes, which helps geneticists identify the individual chromosomes and any abnormal structures.

Grasp—The way a person holds an object.

Gross motor—Involving movements of the large muscles of the body such as those in the legs, arms, and trunk.

Hand-eye coordination—The use of the eyes to guide the hands in movements, such as when picking up an object or catching a ball.

Hearing aid—A device that amplifies sounds for people who have a hearing loss.

Hearing loss—A decrease in the ability to hear sounds of different volume and pitch.

Heart—The organ located in the center of the chest that pumps blood throughout the body. It is divided into four chambers—the two atria, on top, and the two ventricles, on the bottom. The openings between the atria and ventricles are known as valves.

Heart defects—Structural abnormalities of the heart that block blood flow or result in abnormal blood flow through the heart.

Heart failure—A condition of the heart in which it is unable to function at the optimal level and cannot pump enough blood to the lungs and the rest of the body.

Heart valves—Tissue inside the heart that seals off the chambers during heart contractions to force blood to flow in only one direction.

Hirschsprung's disease—A condition in which there are no nerve cells in the colon (large intestine). It appears during early infancy and causes the colon to swell.

Hyperextensive joints—Joints (such as the hips or shoulders) that are unusually flexible.

Hypermetropia—*See* Farsightedness.

Hypothyroidism—The decreased production of thyroid hormone by the thyroid gland. This condition is more common in babies with Down syndrome than in other children. but is easily treated.

Hypotonia—Low muscle tone. Muscle tone that is more relaxed or "floppy" when the person is at rest. *See* Muscle tone.

IDEA—The Individuals with Disabilities Education Act. This law establishes the right of children with Down syndrome and other disabilities who live in the United States to a "free appropriate public education" and specifies the school system's responsibilities in providing that education.

Identification—The determination that a baby or child should be evaluated as a possible candidate for special education services.

IEP—See Individualized Education Program.

IFSP—See Individualized Family Service Plan.

Imitation—The ability to observe the actions of others and to copy them in one's own actions.

Immunization—The process of making a person immune to certain diseases, using injections or other methods.

Imperforate anus—A congenital condition in which the anal opening is either absent or obstructed.

Inclusion—The practice of providing necessary supports and services so that students with disabilities can learn alongside students without disabilities in general education classrooms.

Individualized Education Program (IEP)—A written document that details the special education program to be provided a child aged three and older with a disability. The document specifies individualized education goals for the student, the services that will be provided to enable the student to meet those goals, the setting where services will be provided, accommodations and modifications to be provided to the child, etc. IEPs are required under the Individuals with Disabilities Education Act.

Individualized Family Service Plan (IFSP)—A written report that details the early intervention services to be provided to an infant with Down syndrome or other disability and his or her family.

Individuals with Disabilities Education Act—*See* IDEA.

Infant—A child under 12 months of age.

Infant educator—A teacher with special training in helping with the overall development of infants, and specifically with cognitive development.

Input—Information that a child receives through any of the senses such as vision, hearing, touch, or feeling that helps him or her develop new skills or respond to his environment.

Insulin—A hormone produced by the pancreas that regulates the metabolism of blood sugar.

Intellectual disability—A condition that results in cognitive skills that fall below the average range as well as significant difficulties in acquiring the skills needed to function independently in the environment. Also known as cognitive disability, or in other English-speaking countries, learning disability. In the U.S., this term is replacing the older term *mental retardation.*

Intelligence quotient (IQ)—A numerical measure of a person's intelligence or cognitive ability as determined by standardized tests. Usually a score of 100 is considered exactly "average," with scores from approximately 85 to 115 considered to be in the "average range," scores from 70 to 85 considered to be "low average," and scores below about 70 considered to be in the range of intellectual disability.

Intelligibility—The understandability of someone's speech; how easy or difficult it is for others to comprehend her spoken words.

Interactive play—Children playing with each other.

Intestinal malformation—A condition of the intestine, such as a blockage, that prevents the normal function of the gastrointestinal tract.

Jargon—The usually-unintelligible speech of infants and young children that is a stage in the development of full expressive speech.

Joint tenancy—Property that is owned equally by each spouse; when one spouse dies, the survivor automatically becomes the sole owner.

Karyotype—A picture of human chromosomes made after culturing of cells from a fetus or person. These can reveal the presence of chromosomal disorders such as Down syndrome.

Language—The spoken or written words or symbols used to express and understand human communication.

Large muscles—Muscles such as those in the arms, legs, and abdomen.

Lazy eye—*See* Amblyopia.

Learning disability—In the U.S., this term is used to refer to difficulties learning in one or more specific academic areas (such as math or reading) that would not be expected based on the child's overall intellectual abilities. That is, the child's performance in one or more areas of learning is notably lower than in other areas of learning. Usually, but not always, the term is applied to people with overall intelligence in the average range. In some other English-speaking countries, the term is used to mean intellectual disability (mental retardation).

Least Restrictive Environment (LRE)—The requirement under the IDEA that children with disabilities receiving special education must be made a part of a general education class in the neighborhood school to the fullest extent possible. This requirement was included in the law as a way of ending the traditional practice of isolating children with disabilities.

Leukemia—A type of cancer that attacks the red blood cells. This disease is slightly more common among children with Down syndrome.

Local education agency (LEA)—The agency responsible for providing educational services on the local (city, county, school district) level.

Luxury trust—A trust that describes the kind of allowable expenses in a way that excludes the cost of care in a state-funded program in order to avoid cost-of-care liability.

Mainstream—An older term for the practice of involving children with disabilities in regular school and preschool environments. This term (and practice) has largely been replaced by *Inclusion*.

Medicaid—A federal program that provides payments for medical care to people who are entitled to receive Supplementary Security Income.

Medicare—A federal program that provides payments for medical care to people who are receiving Social Security payments.

Meiosis—The process of the development of reproductive (sex) cells (egg and sperm) during which the number of chromosomes is usually reduced by half to 23. Upon conception, the fertilized egg usually has 46 chromosomes.

Mental retardation—Older terminology synonymous with *intellectual disability*. Although the term has fallen out of favor with families and people who have intellectual disabilities, in the U.S. the term is still used in some federal laws and many school systems, and it is one of the qualifying conditions under IDEA.

Metabolism—The chemical processes carried out by cells in the body that are necessary for life.

Metatarsus varus—Abnormal toeing-in of the foot.

Microcephaly—Head size that is at or below the third percentile on "normal" growth charts.

Middle ear—The portion of the ear that transmits sound from the outer ear canal to the inner ear. It is behind the tympanic membrane (eardrum). The middle ear includes the eardrum, auditory ossicles (malleus, incus, and stapes, also known by their shape as the hammer, anvil, and stirrup), facial nerve, and Eustachian tube. When physicians examine the ear for fluid, they are looking for fluid through the tympanic membrane.

Middle ear fluid—Fluid that accumulates in the middle ear, behind the eardrum, usually as a consequence of ear infections, allergies, and/or Eustachian tube dysfunction. It interferes with hearing, and can lead to hearing loss if not treated.

Midline—The vertical center of the body. Development progresses from the midline (proximal) to the extremities (distal). Therapists may encourage babies to do activities at the midline (e.g., bringing hands together at the midline) because they allow for other important developmental gains.

Mitosis—The process of cell division during which a cell produces an exact copy of itself, including a duplicate set of chromosomes.

Modification—A change made to the content of what a student learns. Examples include learning less material or simplified material (e.g., being responsible for learning half of the vocabulary words rather than all of them).

Morphology— Morphology describes how an individual uses mor-phemes in communication. Morphemes are the smallest units of meaning in a language and include word parts such as root words, prefixes, suffixes, and verb endings (does the child use "ed" to form the past tense? does he understand what the prefix "un" does to a verb or adjective?). Morphology is an important part of grammar, along with syntax, so you may hear the two spoken of together as "morphosyntax." *See also* Syntax.

Mosaicism—A relatively rare type of Down syndrome in which a faulty cell division occurs in one of the first cell divisions after fertilization. The result is that some but not all of the baby's cells contain extra ge-netic material.

Mottled skin—Spotted or blotchy skin color with variable color.

MRI—Magnetic resonance imaging. A procedure used to visualize the interior of the body by using electromagnets to magnetize the body and then making recordings of the radio frequencies given off. Also known as a PET scan.

Multidisciplinary Team—In relation to early intervention, a team of two or more professionals from different disciplines (e.g., physical therapy, speech-language pathology) who collaborate in providing assessment and/or treatment.

Muscle tone—The degree of elasticity or tension of muscles when at rest. Muscle tone can be too low (hypotonia) or too high (hypertonia); either condition causes developmental problems, particularly in motor areas. Children with Down syndrome commonly have low muscle tone.

Myopia—See nearsightedness.

Myringotomy—A surgical procedure to create a small opening in the eardrum to allow fluid to drain from the middle ear. Often, an *ear tube* is placed to maintain the opening.

Nasal bridge—The bony structure at the top of the nose between the eyes. Usually flatter in babies with Down syndrome.

Naso lacrimal duct obstruction—Blocked tear ducts.

Nearsightedness—A condition of the eye in which images of distant objects are not focused precisely on the retina, but in front of it. This results in blurred vision, with distant objects appearing more blurred than near objects. Technically known as myopia, this condition can be corrected with eyeglasses or contacts.

Neurons—Nerve cells. Nerve cells release neurotransmitters (chemical substances) to signal other neurons and organs of the body to function.

Nondisjunction—The failure of sex cell (egg and sperm) chromosomes to separate properly during meiosis. This can be a cause of Nondisjunction Trisomy 21.

Nondisjunction Trisomy 21—The most common type of Down syndrome, caused by the failure of chromosome number 21 to separate during *meiosis* in the egg (female) or sperm (male).

Nucleotides—The chemical building blocks of DNA.

Nutritionist—An individual who provides advice about diet and nutrition.

Obesity—Excessive weight or fat; when a person exceeds their recommended weight by 20 percent.

Object permanence—The cognitive understanding that objects exist even when they are out of sight. When a baby can play peek-a-boo, he is demonstrating that he understands object permanence.

Occupational therapist (OT)—A therapist who specializes in improving the development of fine motor and adaptive skills such as using utensils, writing, drawing, cutting with scissors, zipping a jacket, and tying shoes.

Oncogene—A gene that is linked to cancer.

Open heart surgery—Surgery during which the chest and heart are opened to enable surgeons to make repairs to the heart.

Ophthalmologist—A medical doctor who has specialized training in diagnosing and treating diseases and conditions of the eye and can also prescribe eyeglasses and contacts.

Optometrist—A doctor of optometry (not a medical doctor) who is qualified to measure visual acuity (nearsightedness, farsightedness, astigmatism) and visual fields (how far to the sides and above and below the eyes someone can see) and to prescribe eyeglasses and contacts.

Oral motor—Relating to the use of the muscles in and around the mouth and face. Oral motor skills are important for learning to eat and talk properly.

Orthopedic inserts—Small devices placed in shoes to help stabilize the ankles and feet. Sometimes used to help children with Down syndrome because of low muscle tone and flexible joints. Also called orthotics.

Other Health Impaired (OHI)—A disability category used in IDEA and defined as: "having limited strength, vitality, or alertness, including a heightened alertness of environmental stimuli, that results in limited alertness with respect to the educational environment." Some children with Down syndrome may qualify for special education services under this category.

Otitis Media—Inflammation of the middle ear.

Otitis Media with Effusion (OME)—In addition to inflammation of the middle ear, fluid is present, but there are signs or symptoms of ear infection. Other terms used to describe this condition are serous otitis media (SOM) and "glue ear" (in UK).

Oxygenate—The process of tissue absorbing oxygen delivered by the blood.

Parallel play—Children playing near each other and in the same way, but without interacting.

Parent-professional partnership—The teaming of parents and teachers (or doctors, nurses, or other professionals) to work together to facilitate the development of babies and children with special needs.

Part C of IDEA—The provisions in IDEA that make early intervention services available to babies with Down syndrome and other disabilities.

Partial Trisomy 21—A rare condition in which the extra 21st chromosome in the cells of a child with Down syndrome is missing part of its genetic material. The child has two whole 21st chromosomes and a portion of a third one. Which characteristics of Down syndrome are present depend on which portion of the 21st chromosome is present.

Patching—One treatment for amblyopia, in which a child's stronger eye is covered or blurred with eye drops in order to force the weaker eye to develop.

Patellar instability—Instability of the kneecap.

Pediatric cardiologist—A medical doctor who specializes in diagnosing and treating heart conditions in children.

Pediatric geneticist—A medical doctor who studies genes and the effects of genetic conditions in children.

Pediatric ophthalmologist—A medical doctor who specializes in the care and treatment of the eyes of children.

Periodontal disease—Disease of the gums and bones surrounding the teeth.

Pes planus—Flat feet.

Phenotype—A person's observable characteristics, as determined by his genes and their interaction with the environment. *See also* Phenotype.

Phonology—The rules followed in a particular language when combining speech sounds (e.g., "show" is a valid combination in English, but "sprlow" is not).

Physical therapist (PT)—A therapist who works with a baby or child to help him overcome physical problems such as low muscle tone that affect the development of gross motor skills such as sitting, crawling, walking, jumping, or riding a tricyle.

Pincer grasp—The use of the thumb and forefinger to grasp small objects.

Placement—The selection of the educational program (school, classroom) for a child who needs special education services.

Pneumonia—An inflammation of the lungs resulting from an infection.

Posture—How a person stands or carries him- or herself.

Pragmatics—The social and interactional uses of language in real-life communication situations. Pragmatics skills include verbal and non-verbal skills such as facial expressions, eye contact, using gestures, making requests, and conversational skills such as taking turns and staying on topic.

Precursors—Behaviors or skills that precede the development of more sophisticated behaviors or skills.

Prompt—Input (such as a word or gesture) that encourages a child to perform a movement or activity.

Protection & Advocacy (P&A)—A nationwide system providing legal services for families of children with disabilities, including Down syndrome.

Public Accommodation—A place, such as a school, restaurant, or theater, generally open to the public. The ADA prohibits discrimination against people with disabilities by public accommodations.

Pulmonary hypertension—High blood pressure in the blood vessels in the lungs. This condition can result from heart defects that cause excessive amounts of blood to be pumped to the lungs, and can be fatal if not corrected.

Pyloric stenosis—A narrowing of the opening between the stomach and the duodenum, the first section of the small intestine.

Quadruple Screen—A prenatal test of the mother's blood that measures four substances and provides an estimate of the chances that the baby has Down syndrome or spina bifida.

Radiation therapy—A treatment for leukemia and other cancers.

Receptive language—The ability to understand spoken or written communication as well as gestures.

Receptive vocabulary—The words a child is able to understand.

Reciprocal movement—Moving one side of the body and then the other in a coordinated, alternate fashion, such as when hearing a drum or pedaling a tricycle.

Refraction—The bending of light waves. In vision, the lens of the eye bends light rays so that they focus on one point on the retina.

Regression—The loss of skills that have been previously acquired.

Reinforcement—Responding to behavior in a way that is designed to increase the behavior. Positive reinforcement involves adding something to the environment (e.g., giving the child a pretzel, praise, or computer time), while negative reinforcement involves taking something away from the environment (e.g., reducing the amount of work the child must do).

Related services—Transportation and other developmental, corrective, or supportive services such as physical or occupational therapy or counseling needed to enable a child to make progress in the general education curriculum. Under IDEA, a child is entitled to receive these services as part of his special education program.

Respiratory infection—An infection, usually viral or bacterial, of the nasal passages, throat, bronchial tubes, or lungs.

Respite care—Care provided by trained adults to enable parents to have time away from their child with Down syndrome or other disability.

Retina—The inner layer of the eye, which consists of millions of specialized cells which act as light receptors.

Reward chart—A chart that keeps track of a child's behavior as part of a behavior modification program. The child accumulates points, stickers, or "stars" on the chart to earn a reward.

Rooting—The instinctive searching for a breast or bottle nipple by a hungry baby.

Rotation (external)—Turning out of the feet, legs, hips, or hands. Seen in babies and children with Down syndrome because of their low muscle tone and joint flexibility.

Section 504 of the Rehabilitation Act—A federal law that prohibits discrimination on the basis of disability in programs receiving federal funds.

Seizure—A sudden loss of consciousness or convulsion resulting from abnormal electrical activity in the brain.

Self-help skills—Skills needed to take care of one's self, including eating, dressing, bathing, and grooming activities.

Sensorineural Hearing Loss—Hearing impairment that occurs as the result of permanent damage to the inner ear or to the auditory nerve (which transmits sound impulses to the brain).

Sensory processing—The ability to process sensations, such as touch, sound, light, smell, and movement.

Septa (septum)—The wall of cardiac tissue between the chambers of the heart.

Shared risk—An insurance practice of grouping a large number of people together for purposes of spreading insurance risks.

Slanting palpebral fissures—The term describing the upward slanting appearance of the eyes of children with Down syndrome.

Sleep apnea—A condition in which breathing stops momentarily (for more than 5 seconds) during sleep. It may be due to blockage in the mouth, nose, or throat (e.g., enlarged tonsils), or to a neurological problem in the brain.

Social Security Disability Insurance (SSDI)—A federal disability insurance system to provide financial assistance to qualified people with disabilities.

Social skills—The ability to function in groups, to interact with other people.

Special education—The term commonly used to refer to the education of children with disabilities such as Down syndrome; it includes instruction individually designed to help children with disabilities learn and is mandated by IDEA in the U.S.

Special needs trust—A trust where money can be deposited for the use of a person with disabilities and that is administered by a trustee for the benefit of the person with disabilities. If the trust is drawn up properly, the money cannot be tapped by the government to pay for care of the person with disabilities.

Specific Learning Disability (SLD)—The term used for *learning disabilities* in IDEA.

Speech-language therapist (pathologist)—A therapist who is trained to diagnose and treat difficulties with speech and language skills. Some may also helping with feeding difficulties.

Sperm—The male reproductive (sex) cell.

Spinal column—The bones that form the spine. The spinal cord runs in the middle of this column.

Spinal cord—The nerve tissue that runs up and down the spinal column.

SSDI—*See* Social Security Disability Insurance.

SSDI—*See* Supplemental Security Income.

Standardized test—A test in which a child's performance is compared to the performance of other children of the same age on the same test.

Strabismus—Misaligned or "crossed" eyes; typically one or both eyes look inward or outward.

Supplemental Security Income (SSI)—A federal public assistance program that provides funds for qualified people with disabilities.

Support trust—A trust that requires that funds be expended to pay for the beneficiary's expenses of living, such as housing, food, and transportation.

Synapse—The microscopic space between adjoining nerve cells in the brain; signals travel from one cell to another by releasing chemicals (neurotransmitters) that cross the synapse and cause an electrical charge in the next cell.

Syndrome—A group of symptoms or traits that are characteristic of a particular condition.

Syntax—The rules governing the way words are sequenced to form meaningful phrases and sentences; grammar. For example, "He not do it" is an example of incorrect syntax, while "He did not do it" is correct. *See also* Morphology.

Tactile—Having to do with the sense of touch.

Tactile defensiveness—An overreaction to or avoidance of touch.

Tear ducts—The glands above the eyes that secrete tears.

Therapist—A trained professional who works with children or adults to overcome the effects of developmental problems or to help them master skills.

Thyroid—The gland located in the front of the neck that produces thyroid hormone, which plays a role in controlling body metabolism.

Toddler—A child between the ages of about one and three.

Tonsils—The two small masses of lymph tissue located at the back of the throat that help to ward off respiratory diseases.

Transdisciplinary—In relation to early intervention services, describes a team approach to providing therapies, instruction, and family support in which professionals from different disciplines collaborate to provide needed services, sometimes consulting with one another to provide services outside their usual area of expertise.

Translocation Trisomy 21—A rare form of Down syndrome in which an extra number-21 chromosome is attached to another chromosome.

Transverse palmar crease—A single crease across the palm of the hands of some children with Down syndrome. One of the physical traits used to identify Down syndrome.

Triple test—A prenatal combined screening for the genetic markers of Down syndrome.

Trisomy—The presence of an extra (third) chromosome in the body's cells (ordinarily, there are two copies of each chromosome per cell, not three).

Tympanometry—A test that measures fluid that may be present behind the ear drum or detects a blockage of the Eustachian tube.

Ultrasound—The use of high pitched sound waves to create a picture of internal organs or a fetus. This procedure is used to examine babies before birth and to help guide medical instruments during amniocentesis and chorionic villus sampling (CVS).

Umbilical hernia—A protrusion of the navel caused by incomplete muscle development around the navel. Umbilical hernias usually close by themselves.

Ventricles—The lower chambers of the heart.

Ventricular septal defect (VSD)—A hole in the wall separating the two lower chambers of the heart.

Vertebrae—The bones of the spinal column.

Vestibular—Pertaining to the sensory system located in the inner ear that allows the body to maintain balance and enjoyably participate in movement such as swinging and roughhousing.

X-chromosome—One of the so-called "sex chromosomes" that determine a person's gender. The other sex chromosome is the Y chromosome. Females have two X-chromosomes; males have one X-chromosome and one Y-chromosome.

Y-chromosome—*See* X-chromosome.

Zygote—The cell formed when an egg is fertilized by a sperm. Once the zygote begins to divide and multiply, it becomes an embryo.

READING LIST

This Reading List is designed especially for parents of babies and young children with Down syndrome. The publications, online articles, and DVDs listed here were either created expressly for parents or are included because they use nontechnical, respectful, reader-friendly language. The list is roughly divided according to the topics covered in each chapter of the book, although some materials cover subjects from several chapters.

This list does not pretend to be complete. There may be many other worthy books available. You can find other suggested readings by visiting some of the organizations included in the Resource Guide, by searching online, or by asking other parents, teachers, or your librarian for recommendations.

◾ Foreword: Books by Authors with Down Syndrome

Burke, Chris and McDaniel, Jo Beth. **A Special Kind of Hero.** Lincoln, NE: Backinprint.com, 2001.

Chris Burke, the first actor with Down syndrome to star in a prime time TV series (Life Goes On), contributed three chapters about his life and aspirations to this combination autobiography/biography, while his co-author filled in background information.

Josephson, Gretchen. **Bus Girl.** Cambridge, MA: Brookline Books, 1997.

Gretchen Josephson, who has Down syndrome, wrote the poems in this collection over the course of 25 years, between her teens and early forties. Some of the poems are autobiographical; others deal with universal themes such as love, nature, and death.

Kingsley, Jason and Levitz, Mitchell. **Count Us In: Growing Up with Down Syndrome.** 2nd ed. New York, NY: Harvest Books, 2007.

In this unique book, Jason Kingsley and Mitchell Levitz, two accomplished men with Down syndrome, share their life stories and their dreams for the future. Kingsley and Levitz discuss a variety of issues that affect their lives, including society's perception of people with Down syndrome, politics, independence, and relationships. The book was originally written when the authors were 19 and 22 and updated when they were in their 30s.

▪▪ Chapter 1: What is Down Syndrome?

Batshaw, Mark L., Pelligrino, Louis, and Roizen, Nancy, eds. **Children with Disabilities.** 6th ed. Baltimore: Brookes Publishing Co., 2007.

This comprehensive reference book includes chapters on genetics, the brain, Down syndrome, developmental delay and intellectual disability, Down syndrome, and early intervention. The book is pricey, but you may be able to find a copy in your library.

"Brain Basics: Know Your Brain." Bethesda, MD: National Institute of Neurological Disorders and Stroke, 2007.
www.ninds.nih.gov/disorders/brain_basics/know_your_brain.htm

Brief explanations of the parts of the brain and what they do. The booklet can be downloaded for free or request NIH Publication No. 01-3440a by phone at: 800-352-9424.

Centre for Genetics Education. **"Fact Sheets."** Sydney, NSW: Royal North Shore Hospital. www.genetics.com.au.

A number of useful fact sheets are available for free download, including: "Genes and Chromosomes"; "Mosaicism"; "Prenatal Testing"; "Some Ethical Issues in Human Genetics."

Leshin, Len. **"Prenatal Screening for Down Syndrome."**
www.ds health.com/prental.htm.

A thorough discussion of the prenatal tests available for Down syndrome, their risks, and how the results are interpreted.

National Institutes of Health. **"Research Plan on Down Syndrome."** Bethesda, MD: 2007.
www.nichd.nih.gov/publications/pubs/upload/NIH_Downsyndrome_plan.pdf

This paper details the short-, medium-, and long-term objectives of the federal agencies working together on the ten-year research plan intended to produce new insights into, and treatments for, Down syndrome.

National Library of Medicine. **"Genetics Home Reference: Your Guide to Understanding Genetic Conditions."** Bethesda, MD: NLM. http://ghr.nlm.nih.gov.

Reader-friendly information on such topics as "Cells and DNA"; "How Genes Work"; and "Genomic Research."

Pueschel, Siegfried. **A Parent's Guide to Down Syndrome: Toward a Brighter Future.** 2ⁿᵈ edition. Baltimore: Paul Brookes Publishing Co., 2000.

This book provides an overview of raising a child with Down syndrome from birth to young adulthood. Chapters are contributed by experts in different fields and include many suggestions aimed at optimizing development.

Schermerhorn, Will. **Down Syndrome: The First 18 Months.** Blueberry Shoes Productions, 2004.

Will Schermerhorn, the father of a child with Down syndrome, produced this DVD to give other new parents a positive overview of the key issues confronting them after their baby's birth. The DVD incorporates interviews with professionals and parents with footage of infants and toddlers with Down syndrome to cover common concerns related to diagnosis, health care, feeding and nutrition, therapies, and expectations.

Understanding Genetics: A Guide for Parents and Health Professionals. Washington, DC: Alliance of Genetic Support Groups, no date.

In reader-friendly language, this illustrated manual covers the basics about genetics and genetic testing. It can be downloaded for free from www.geneticalliance.org (click on "Publications").

WikiGenetics
www.wikigenetics.org

This is a web-based encyclopedia on human genetics created by its users. It includes reader-friendly explanations of such topics as chromosomes and genes, genetic testing, genetic counseling, and the human genome.

Wilson, Pamela. **"Welcoming Babies with Down Syndrome."** www.bellaonline.com/articles/art32534.asp (in English)
www.bellaonline.com/articles/art32537.asp (in Spanish)
www.bellaonline.com/articles/art32538.asp (in French)

This is a good, short overview about the joys and challenges of raising a child with Down syndrome written by Pam Wilson, the mother of a young adult with Down syndrome and BellaOnline's Special Needs Children's Editor. This article may be useful to send to friends and relatives who need to get up-to-speed about the major issues you are facing. You can get to many other helpful, positive articles about Down syndrome on BellaOnline by following the links at the bottom of the page.

▪▪ Chapter 2: Adjusting to Your Baby

Note: Resources especially helpful for parents who have received a prenatal diagnosis of Down syndrome are indicated with ✳.

Assimotos-McElwee, Sandra. **"What to Say."** http://leeworks.net/DDS/speech.html.

Advice (from a Christian perspective) to friends and family from the mother of a child with Down syndrome about what to say and not say to the new parent of a child with Down syndrome.

*Beck, Martha. **Expecting Adam: A True Story of Birth, Rebirth, and Everyday Magic.** New York, NY: Berkley, 2000.

A prominent magazine columnist and writer chronicled her experiences with a prenatal diagnosis of Down syndrome in this autobiographical account. During the course of her pregnancy, the author wrestled with her previous beliefs that the worth of individuals is inextricably linked with their intellectual abilities and came to believe that the son she was carrying was the one she was meant to have. The author's change of heart was, in part, precipitated by premonitions and other supernatural occurrences during her pregnancy.

Beckham, Beverly. "**Columns.**" www.grandparents.com.

Click on "Columns," then "Beverly Beckham," to read several first-rate essays about being the grandmother of a little girl with Down syndrome, written by a doting grandmother who happens to be an award-winning columnist for the *Boston Globe*.

Berube, Michael. *Life As We Know It: A Father, a Family, and an Exceptional Child.* New York, NY: Vintage Books, 2006.

A university professor writes of the first four years of his son with Down syndrome. Interspersed with interesting scenes of family life and snapshots of the little boy's development are lengthy passages in which the author reflects upon society's treatment of people with disabilities, eugenics, and abortion.

Featherstone, Helen. **A Difference in the Family: Living with a Disabled Child.** New York, NY: Penguin Books, 1980.

In this classic book, the mother of a child with multiple disabilities takes a compassionate look at her own and others' emotions related to raising a child with a disability. Although the language used to refer to disabilities has changed somewhat over the years, many of the author's insights and experiences still ring true.

Gill, Barbara. **Changed by a Child: Companion Notes for Parents of a Child with a Disability.** New York, NY: Doubleday, 1997.

This book consists of very short meditative pieces about topics that parents of children with disabilities often find themselves musing about—for example, Fault, Labels, Losing It, Recurring Sorrow, and In-Jokes. Some end with an affirmation ("Today I will….) but most just provide interesting, empathetic food for thought.

Groneburg, Jennifer Graf. **Road Map to Holland: How I Found My Way through My Son's First Two Years with Down Syndrome.** New York, NY: New American Library, 2008.

When one of the author's twin sons was born with Down syndrome, she blamed herself for spoiling the idyllic life she and her husband had built on the shores of a lake in Montana. Her book chronicles how she slowly came to terms with her own and others' feelings and found forgiveness for herself and love and acceptance for her child.

Kidder, Cynthia S. and Skotko, Brian. **Common Threads: Celebrating Life with Down Syndrome.** Rochester Hills, MI: Band of Angels Press, 2001.

This oversized coffee table book includes mini-biographies and large black-and-white photographs of almost 60 children and young people with Down syndrome. Some of the people profiled are quite accomplished individuals and well known in the Down syndrome field; others are people with more ordinary, but still interesting, lives.

Klein, Stanley & Schive, Kim. **You Will Dream New Dreams: Inspiring Personal Stories by Parents of Children with Disabilities.** New York: Kensington, 2006.

A collection of essays by parents of children with a variety of special needs, including Down syndrome. The writers have newly diagnosed children, adult children, and everything in between.

✳ **"Light at the End of the Tunnel: Reflections from Parents Whose Child with Down Syndrome was Diagnosed before Birth."**
www.dsaoc.org/programs/tunnelEnglish.pdf

An online, illustrated booklet with thoughts, advice, and encouragement from parents of children who were prenatally diagnosed with Down syndrome.

Meyer, Donald. **Uncommon Fathers: Reflections on Raising a Child with a Disability.** Bethesda, MD: Woodbine House, 1995.

This book is a collection of heartfelt essays written by fathers of children, teens, and young adults with a variety of disabilities. Several of the writers are fathers of children with Down syndrome.

✳ Soper, Kathryn Lynn, ed. **Gifts: Mothers Reflect on How Children with Down Syndrome Enrich Their Lives.** Bethesda, MD: Woodbine House, 2007.

In this engrossing and uplifting essay collection, over 60 mothers of children with Down syndrome reflect on the intangible gifts they have received from parenting their child. Many of the mothers received news of their child's diagnosis before birth and give candid accounts of the thoughts and emotions they wrestled with before deciding to continue their pregnancies. Others write of the shock of discovering only after birth that their baby had Down syndrome, or of their decision to adopt a child with Down syndrome, or of another aspect of their journey with their child.

✳ Zuckoff, Mitchell. **Choosing Naia: A Family's Journey.** Boston: Beacon Press, 2003.

Naia was prenatally diagnosed with Down syndrome. This book is an account of how her parents dealt with that diagnosis and ultimately made the decision to continue the pregnancy and then do their utmost to give their daughter the medical and developmental help she needed to blossom as an infant and toddler. The author, a newspaper journalist, interweaves the family's story with information about prenatal testing, how people with developmental disabilities have historically been treated, and other background information.

** Chapter 3: Medical Concerns and Treatments

Down Syndrome: Health Issues: News and Information for Parents and Professionals
www.ds-health.com

This website, maintained by Dr. Len Leshin, the author of Chapter 3 in this book, is a goldmine of information about Down syndrome in general, as well as medical and health issues in specific. The website includes articles written by Dr. Leshin about common health problems and controversies, as well as articles written by other specialists, abstracts of research studies of interest to parents, and links to Down syndrome clinics, support groups, blogs, and other resources.

Freeman, John, Vining, Eileen, and Pillas, Diana. **Seizures and Epilepsy in Children: A Guide.** Baltimore: Johns Hopkins Press, 2002.

A parent-friendly guide which discusses the types of seizures, their diagnosis, and treatment, including medications, the Ketogenic diet, and surgical options.

"Health Care Guidelines for Individuals with Down Syndrome." (Sept. 1999). Down Syndrome Quarterly Vol. 4, No. 3. Available online at: www.ds-health.com/health99.htm

These guidelines, compiled by medical professionals with experience caring for people with Down syndrome, provide an overview of medical and developmental concerns, recommended medical tests, nutritional concerns, etc. for people with Down syndrome. The guidelines address concerns by age range, from birth to adulthood. An essential resource to provide your pediatrician if he or she has had little experience with patients with Down syndrome.

Korn, Dana. **Kids with Celiac Disease: A Family Guide to Raising Happy, Healthy, Gluten-Free Children.** Bethesda, MD: Woodbine House, 2001.

For parents of children diagnosed with celiac disease, this guide provides helpful advice on managing your child's diet and preventing exposure to gluten in foods at home and when out in the community.

Kramer, Gerri and Mauer, Shari. **The Parent's Guide to Congenital Heart Defects: What They Are, How to Treat Them, How to Cope with Them.** New York, NY: Three Rivers Press, 2001.

Written by two mothers of children born with heart defects, this guide covers types and causes of common heart defects in children, diagnosis, treatment, recovery, and life after surgery. Medical experts contribute answers to common questions parents have.

National Center of Medical Home Initiatives. **Build Your Own Care Notebook.** www.medicalhomeinfo.org/toos/care_notebook.html.

From this website, you can download pages for medical care notebooks for your child (or fill them out online and then print them out). There are several free versions of notebooks available, including one in Spanish and one specifically for parents of children with special needs. Blank pages cover information such as height and weight, immunizations, hospitalizations, therapies, insurance information, how your child eats and sleeps, etc.

Neill, Catherine, Clark, Edward, and Clark, Carleen. **The Heart of a Child: What Families Need to Know about Heart Disorders in Children.** Baltimore: Johns Hopkins University Press, 2001.

Two physicians and a nurse teamed together to write this comprehensive and readable guide. The book includes a chapter on children with multiple disabilities, which lists syndromes commonly associated with heart defects and discusses special considerations in planning treatment and long-term care.

Shelov, Steven, ed. **Caring for Your Baby and Young Child: Birth to Age 5.** New York: Bantam Books, 2004.

This comprehensive guide from the American Academy of Pediatrics covers many childrearing and healthcare topics of concern to new parents. It's a good book to have on hand when you are wondering what a particular symptom could mean and whether you should call a doctor. There is also information and advice on feeding, infant care, behavior, and developmental issues.

:: Chapter 4: Daily Care of Your Baby

Anderson, Stephen et al. **Self-Help Skills for People with Autism: A Systematic Teaching Approach.** Bethesda, MD: Woodbine House, 2007.

Despite the title, this book can be helpful in teaching self-care skills to any child who is experiencing learning delays. The authors explain a systematic method to help children master eating, dressing, toileting, and personal hygiene skills.

Baker, Bruce L. **Steps to Independence: Teaching Everyday Skills to Children with Special Needs.** 4th ed. Baltimore: Brookes Publishing Co., 2003.

The authors explain step by step how to teach skills such as toilet training, dressing, and feeding and also offer advice on behavior management. Charts for monitoring and assessing improvement are included.

Coucouvanis, Judith. **The Potty Journey: Guide to Toilet Training Children with Special Needs, Including Autism and Related Disorders.** Shawnee Mission, KS: Autism Asperger Publishing Company, 2008.

This guide espouses a relaxed approach to toilet training children who have language delays and sensory issues. The authors detail how to determine whether a child is ready, how to gradually introduce potty training, and how to make the procedure rewarding.

Durand, V. Mark. **Sleep Better! A Guide to Improving Sleep for Children with Special Needs.** Baltimore: Brookes Publishing Co., 1998.

In this book, the author not only discusses helping children with disabilities get to sleep and stay asleep, but also problems such as sleep-phase problems, nightmares, bedwetting, and apnea. Several methods for improving sleep are explained, along with medications that can be helpful.

Faull, Jan. **Mommy! I Have to Go Potty!** Parenting Press, 1996.

This book offers a gradual approach to toilet training, and includes information on determining whether your child is ready, tips on getting your child to "buy in" to the potty training routine, dealing with power struggles, using rewards, and handling accidents.

Huggins, Kathleen. **The Nursing Mother's Companion.** Revised ed. Boston: Harvard Common Press, 2005.

The author offers a straightforward, problem solving approach to breastfeeding babies from birth through toddler age. A chapter on nursing babies with special needs is included.

"Is it Possible to Breastfeed My Baby Who Was Born with Down Syndrome?" Schaumberg, IL: La Leche League. www.lalecheleague.org/FAQ/down.html

This online fact sheet offers basic guidance on positioning a baby with Down syndrome so he can successfully breastfeed and provides links for further information.

KidsHealth
www.kidshealth.com

This comprehensive parenting website offers parent-friendly articles on a wide range of subjects, including positive parenting, fitness and health, emotions and behavior, first aid and safety, and medical problems. Information is available in Spanish as well as English.

Medlen, Joan Guthrie. **The Down Syndrome Nutrition Handbook: A Guide to Promoting Healthy Lifestyles.** Portland, OR: Phronesis Publishing, 2005.

A comprehensive guide to feeding and nutritional issues for people with Down syndrome from birth to adulthood. For parents of babies and young children, there is helpful information on breastfeeding/bottle feeding, introducing textures, helping the young child make choices, helping mealtimes go smoothly, and meeting nutritional needs.

Murphy, Jana. **The Secret Lives of Toddlers: A Parent's Guide to the Wonderful, Terrible, Fascinating Behavior of Children Ages 1 to 3.** New York, NY: Berkley, 2004.

Why do toddlers like to read the same books over and over again? Why do toddlers spit out food? Why do toddlers wake up so darned early? If you have reached a stage where you are wondering about these types of questions, this is the book for you. It explains the underlying reasons for common toddler behaviors and explains when to ignore or even encourage these things and when and how to discourage them.

Myrelid, A., Gustafsson, J., Ollars, B., and Anneren, G. (2002). **"Growth Charts for Down's syndrome from Birth to 18 years of Age."** Archives of Disease in Childhood. Vol. 87, No. 2 (2002), pp. 97-103.

The authors gathered data to produce growth charts specific to children with Down syndrome in Sweden. You can read the article and see the charts online at: http://www.pubmedcentral.nih.gov/articlerender.fcgi?artid=1719180

Satter, Ellyn. **Child of Mine: Feeding with Love and Good Sense.** 3rd ed. Palo Alto, CA: Bull Publishing, 2000.

Written by a dietitian, this book offers advice on feeding and nutrition from birth through age five. The author explains the parent's and child's roles in the feeding relationship, as well as nitty gritty information about breastfeeding, formula feeding, and progressing to solid foods.

Styles, M., Cole, T., Dennis, J., and Preece, M. **"New Cross Sectional Stature, Weight, and Head Circumference References for Down's Syndrome in the UK and Republic of Ireland."** Archives of Disease in Childhood. Vol. 87, No. 2 (2002), pp. 104-108.

The authors gathered data to produce growth charts specific to children with Down syndrome in the UK. You can read the article and see the charts online at: www.pubmedcentral.nih.gov/articlerender.fcgi?artid=1719181.

Wolraich, Mark and Tippins, Sherill (ed). **American Academy of Pediatrics Guide to Toilet Training.** New York: Bantam Books, 2003.

This book covers all the typical issues related to toilet training, including determining when your child is ready and handling accidents, and includes chapters on training children with special needs and older children.

:: Chapter 5: Family Life with Your Baby

Note: Books appropriate for siblings, as well as children with Down syndrome themselves, are listed in a separate section at the end of the Reading List.

Fawcett, Heather and Baskin, Amy. **More Than a Mom: Living a Full and Balanced Life When Your Child Has Special Needs.** Bethesda, MD: Woodbine House, 2006.

More Than a Mom explores how women can live rich, fulfilling lives when they have a child who needs more time and attention than usual. The book covers such topics as juggling a job with motherhood, staying physically and emotionally healthy, finding specialized childcare, and nurturing your own interests and goals.

Glasberg, Beth. **Functional Behavior Assessments for People with Autism: Making Sense of Seemingly Senseless Behavior.** Bethesda, MD: Woodbine House, 2006.

Although this book focuses on children with autism, it can also be helpful for parents of children with other disabilities, including Down syndrome. Step by step, the book outlines a procedure for pinpointing the causes of a child's challenging behavior as the first step to improving it. Especially useful for families of children who are not yet verbal or have difficulties expressing their feelings.

Marshak, Laura and Prezant, Fran. **Married with (Special-Needs) Children: A Couples' Guide to Keeping Connected.** Bethesda, MD: Woodbine House, 2006.

Based on interviews with hundreds of parents of children with special needs, this is a guide to keeping your marriage strong or deciding whether it is worth sustaining when you have a child with a disability or significant health care needs. The authors cover such topics as keeping the romance in your marriage, communication skills, and troubleshooting potentially serious marital difficulties.

Meyer, Don. **The Sibling Slam Book: What It's Really Like to Have a Brother or Sister with Special Needs.** Bethesda, MD: Woodbine House, 2005.

In this book targeted at teenaged siblings of children with special needs, 81 young people answer short questions related to their own and their siblings' lives. Examples of questions: Does your sib every frustrate you? What do you see for your sibling's future? What do you tell your friends about your sib's disability? Many of the participants have a sibling with Down syndrome. Reading their thoughts may help parents understand their other children's perspectives and needs.

Pantley, Elizabeth. **The No-Cry Discipline Solution: Gentle Ways to Encourage Good Behavior without Whining, Tantrums & Tears.** New York, NY: McGraw-Hill, 2007.

This guide to managing the behavior of children ages two to eight emphasizes using discipline to teach better behavior. The author includes specific advice for many common problems such as biting and not wanting to get out of the bath, as well as suggestions to help parents keep their cool.

Phelan, Thomas. **1-2-3 Magic: Effective Discipline for Children 2-12.** 3rd ed. Glen Ellyn, IL: Parentmagic, 2003.

The author describes a method of discipline that is especially useful in managing the behavior of children with attention deficit disorders, but has been used for children with other disabilities as well.

Smith, Karen, and Gouze, Karen. **The Sensory-Sensitive Child: Practical Solutions for Out-of-Bounds Behavior.** New York, NY: Harper Collins, 2004.

This book explains how sensory sensitivities can contribute to problem behavior, and offers an insight into the child's perspective. Included are solutions (including OT) for helping deal with, and prevent behavior related to sensory issues.

Strohm, Kate. **Being the Other One: Growing Up with a Brother or Sister Who Has Special Needs.** Boston: Shambhala Publications, 2005.

The author, herself the sibling of a woman with cerebral palsy, interviewed many brothers and sisters of people with various disabilities (including Down syndrome) in writing this book. The book includes information about the effects of having a sibling with disabilities, as well as advice that parents and adult siblings can use to help with emotional coping.

▪▪ Chapter 6: The Development of Babies with Down Syndrome

Acredolo, Linda and Goodwyn, Susan. **Baby Signs.** New York, NY: McGraw-Hill, 2002.

The authors believe in teaching sign language to all babies before they can talk in order to lessen frustration. The book covers the advantages of using sign language with hearing babies and illustrates approximately 50 useful signs.

Beyer, Monica. **Baby Talk: A Guide to Using Basic Sign Language to Communicate with Your Baby.** New York, NY: Jeremy Tarcher, 2006.

Another popular, parent-friendly guide to using sign language with hearing babies before they are ready to use speech.

Bruni, Maryanne. **Fine Motor Skills for Children with Down Syndrome: A Guide for Parents and Professionals.** 2nd edition. Bethesda, MD: Woodbine House, 2006.

Maryanne Bruni is an occupational therapist who specializes in diagnosing and treating fine motor delays in children with Down syndrome and other disabilities. Her parent-friendly guide explains why Down syndrome can affect the development of skills such as pointing, grasping, finger-feeding, using utensils and scissors, and writing, and suggests activities for improving fine motor skills that families can do at home with children aged approximately birth to adolescence.

Couwenhoven, Terri. **Teaching Children with Down Syndrome about Their Bodies, Boundaries, and Sexuality: A Guide for Parents and Professionals.** Bethesda, MD: Woodbine House, 2007.

This book by Terri Couwenhoven, a sexuality educator who has a child with Down syndrome, will convince you that it is never too early to begin teaching children with Down syndrome about their bodies, boundaries, and sexuality. In the early years, it is important for children to learn such skills as letting others know when they do or don't want to be touched, respecting personal space, privacy, appropriately expressing affection, and identifying and expressing emotions appropriately. In later childhood, it becomes important to teach about the physical and emotional changes of puberty, relationships, and other issues they will face in adolescence.

Development in Practice DVDs. These DVDs produced by Down Syndrome Education International can be ordered on their website at www.downsed.org/practice.

- Development in Practice—Activities for Babies with Down Syndrome: This DVD focuses on practical activities to promote the development of babies with Down syndrome.
- Development in Practice—Speech and Language Activities for Preschool Children with Down syndrome: This film explores practical activities for promoting the communication, speech, and language skills of preschool children with Down syndrome.

Developmental Journal for Babies and Children with Down Syndrome. Available from: www.earlysupport.org.uk.

A journal developed especially for parents of children with Down syndrome to track their children's progress, note areas of concerns, and celebrate achievements. It was developed for the UK's Early Support program by a team of experts, led by the Down Syndrome Education International. The pages can be downloaded for free, courtesy of the UK government (and parents in the UK can request a paper copy). On the website, click on "Materials" and then "Developmental Journals."

Down Syndrome Issues and Information books. This series of books is published by Down Syndrome Education International (Portsmouth, UK) and can be ordered online at: www.downsed.org. Titles that are especially relevant to parents of babies and young children are:

- Buckley, S. (2000). Living with Down Syndrome.
- Buckley, S. & Sacks, B. (2001). An Overview of the Development of Infants with Down syndrome (0-5 years).
- Buckley, S. & Bird, G. (2001). Speech and Language Development for Infants with Down Syndrome (0-5 years).
- Bird, G. & Buckley, S. (2001). Reading and Writing for Infants with Down Syndrome (0-5 years).
- Bird, G. & Buckley, S. (2001). Number Skills Development for Children with Down Syndrome (0-5 years).
- Sacks, B. & Buckley, S. (2008). Motor Skills Development for Infants with Down Syndrome (0-5 years).
- Buckley, S., & Bird, G. (2008). Social Development for Infants with Down Syndrome (0-5 years).
- Bird, G., Buckley, S.J. & Sacks, B. (in preparation—autumn 2008). Strategies for Changing Behaviour and Developing Social Skills.
- Sacks, B. & Buckley, S.J. (in press—autumn 2008). An Overview of Less Typical Development in Down syndrome.
- Buckley, S. & Bird, G. (2000). Education for Individuals with Down Syndrome—An Overview.

Healy, Jane. **Your Child's Growing Mind: Brain Development and Learning from Birth to Adolescence.** 3rd ed. New York: Broadway, 2004.

This book offers an engrossing look at the development of cognitive skills in children. Although the focus is on typical development, understanding the sequence of development, how skills are interrelated, and differences in learning styles can be useful to any parent in supporting their child's development.

Kranowitz, Carol S. **The Out of Sync Child: Recognizing and Coping with Sensory Processing Disorder.** Revised edition. New York: Perigee, 2006.

The author provides an excellent overview of how sensory processing is supposed to work in children and how difficulties with sensory processing may manifest themselves. The book includes plentiful suggestions for dealing with sensory issues in daily life.

Kumin, Libby. **Early Communication Skills for Children with Down Syndrome: A Guide for Parents and Professionals.** Bethesda, MD: Woodbine House, 2003.

Libby Kumin is a speech-language pathologist who specializes in understanding and treating communication problems in children with Down syndrome. This comprehensive, practical book is devoted to communication issues in children with Down syndrome aged birth until about age five or six (or the stage when they are using two- to three-word phrases). Information covered includes typical difficulties in learning communication skills, reasons for delays and difficulties, finding and working with a speech-language therapist, and many activities and games parents can do with their children at home to teach and reinforce speech and language skills.

Schermerhorn, Will. **Discovery: Pathways to Better Speech for Children with Down Syndrome.** Blueberry Shoes Productions, 2005.

This DVD, produced by the father of a child with Down syndrome, delves into the major issues that affect speech development in children with Down syndrome from birth to about age 7. Through interviews with experts such as Libby Kumin and Sue Buckley and engaging footage of children with Down syndrome communicating, the DVD offers an overview of hearing issues, ways that parents and therapists can encourage speech and increase vocabulary, and the connection between reading and speech.

Schwartz, Sue. **The New Language of Toys: Teaching Communication Skills to Children with Special Needs, a Guide for Parents and Teachers.** 3rd ed. Bethesda, MD: Woodbine House, 2004.

This classic parent's guide describes how to use toys and games (commercially available and homemade) to encourage the development of speech and language skills during play with your child.

Winders, Patricia. **Gross Motor Skills in Children with Down Syndrome.** Bethesda, MD: Woodbine House, 1997.

Patricia Winders is a physical therapist who has worked exclusively with children with Down syndrome for over twenty years. In this parent-friendly, well-illustrated book, she shares her encyclopedic knowledge related to helping children with Down syndrome improve gross motor skills such as sitting, crawling, standing, walking, and jumping. The book is appropriate for parents of children aged birth to approximately five to eight, depending on the child's gross motor skills.

∷ Chapter 7: Early Intervention

Anderson, Winifred, Chitwood, Stephen, Hayden, Deirdre, and Takemoto, Cherie. **Negotiating the Special Education Maze: A Guide for Parents and Teachers.** 4th ed. Bethesda, MD: Woodbine House, 2008.

This practical manual walks parents through every step involved in obtaining and maintaining an appropriate education for a child with disabilities, and includes a separate chapter on early intervention. The emphasis is on rights and requirements under IDEA, with some additional information on Section 504 and the ADA.

Braaten, Ellen and Felopulos, Gretchen. **Straight Talk about Psychological Testing for Kids.** New York, NY: Guilford Press, 2004.

Although not specific to Down syndrome, this book may be useful in explaining what tests are usually used in cognitive testing and what the scores mean. Includes chapters on diagnosing dyslexia, autism, AD/HD, and mental retardation.

Coleman, Jeanine G. **Early Intervention Dictionary: A Multidisciplinary Guide to Terminology.** 3rd ed. Bethesda, MD: Woodbine House, 2006.

This comprehensive guide includes easy-to-understand definitions of terms that parents of young children with disabilities are likely to encounter in their readings and when dealing with therapists, educators, psychologists, medical professionals, etc.

Horstmeier, DeAnna. **Teaching Math to People with Down Syndrome and Other Hands-On Learners, Book 1.** Bethesda, MD: Woodbine House, 2004.

In addition to covering background information on typical difficulties that children with Down syndrome have in learning mathematics and number concepts, this book offers many activities and games to help children aged about two through elementary school learn early concepts about numbers, counting, and shapes, as well as the basics of addition, subtraction, telling time, and money concepts.

Jennings, Jessica (director). **Boy in the World.** Providence, RI: VisionWink Productions, 2007. (Available from the Rhode Island Parent Information Network at www.ripin.org; 401-727-4144).

This DVD shows how a young boy with Down syndrome is successfully included in preschool, as well as in his community.

Oelwein, Patricia. **Teaching Reading to Children with Down Syndrome: A Guide for Parents and Teachers.** Bethesda, MD: Woodbine House, 1995.

One of the best-known experts on teaching young children with Down syndrome here presents a sight-word method that has been successfully used by thousands of parents and teachers to teach their children to read. The book includes background information on how children with Down syndrome learn, suggestions for fun activities and games, and instructional materials that can be photocopied.

▰▰ Chapter 8: Legal Rights and Hurdles

Elias, Stephen. **Special Needs Trusts: Protect Your Child's Financial Future.** 2nd ed. Berkeley, CA: Nolo, 2007.

In plain English, this guide explains how parents can leave money to a child with disabilities without jeopardizing government benefits.

"Medicare and You." Baltimore, MD: U.S. Dept. of Health and Human Services, 2007. www.medicare.gov/publications/pubs/pdf/10050.pdf

The official guide to Medicare benefits can be ordered in English or Spanish from the Dept. of Health and Human Services by calling 800-633-4227 or writing to them at 7500 Security Blvd., Baltimore, MD 21244-1850.

Morton, David. **Nolo's Guide to Social Security Disability: Getting and Keeping Your Benefits.** Berkeley, CA: Nolo Press, 2008.

This comprehensive handbook to understanding, applying for, and appealing denials of SSDI and SSI includes a section specific to benefits for children with disabilities.

Nadworny, John and Haddad, Cynthia. **The Special Needs Planning Guide: How to Prepare for Every Stage in Your Child's Life.** Baltimore: Paul Brookes, 2007.

This book takes a two-pronged approach to financial planning, discussing how parents can plan for their own financial well-being while also planning for the financial future of a family member with disabilities.

Treeby, Graeme. **Removing the Mystery: An Estate Planning Guide for Families of People with Disabilities.** Toronto: Ontario Federation for Cerebral Palsy.
A resource available on CD or in print edition for Canadian readers, the guide covers trusts, wills, and other financial planning issues for families of children with disabilities.

U.S. Department of Justice. **The Americans with Disabilities Act: Questions and Answers; A Guide to Disability Rights Laws; and Commonly Asked Questions about Childcare Centers and the Americans with Disabilities Act.** Available by calling the ADA information line at 800-514-0301 or from website: www.ada.gov.
These free booklets are available online for downloading or in standard print, large print, or Braille if you call the information line.

With Open Arms: Embracing a Bright Financial Future for You and Your Child. Chicago, IL: Easter Seals.
This free booklet can be downloaded from www.easterseals.com (click on "Support"; "Raising a Child with Special Needs") or can be ordered in print format for $5 shipping and handling from Easter Seals, 230 W. Monroe, Suite 1800, Chicago, IL 60606. Topics covered include financial planning, government benefits, estate planning, and insurance.

Wright, P.W.D. & Wright, P.D. **Wrightslaw: IDEA 2004.** Hartfield, VA: Harbor House Law Press, 2005.
Available in a print and e-book edition, this guide includes the full text of the Individuals with Disabilities Act of 2004 with helpful commentary and annotation by the authors designed to help parents use the law to their children's advantage.

:: Children's Books

Bouwkamp, Julie. **Hi, I'm Ben ... and I've Got a Secret.** Rochester Hills, MI: Band of Angels, 2006.
Ben tells about his life, likes, dislikes, and how much he is like any other child before revealing his secret—that he has Down syndrome. A story about a real boy illustrated with color photographs.

Cairo, Shelley. **Our Brother Has Down's Syndrome: An Introduction for Children.** Toronto: Annick Press, 1988.
This book for young siblings shows what life is like for two sisters and their little brother with Down syndrome; illustrated with charming color photographs.

Dodds, Bill. **My Sister Annie.** Honesdale, PA: Boyds Mills Press, 1997.
In this novel for middle grade readers, Charlie, an eleven-year-old, struggles with his feelings about his older sister Annie, who has Down syndrome, as well as with the typical preteen feelings about fitting in and the opposite sex.

Gifaldi, David and Johnson, Layne. **Ben, King of the River.** Morton's Grove, IL: Albert Whitman, 2001.

This realistic picture book focuses on the interactions of two brothers, Chad, aged about 8, and his little brother, Ben, who has a developmental disability and "doesn't like new things." The words and brightly colored illustrations nicely capture the range of emotions Chad feels about his brother on the first day of a family camping trip.

Girnis, Margaret and Leamon Green, Shirley. **1 2 3 for You and Me.** Morton's Grove, IL: Albert Whitman, 2001.

This book features photographs of smiling children with Down syndrome holding objects for young readers to count (numbers one to twenty).

Girnis, Margaret and Leamon Green, Shirley. **ABC for You and Me.** Morton's Grove, IL: Albert Whitman, 2000.

This alphabet book features nice, clear photos of children with Down syndrome posing with objects representing each letter of the alphabet.

Hale, Natalie. **Oh, Brother! Growing Up with a Special Needs Sibling.** Washington, DC: Magination Press, 2004.

In this illustrated story for older elementary school children, younger sister Becca sometimes has trouble dealing with the quirks of her brother Jonathan, who has Down syndrome, but she comes up with some coping strategies that she shares for the benefit of other siblings.

Meyer, Donald. **The Sibling Slam Book: What It's Really Like to Have a Brother or Sister with Special Needs.** Bethesda, MD: Woodbine House, 2005.

This book for teens is structured like a real slam book, with questions posed at the top of each page and the participants' answers scrawled below. Over 80 teenaged brothers and sisters of children with disabilities, including Down syndrome, candidly shared their experiences and thoughts and feelings about their siblings, as well as information about their hopes and dreams, in response to questions posed by the author.

Meyer, Donald. **Views from Our Shoes.** Bethesda, MD: Woodbine House, 1997.

This is a collection of short, positive essays by four dozen children who have a brother or sister with a disability, including Down syndrome; suitable for readers in grades 3-7.

Pitzer, Marjorie. **I Can, Can You?** Bethesda, MD: Woodbine House, 2004.

Color photos of adorable young children with Down syndrome demonstrating what they can do are featured on the pages of this board book, suitable for ages birth to 5.

Pitzer, Marjorie. **My Up and Down and All Around Book.** Bethesda, MD: Woodbine House, 2008.

This board book showcases photos of children with Down syndrome demonstrating the meaning of a variety of pronouns using appealing props such as playground equipment, play houses, and dogs.

Siblings—Growing Up with Your Brother or Sister with Down Syndrome.
Down's Syndrome Scotland. www.dsscotland.org.uk/brothers-and-sisters.

A short, illustrated book for siblings aged about 5 to 10 discussing the emotions that may come along with having a brother or sister with Down syndrome. May be downloaded for free from the website.

Stuve-Bodeen, Stephanie. **We'll Paint the Octopus Red.** Bethesda, MD: Woodbine House, 1998.

While waiting for her baby brother's birth, six-year-old Emma figures out at least a million things she'll do with him. But when Isaac is born with Down syndrome, she worries that that will change everything. As she and her father discuss what "this Down thing" will mean for Isaac, they are both reassured that with time and patience, Isaac will be able to do everything that matters. This whimsically illustrated book concludes with Q&A's about Down syndrome for kids aged 3 to 8.

Stuve-Bodeen, Stephanie. **The Best Worst Brother.** Bethesda, MD: Woodbine House, 2005.

In this sequel to **We'll Paint the Octopus Red**, Isaac is now a toddler and both he and his sister are finding his communication difficulties frustrating. With patience and persistence, both siblings learn a few things by the end of the story and make themselves (and each other proud).

Woloson, Eliza. **My Friend Isabelle.** Bethesda, MD: Woodbine House, 2003.

In spare language perfect for preschoolers, Charlie describes his friendship with Isabelle. Despite some differences, including Isabelle's Down syndrome, the two friends enjoy dancing, snacking, playing in the park, and pretending to shop together. The book's boldly colored, joyous illustrations help underscore the theme that "differences are what make the world so great."

Resource Guide

The organizations, websites, and other resources listed below offer a variety of services that can be helpful to families of children with Down syndrome living in North America and other English-speaking countries. For further information about any of these organizations, call, write, or visit their webpage and request a copy of their newsletter or other publications.

There are now thousands of resources online. Since it can be difficult to determine which ones are reputable, however, you may want to start with some long-established, authoritative websites:

- **PubMed** (a service of the U.S. National Library of Medicine) at www.pubmed.gov—This website enables you to search medical journals and read the "abstracts" of most articles. These are short summaries of the articles. Sometimes you receive the full article. You can go to the website and search for Down syndrome, otitis media, alopecia areata, hypothyroidism, strabismus—whatever specific medical topic you are looking for.
- **Google Scholar** at www.scholar.google.com—This is another good online search engine that searches through scholarly papers on many different topics.
- **Education Resources Information Center (ERIC)** at www.eric. ed.gov —This website, associated with the U.S. Department of Education, enables you to search over a million articles on education topics, and, in many cases, retrieve the full text of the original article.

■■ Down Syndrome-Specific Resources

Canadian Down Syndrome Society
811 14ᵗʰ St., NW
Calgary, Alberta T2N 2A4
Canada
403-270-8500; 800-883-5608
www.cdss.ca

The CDSS advocates for people with Down syndrome, provides information to families, and sponsors conferences. Several parent-friendly publications are available online, as are online forums on a variety of topics, including health and medical issues, education, and community living. Visit the website for links to local affiliates all across Canada.

Center for Research and Treatment of Down Syndrome
Stanford University School of Medicine
http://dsresearch.stanford.edu
dsresearch@med.stanford.edu

This research center is actively researching the basis of the cognitive problems in Down syndrome, in hopes of developing treatments. Check the website for updates on their research findings.

Down Syndrome Education International
The Sarah Duffen Centre
Belmont St.
Southsea, Hampshire PO5 INA
United Kingdom
www.downsed.org

This organization, formerly known as the Down Syndrome Educational Trust, is a nonprofit, charitable organization founded by Sue Buckley and dedicated to advancing research that will lead to helping people with Down syndrome achieve more. It publishes a cutting-edge journal called *Down Syndrome Research and Practice* that is available free of charge online, a series of books called Down Syndrome Issues and Information, and also operates a website, Down Syndrome Online (www.down-syndrome.org), that provides free access to many articles on Down Syndrome.

Down Syndrome Education USA
19900 MacArthur Blvd., Suite 1050
Irvine, CA 92612
www.downsed-usa.org

An offshoot of Down Syndrome Education International, this organization was recently established to offer people with Down syndrome everywhere better educational opportunities. Publications, learning packages, and conventions to help parents and teachers support learning are planned.

Down Syndrome: Health Issues: News and Information for Parents and Professionals
www.ds-health.com

This website, maintained by Dr. Len Leshin, the author of Chapter 3 in this book, is a goldmine of information about Down syndrome in general, as well as medical and health issues in specific. The website includes articles written by Dr. Leshin about common health problems and controversies, as well as articles written by other specialists and abstracts of research studies of interest to parents. There are many links to Down syndrome support groups, blogs, and informational websites; Down syndrome clinics; and other resources.

Down Syndrome Listserv
listserv@listserv.nodak.edu

This is a longstanding online newsgroup for parents and other family members of children with Down syndrome. Members post news items related to Down syndrome and special education; pose questions about education, development, family life, medical treatments; seek support from one another; share good news related to their child with Down syndrome, etc. Subscribers to the newsgroup can elect to receive a daily email digest of all posts, or to receive each message as an individual email. To subscribe, send an email to the above address and write: *subscribe downsyn [your real name]* in the body of the message (you don't have to fill in the subject line). Then do as the return email instructs to finish the subscription process.

Down Syndrome Research Foundation
1409 Sperling Ave.
Burnaby, BC V5B 4J8
694-444-3773; 888-464-3773 (toll-free in Canada only)
www.dsrf.org

The DSRF conducts research with the aim of improving the quality of life for people with Down syndrome and their families and disseminates information. A number of papers are available online and the organization also publishes the *Down Syndrome Quarterly*.

Eleanor Roosevelt Institute
University of Denver
2101 E. Wesley Ave.
Denver, CO 80208
www.eri.du.edu

The Eleanor Roosevelt Institute hosts several research programs that are currently looking into causes and treatments for Down syndrome and other cognitive disabilities. You can read about the latest findings on their website, under "Research Programs."

International Mosaic Down Syndrome Association
P.O. Box 1052
Franklin, TX 77856
www.imdsa.com

IMSDA is a nonprofit organization that provides information and support to families touched by mosaic Down syndrome. It publishes a newsletter and sponsors a conference every two years; the website includes a link to an online support group and other resources.

National Down Syndrome Congress
1370 Center Dr., Suite 102
Atlanta, GA 30338
770-604-9599; 800-232-6372
www.ndsccenter.org
The NDSC is a national organization of parents and professionals dedicated to improving the lives of people with Down syndrome and their families. It provides information and referral online and over the phone; holds an annual conference for family members and professionals; advocates for issues of concern to members. For contact information for the nearest local chapter, call the NDSC or visit their website and click on "Expectant Parents" and then "Directory of Organizations." You can get a "New Parent Package" by calling the toll-free number or clicking on "Parent Resources" on the website.

National Down Syndrome Cytogenic Registry
www.wolfson.qmul.ac.uk.ndscr
This website includes official statistics about the numbers of children with Down syndrome prenatally diagnosed and born in the UK, as well as statistics on the risk of Down syndrome based on maternal age and other statistics.

National Down Syndrome Society
666 Broadway, 8th floor
New York, NY 10012
212-460-9330; 800-221-4602
www.ndss.org
The NDSS is a national organization that works to promote a better understanding of Down syndrome. It sponsors scientific and educational research into Down syndrome, provides an extensive offering of online and print publications, sponsors "Buddy Walks" to raise money and promote Down syndrome awareness, and operates a website with numerous links. Call the NDSS or visit their website for contact information for the nearest local chapter.

Yahoo! Groups
http://groups.yahoo.com
There are many different Yahoo Groups (online forums) for parents and others who are interested in exchanging information and support related to raising a child with Down syndrome. For example, Dads Appreciating Down Syndrome (fathers' concerns); Downs-Heart (for families of children with heart defects); down-syndrome-adoption; Down syndrome Canadian parents; Homeschooling and Down Syndrome; Down Syndrome and Autistic Spectrum. To see a complete list of groups that are available to join, go to the above website and type *Down syndrome* into the box that says "Find a Yahoo! Group."

■■ Adoption

Child Welfare Information Gateway
Children's Bureau/ACYF
1250 Maryland Ave., SW
Washington, DC 20024
703-385-7565; 800-394-3366
www.childwelfare.gov

Among other services, the CWIG provides comprehensive information about adoption and foster care, including information on individual state statutes. The National Adoption Information Clearinghouse was absorbed into this organization.

Down Syndrome Association of Greater Cincinnati
Adoption Awareness Program
644 Linn St., Ste. 1128
Cincinnati, OH 45203
513-761-5400; 888-796-5504
www.dsagc.com

In addition to providing information and support to families of children with Down syndrome in the Cincinnati area, the DSAGC runs a national Adoption Awareness Program. The program helps families who want to adopt a child with Down syndrome locate a child to adopt and also provides information and support to birth families who might wish to consider an adoption plan for their baby with Down syndrome.

Reece's Rainbow
www.reecesrainbow.com

Reece's Rainbow attempts to help prospective adoptive families locate orphans with Down syndrome around the world who are up for adoption and provide financial assistance to facilitate adoption of orphans with Down syndrome. Visitors to the website can pledge money to support these goals as well as locate available children in specific countries.

■■ Child Care & Respite

ChildCareAware
3101 Wilson Blvd., Suite 350
Arlington, VA 22201
800-424-2246
www.childcareaware.org

This organization offers information on finding quality childcare in general, as well as some on children with special needs in particular. Operates child care resource and referral centers across the U.S.

ARCH National Respite Network
Chapel Hill Training-Outreach Project
800 Eastowne Dr., Ste. 105
Chapel Hill, NC 27514

919-490-5577
www.chtop.org/ARCH.html
　　ARCH operates a Respite Locator Service which enables families in need of respite care in the U.S. and Canada to search for sources of respite services in their state or province. Fact sheets about respite care are also available.

▋ Education & Therapies

American Physical Therapy Association
1111 North Fairfax Street
Alexandria, VA 22314
703-684-APTA (2782) or 800-999-APTA (2782); 703-684-7343 (fax)
www.apta.org
　　This professional organization for physical therapists offers publications of interest to parents and educators and has an online searchable database of physical therapists to help you find a PT in your area.

American Speech-Language-Hearing Association
2200 Research Blvd.
Rockville, MD 20850
800-498-2071
www.asha.org
　　ASHA can provide information on speech and language therapists and audiologists in your area. It also distributes brochures on speech and hearing disorders.

CAST
40 Harvard Mills Square
Suite 3
Wakefield, MA 01880
781-245-2212
www.cast.org
　　This organization, formerly known as the Center for Applied Special Technology, is a premier source of information about universal design for learning—a way of designing curricula that reduces the barriers to learning that people with disabilities often face. Offers free guidelines to UDL, as well as conferences and publications.

Center on Education Policy
1001 Connecticut Ave., NW
Suite 522
Washington, DC 20036
202-822-8065
www.cep-dc.org
　　A national, independent advocate for public education and for improving public schools. Information is available on the website related to special education, the NCLB act, testing, Title 1 programs, etc.

The Council for Exceptional Children (CEC)
1110 North Glebe Road, Suite 300
Arlington, VA 22201
703-620-3660; 703-264-9494 (fax)
www.cec.sped.org
    This is a membership organization for educators in the U.S. and Canada who are interested in the needs of children who have disabilities or are gifted. Their publication catalog offers a number of books and other materials on education-related topics.

IDEA Website
U.S. Dept. of Education
Office of Special Education Programs
http://IDEA.ed.gov
    The U.S. government's "one-stop shop" for information about IDEA, including the complete searchable text of the law and regulations.

Inclusion Network
www.inclusion.com/inclusionnetwork.html
    A number of articles on the topic of inclusion are available for download on the Inclusion Network's website. There is also a listing of hundreds of resources on inclusion, including links to websites, books, DVDs, and school resources.

LD Online website
www.ldonline.com
    This website offers articles, resources, and forums to help parents, teachers, and people with learning disabilities or other academic learning problems learn strategies and information to help individuals with LD be more successful at home, school, and on the job.

National Early Childhood Technical Assistance Center
Campus Box 8040, UNC-CH
Chapel Hill, NC 27599-8040
919-962-2001
www.nectac.org
    Provides information with the goal of ensuring that young children with disabilities (birth to 5) and their families receive and benefit from high quality, family-centered services. Has an online clearinghouse of information and resources. Some information available in Spanish. Those without Internet access can call for a print copy of publications available.

U.S. Department of Education
Clearinghouse on Disability Information
400 Maryland Ave., SW
Washington, DC 20202
800-USA-LEARN; 202-205-8245www.ed.gov/index/html
    Useful links and articles are provided under "My Child's Special Needs." The site also offers information on topics such as school readiness, the importance of reading, the "achievement gap," and the No Child Life Behind Act.

Zero to Three
National Center for Infants, Toddlers, and Families
2000 M St. NW, Suite 200
Washington, DC 20036
202-638-1144
www.zerotothree.org
   This organization educates and supports adults who influence the lives of infants and toddlers. Offers online fact sheets about childcare, early development, nutrition, etc.

■■ Family Support

Abiding Hearts
abidinghearts@yahoo.com
   Abiding Hearts is a not-for-profit organization dedicated to providing support and information to parents continuing their pregnancies after prenatal testing has revealed the presence of birth defects, some of which may be life-threatening. Provides a network of contact parents in a growing number of areas across the United States; promotes patient advocacy; provides referrals to support groups and other services; and offers educational and support materials.

Parent to Parent—USA (P2P USA)
www.p2pusa.org
   Parent to Parent is a national nonprofit organization that helps ensure that local P2P programs can provide emotional and information support to parents of children with special needs by matching new parents with experienced support parents. Visit the website to find the Parent to Parent program serving your state or community.

Sibling Support Project
www.siblingsupport.org
   This website has a variety of useful links for families, including information on finding events for siblings of children with disabilities of all ages, separate listservs for adult and child siblings, and thoughts from siblings about what it is like to have a brother or sister with special needs.

Technical Assistance Alliance for Parent Centers
c/o Pacer Center
8161 Normandale Blvd.
Minneapolis, MN 55437
888-248-0822
www.taalliance.org
   Parent centers serve families of children with disabilities aged birth to 22, helping families obtain education and services, offering parent training, connecting families with community resources, resolving problems between families and schools or other agencies. Contact the National Technical Assistance center above (or visit the website) for the location of the parent center nearest you.

▌▌ General Disability Information

Autism Society of America
7910 Woodmont Ave., Suite 300
Bethesda, MD 20814
800-328-8476; 301-657-0881
www.autism-society.org

The ASA is a national organization of parents and professionals that promotes a better understanding of autism spectrum disorders. It acts as an information clearinghouse about autism and services for people who have autism.

Canadian Abilities Foundation
340 College Street, Suite 401
Toronto, ON M5T 3A9
CANADA
416-923-1885
www.abilities.ca

Provides links to disability organizations in Canada and throughout the world, as well as information/message boards about disability issues. Subscriptions to *Abilities* magazine are available here.

Canadian Association for Community Living
Kinsmen Building, York University
4700 Keele Street
Toronto, Ontario M3J 1P3
Canada
416-661-9611; 416-661-5701 (fax)
www.cacl.ca

An association of family members and others working for the benefit of Canadians with intellectual disabilities. Offers a newsletter and other publications.

ClinicalTrials.gov
www.clinicaltrials.gov

A service of the U.S. National Institutes of Health, this site is a registry of clinical trials conducted in the U.S. and around the world. The site gives information about the purpose of trials, who can qualify to participate, and contact information. You can search by subject (such as Down Syndrome or Alopecia) to locate federally and privately sponsored research studies that are currently being conducted. Families sometimes choose to participate in clinical trials to help advance research into their child's condition, to get free treatment for their child, or for other reasons.

DisabilityInfo.Gov
www.disabilityinfo.gov

DisabilityInfo.gov is the U.S. government's one-stop website for information for people with disabilities, bringing together information from twenty-two federal agencies. Major topics covered are education, employment, benefits, housing, transportation, health, technology, community life, and civil rights.

Disability News

www.patriciaebauer.com

Journalist Patricia Bauer, the mother of a young adult with Down syndrome, created this website as a one-stop source of current media stories on disability issues. The website has summaries of disability-related stories in newspapers, magazines, and other publications, with links to the original story, and allows readers to comment on the stories.

Family Village

www.familyvillage.wisc.edu

This website describes itself as "a global village of disability-related resources." It includes full text articles on specific disabilities, education issues, legal issues, recreation, and more, as well as opportunities to connect with others and extensive links to information, products, and resources.

National Disability Rights Network

900 Second St., NE, Ste. 211
Washington, DC 20002
202-408-9514
www.ndrn.org

A nonprofit organization that uses training and technical assistance, legal support, and legislative advocacy to enforce and expand the rights of people with disabilities. You can locate your state Protection and Advocacy agency on the website, as well as read articles about "hot topics" related to disabilities.

National Dissemination Center for Children with Disabilities (NICHCY)

P.O. Box 1492
Washington, DC 20013-1492
800-695-0285
www.nichcy.org

This clearinghouse specializes in providing information on educational programs and laws and other issues of importance to families of children with disabilities. Publications can be downloaded from the website or ordered in hard copy (usually for no charge). Especially useful are NICHCY's "State Sheets," which list a variety of support and other organizations in each state.

National Easter Seal Society

230 W. Monroe
Suite 1800
Chicago, IL 60606
800-221-6827; 312-726-1494 (fax)
www.easterseals.com

Easter Seals supports families of children with disabilities by offering direct services such as screening and therapy through local affiliates; through public education; and through advocacy. Some local affiliates provide childcare and sponsor summer camps.

National Rehabilitation Information Center (NARIC)
4200 Forbes Blvd., Suite 202
Lanham, MD 20706
800-346-2742; 301-459-5900
www.naric.com
 An online source of disability and rehabilitation-oriented information on education, advocacy, financial assistance and benefits, resources, etc. for people with disabilities, their families, and researchers.

TASH
29 W. Susquehanna Avenue, Suite 210
Baltimore, MD 21204
410-828-8274; 410-828-6706 (fax)
www.tash.org
 TASH is an international association of people with disabilities, their family members, other advocates, and professionals fighting for a society in which inclusion of all people in all aspects of society is the norm. Publishes a newsletter and sponsors conferences.

The Arc
1010 Wayne Ave., Ste. 650
Silver Spring, MD 20910
301-565-3842; 800-433-5255
www.thearc.org
 The Arc is a national organization that advocates on behalf of people with developmental disabilities, including Down syndrome. Publications and an online Discussion Board are available from the national office, above. There are local affiliates in many communities that offer parent training, lending libraries, support and information, and other services (you can locate your nearest affiliate online).

∷ Health & Medical Concerns

American Academy of Otolaryngology—Head and Neck Surgery
1 Prince St.
Alexandria, VA 22314
703-836-4444
www.entnet.org
 The academy is a membership organization for specialists who treat disorders of the ear, nose, and throat. The website offers many fact sheets and articles written for parents about these disorders and their treatment (including some in Spanish), and also has an online searchable database of ENT specialists in the U.S.

American Academy of Pediatrics
141 Northwest Point Blvd.
Elk Grove Village, IL 60007
847-434-4000
www.aap.org

The AAP is a membership organization for pediatricians. The official public website of the AAP includes an online Pediatrician Referral Service and a variety of articles and links on topics related to children's health and safety.

American Heart Association
7272 Greenville Ave.
Dallas, TX 75231
800-242-8721

The American Heart Association provides information on issues related to congenital heart defects and their diagnosis and treatment through online articles (some in Spanish) and brochures that can be ordered by calling the number above. The website also provides links to child exercise and nutrition resources.

American Sleep Apnea Association
1424 K St., NW
Washington, DC 20005
202-293-3650
www.sleepapnea.org

This nonprofit organization informs the public about sleep apnea and works to enhances the well-being of people with the disorder. It sponsors an online forum and has print and online publications available.

Celiac Disease and Kids
www.celiackids.com

This is a special page on the larger website, celiac.com, devoted to issues related to celiac disease in children.

Celiac Disease Foundation
13251 Ventura Blvd., Ste. 1
Studio City, CA 91604
818-990-2354
www.celiac.org

A nonprofit organization that is dedicated to providing services and support to people with celiac disease, the CDF has a number of useful online articles on topics such as label reading, grocery shopping, and dining out, and offers a downloadable "Quick Start Guide" to the gluten-free diet. Sponsors local support chapters.

Epilepsy Canada
2255B Queen Street
Suite 336
Toronto, Ontario M4E 1G3
877-734-0873; 905-764-1231 (fax)
www.epilepsy.ca

Dedicated to improving the quality of life for people with epilepsy and their families, Epilepsy Canada offers a variety of fact sheets and brochures in English and French; website includes a list of treatment centers in Canada.

Epilepsy Foundation of America
4351 Garden City Drive
Landover, MD 20785-7223
800-332-1000; 301-577-2684 (fax)
www.efa.org

A national organization that works for the prevention and cure of seizure disorders and promotes independence and optimal quality of life for people with epilepsy. Services commonly provided in local communities are information and referral, counseling, patient and family advocacy, school alert, community education, support groups and camps for children.

Families USA—The Voice for Health Care Consumers
1201 New York Ave NW, Ste 1100
Washington, DC 20005
202-628-3030; 202-347-2417 (fax)
www.familiesusa.org/index.html

This national nonprofit, nonpartisan organization provides information and resources related to healthcare public policy and tracks the progress of legislation affecting managed care, Medicaid, and SCHIP (Children's Health Insurance Program). The organization has publications, which can be mailed or downloaded on computer, regarding health insurance, especially Medicaid, and prescription medications. Lists relevant information state by state.

Healthfinder.gov
U.S. Department of Health and Human Services
www.healthfinder.gov

This website is designed to help you find reliable health information on the Internet. Clicking on "Consumer Guides" takes you to reader-friendly links on a variety of topics such as Medicare, Medicaid, health insurance, and prescription drugs.

Heart and Stroke Foundation of Canada
222 Queen St., Suite 1402
Ottawa, ONT K1P 5V9
Canada
613-569-4361
www.heartandstroke.com

The Foundation offers Canada-specific current information on heart disease, treatment, and tests. *Heart & Soul: A Guide to Living with Congenital Heart Disease* is available as a free download.

Insure Kids Now!
U.S. Dept. of Health and Human Services
877-KIDS-NOW (543-7669)
www.insurekidsnow

A source for easy-to-understand information about the SCHIP health insurance program, together with links to state programs.

KidsHealth website

www.kidshealth.org

This website offers parent-friendly articles on issues of interest to all parents, such as visiting the doctor, nutrition, and childhood medical problems. There are also some articles on disability-related issues.

Lotsa Helping Hands

www.lotsahelpinghands.com

This website enables you to create an online community of friends and family members to help out during a time of medical crisis or another situation where your family could use some help. You (or another "coordinator") can easily create a free, private group calendar, list the tasks that need to be done each day, and send emails to people who might be interested in helping out. Community members can then click on the tasks they volunteer to do. You can also use a message board and create photo galleries to keep your friends and family updated about your loved one's progress.

MedCalc Interactive Growth Charts

www.medcalc.com/growth

This website enables you to type in your child's height and weight measurements (in English or metric terms) and then shows you where he or she falls on the (U.S.) Down syndrome growth chart. You can also see where your child falls on the regular growth charts produced by the CDC.

National Alopecia Areata Foundation

14 Mitchell Blvd.
San Rafael, CA 94903
415-472-3780
www.naaf.org

The NAAF provides information and support and supports research into a cure and treatments for alopecia areata. Information packets are available. The website provides a forum for children with alopecia areata to connect with other children.

National Health Information Center

P.O. Box 1133
Washington, DC 20013-1133
800-336-4797; 301-565-4167; 301-984-4256 (fax)
www.health.gov/nhic

The National Health Information Center (NHIC) is a health information referral service. NHIC links consumers and health professionals who have health questions to organizations best able to provide answers.

State Children's Health Insurance Program (SCHIP)

Centers for Medicare & Medicaid Services
7500 Security Blvd.
Baltimore, MD 21244
877-543-7669

www.cms.hhs.gov/home/schip.asp
Contact this office for information on the SCHIP program, including information about individual state programs and benefits for qualifying children.

U.S. Department of Labor
Employee Benefits Security Administration
200 Constitution Ave., NW
Washington, DC 20210
866-444-EBSA
www.dol.gov/ebsa/newsroom/fsmain/html
The U.S. DOL can provide information about regulations and laws related to health insurance and HIPPA, as well as employee benefits. Fact sheets are available on the website.

▪▪ Legal & Financial Issues
Canada Benefits
www.canadabenefits.ca
800-622-6232
A one-stop gateway to information about government benefits and services for Canadians, including those specific to individuals with disabilities.

Canadian Life and Health Insurance Association
1 Queen St., East, Suite 1700
Toronto, ON M5C 2X9
Canada
800-268-8099
www.clhia.ca
The CLHIA offers consumer assistance through online and print publications about life insurance and supplementary health insurance in Canada.

Centers for Medicare & Medicaid Services
7500 Security Blvd.
Baltimore, MD 21244
800-633-4227 (Medicare Service Center)
800-772-1213 (Social Security or SSI questions)
www.cms.hhs.gov
The official government source for information on Medicare, Medicaid, and SCHIP eligibility, coverage, grievances, etc.

Internal Revenue Service (IRS)
800-829-1040
www.irs.gov
U.S. residents can request publications such as "Tax Highlights for Persons with Disabilities" (#907) to find out whether medical, childcare, or other expenses related to a child with Down syndrome are deductible or get live help with tax questions by calling the toll-free number. Forms can also be downloaded online.

Office of the Americans with Disabilities Act

U.S. Department of Justice
950 Pennsylvania Avenue, NW
Disability Rights Section—NYAV
Washington, DC 20530
800-514-0301; 800-514-0383 (TDD)
202-307-1198 (fax)
www.ada.gov

The U.S. Department of Justice provides free materials about the Americans with Disabilities Act. Printed materials may be ordered by calling the phone numbers above. Automated service is available 24 hours a day for recorded information and to order publications.

PAS Center for Personal Assistance Services

www.pascenter.org

Of interest to some families of children with Down syndrome in the U.S., the website of this organization provides information on the Medicaid waivers available in each state, along with links for more information. Click on "State Information."

Senate Printing and Document Services

B-04, Hart Senate Office Building
Washington, DC 20510-7106
9:00 a.m.—5:30 p.m., Monday—Friday
202-224-7701 (availability inquiries only); 202-228-2815 (fax)
E-mail: orders@sec.senate.gov

The Senate document room provides copies of publications generated by the Senate, including bills and resolutions; legislative and executive reports, including conference reports; documents; and committee assignment lists (pdf). The document room also supplies copies of public laws and treaties. Bills, resolutions, and committee rosters are available for the current Congress only. All other items are held 10 years or more. You can request documents in person, in writing, via e-mail, or via fax.

Social Security Administration

Office of Public Inquiries
6401 Security Boulevard
Room 4-C-5 Annex
Baltimore, MD 21235-6401
800-777-1213; 800-325-0778
www.ssa.gov

Social Security is a U.S. Government program offering economic protection to retirees and people with disabilities, as well as their survivors. The website offers online application for SSI and Medicare, downloadable forms and many pertinent publications, and an explanation of Social Security statements. You can get recorded information by calling the toll-free number or speak to a SSA representative.

United Healthcare Children's Foundation
MN012-S286
P.O. Box 41
Minneapolis, MN 55440-0041
800-328-5979, ext. 24459
www.uhccf.org
Financial assistance in paying for medical-related services is available through this foundation for U.S. children aged 16 and under whose families meet income guidelines and other criteria. Financial grants are available for services that have "the potential to significantly enhance either the clinical condition or the quality of life of the child."

Wrightslaw
877-529-4332
www.wrightslaw.com
Many informative articles on special education and early intervention issues and laws are available free on this website. The founders of the website, Pete and Pam Wright, are also the authors of several comprehensive books on special education advocacy, which can be ordered online.

▪▪ Other Helpful Resources

Babycenter
www.babycenter.com
This website provides information of interest to all new parents (such as tips on bathing or feeding a baby or dealing with colic) and also offers basic information on Down syndrome. There are several Down syndrome bulletin board where parents can discuss concerns and seek information from other parents of children with Down syndrome (click on "boards" and then search under *Down syndrome*).

ABLEDATA
8630 Fenton Street, Suite 930
Silver Spring, MD 20910
800-227-0216; 301-608-8958 (fax)
www.abledata.com
ABLEDATA provides objective information about assistive technology products (communication devices, keyboards, touch screens, etc.) and rehabilitation equipment available from domestic and international sources. Although ABLEDATA does not sell any products, they can help locate the companies that do.

AblePlay
www.ableplay.org
This website is designed to help parents of children with disabilities locate appropriate toys for their abilities as well as toys that will help their child improve skills in specific developmental areas.

National Human Genome Research Institute
National Institutes of Health
Building 31, Room 4B09
31 Center Dr., MSC2152
Bethesda, MD 20892-2152
301-402-2218
www.genome.gov

This organization led the Human Genome Project for the National Institutes of Health. Information about the Genome Project is available on the website, and under "Educational Resources" there are several very easy-to-read explanations about DNA, chromosomes, and other genetics topics that may be of interest to parents.

CONTRIBUTORS

Sue Buckley, OBE, BA, CPsychol, AFBPsS, is a Chartered Psychologist with some 40 years experience in services for children and adults with intellectual disabilities. In her early career, she trained and worked as a clinical psychologist in the National Health Service of Great Britain. For 25 years from 1975, she taught psychology at the University of Portsmouth, and, from 1980, developed a research team which specialized in research into the developmental and educational needs of children with Down syndrome. She is currently Director for Science and Research at Down Syndrome Education International, Portsmouth, England. Professor Buckley is the author of a wide range of books, chapters, and papers on Down syndrome and in wide demand to lecture worldwide on all aspects of early intervention and education for children with Down syndrome. She and her research colleagues have published a number of research papers, but she has also always made a priority of disseminating information to parents and practitioners in a variety of ways. She is the Founding Editor of the specialized international peer reviewed journal *Down Syndrome Research and Practice.* In 2004, she was awarded an OBE (Officer of the Order of the British Empire) for her services to special needs education. One of Sue's three adult children is an adopted daughter with Down syndrome.

Jean Nelson Farley, MSN, RN, CPNP, CRRN, is a clinical instructor at Georgetown University School of Nursing & Health Studies. She also holds a faculty practice appointment as a nurse educator at The HSC Pediatric Center (formerly, The Hospital for Sick Children) in Washington, DC. Ms. Farley has practiced pediatric nursing for 35 years, and her areas of clinical interest and expertise are developmental disabilities, genetic disorders, and pediatric palliative care.

Marian H. Jarrett, Ed.D., is Associate Professor of Special Education at The George Washington University in Washington, DC.

Emily Perl Kingsley joined the Children's Television Workshop as a writer for *Sesame Street* in 1970. She has been writing scripts and songs for *Sesame Street* ever since, and has written about 20 children's books and many home videos (including *Elmo Learns to Share* and several editions of *Elmo's World*). She has received 17 Emmy Awards for her work on *Sesame Street*. The mother of a child with Down syndrome, Ms. Kingsley is a frequent lecturer on that subject and on disability rights. In 1976 she was elected to the Board of Directors of the National Down Syndrome Congress and served on the Board for 9 years. The story of her son, Jason, was the subject of a drama special, *This Is My Son,* on NBC-TV in 1977. Since then, Jason and his mother have appeared on such television shows as *Good Morning America, Dateline NBC,* the soap opera *All My Children, Hour Magazine, CBS Sunday, CNN News,* and many others. (And Jason and his friend, Mitchell Levitz, have told their own stories in the book *Count Us In: Growing Up with Down Syndrome.*) Ms. Kingsley, in collaboration with Allan Sloane, coauthored a teleplay for the movie *Kids Like These,* which dealt with her family's experiences. The movie aired on CBS-TV in 1987 and 1988, has won multiple awards, and is still frequently shown on cable TV. In 1994, Ms. Kingsley received an EDI Award (her first of three) from the National Easter Seal Society in recognition of her *Sesame Street* scripts which have treated disability issues and enhanced the "equality, dignity and independence" of individuals with disabilities. In July 1990, Ms. Kingsley, her husband, Charles, and Jason received the Special Achievement Award for Families from the Joseph P. Kennedy, Jr. Foundation for "contributing in an extraordinary way to improving the quality of life of people with mental retardation." In 2006, Ms. Kingsley was honored in Los Angeles with a Lifetime Achievement Award for her decades of work promoting understanding and inclusion of people with disabilities in the media. In 2008, her video *Learning Is Everywhere* won a Gold Medal at the New York Video/Film Festival.

Ms. Kingsley's essay "Welcome to Holland" has been reprinted in many languages and in many forms all over the world. *Dear Abby* runs this piece every October to commemorate National Down Syndrome Awareness Month and it has been reprinted in *Chicken Soup for the Mother's Soul* and dozens of other books.

Chahira Kozma is an Associate Professor of Pediatrics at Georgetown University Medical Center in Washington, DC. She is board certified in Pediatrics and Clinical Genetics. She has lectured and published widely on genetic conditions, the ethical, legal, and social implications of the Human Genome Project, and fetal alcohol syndrome, among other interests.

Dr. Len Leshin is a board-certified pediatrician in Corpus Christi, Texas. He practices general pediatrics but has a special interest in children with Down syndrome, which developed after the birth of his son with Down syndrome. He is a member of the Down Syndrome Medical Interest Group and is a clinical advisor to the National Down Syndrome Society. He writes and manages a website entitled "Down Syndrome: Health Issues," which is located at www.ds-health.com.

Mitchell Levitz is a Disability Specialist for the Westchester Institute for Human Development/University Center for Excellence in Disabilities and Administrative Liaison to the New York State Self-Advocacy Association. He is also coauthor (with Jason Kingsley) of *Count Us In: Growing Up with Down Syndrome,* and has contributed to eight other books, including a chapter, "Voices of Self-Advocates" in *Human Rights of Persons with Intellectual Disabilities: Different but Equal.* In addition, he is a member of the Board of Directors of the National Down Syndrome Society (NDSS) and the Steering Committee of the Council on Community Advocacy (COCA) for the Association of University Centers on Disabilities (AUCD). His current work is in the areas of health and wellness training, self-advocacy leadership, self-determination and individualized supports, a national service inclusion project, and emergency preparedness.

Joan B. Riley, MS, MSN, CFNP, is an Assistant Professor at Georgetown University School of Nursing & Health Studies. She is also a Nurse Practitioner in the Department of Family Medicine at Georgetown University Hospital. Joan's research interest is in health promotion and health literacy. She is the parent of two young adult women, the oldest with Down syndrome.

Jo Ann Simons, MSW, is a parent-professional well known in the area of intellectual disability who constantly challenges herself and those around her to turn problems into answers and challenges into opportunities. Currently she is President/CEO of the St. Coletta and Cardinal Cushing Schools of Massachusetts, a Board member of the National Down Syndrome Society, and a Trustee of LIFE, Inc. of Cape Cod. Jo Ann also serves as a consultant to Special Olympics, Inc., and lectures throughout the world on issues related to transition and future planning. Previously, she was the Executive Director of the Arc of East Middlesex, the Deputy Superintendent of the Walter E. Fernald State School, the Director of Policy for the Massachusetts Department of Mental Retardation, President of the National Down Syndrome Congress (1983-1991), and on the Board of Directors of Special Olympics International. Jo Ann has two adult children: Jonathan, who has Down syndrome, is a graduate of Swampscott (MA) High School, Riverview School's post-graduate program, GROW, and Cape Cod Community College. Jon lives independently in his own home and has a life filled with meaningful paid work, important volunteer activities, many leisure pursuits, and close friends. Emily, who reminds her that being "typical" is special, too, is a graduate of Cornell University and its law school.

Susan J. Skallerup is a writer and editor who lives in the suburban Washington, D.C. area. She has a master's degree in creative writing from American University. In the distant past, before kids (BK), she aspired to be a professional flutist, wrote music reviews for the *Las Vegas Sun,* and served in the army as a Russian linguist. She and her husband have two music-loving daughters, one with and one without Down syndrome.

Marilyn Trainer is the parent of four children, including an adult son with Down syndrome. She has been active for many years with The Arc and co-founded a support group for parents of children with Down syndrome in Maryland. She holds a degree in English from American University and is the author of a collection of essays about Down syndrome called *Differences in Common* (Woodbine House, 1991). Her writing has appeared in the *Washington Post* and other publications. The Trainers are now the proud grandparents of four. The youngest, Alexandra, was born four months prematurely. The challenges faced by the parents of such a fragile little life are not unlike those faced by parents of babies with Down syndrome. Against the odds, she clung tenaciously to life, a formidable mite of a fighter. As with her Uncle Ben years before, her birth brought joy tempered by sorrow (her twin sister, Helen, died at 17 days), hope tempered by fear, peaceful moments tempered by debilitating anxiety. Today, Alexa is a spunky little girl, her parents' "Wild Fairy Child." And again, like her Uncle Ben, she holds her own very special place within the family circle.

Mary Wilt has many years experience in case management/service coordination for children with special needs, and was Early Intervention Service Coordinator for seven years. At the time this chapter was written, Mary was a Care Coordinator in Virginia's program for children and youth with special health care needs and a member of Virginia's Early Intervention Training Team for new service coordinators. She has three wonderful daughters, the youngest of whom (Emily, age 17) has Down syndrome.

INDEX